W. H. AUDEN

Also by Rainer Emig

MODERNISM IN POETRY: Motivations, Structures and Limits

W. H. Auden

Towards a Postmodern Poetics

Rainer Emig

First published in Great Britain 2000 by
MACMILLAN PRESS LTD
Houndmills, Basingstoke, Hampshire RG21 6XS and London
Companies and representatives throughout the world

A catalogue record for this book is available from the British Library.

ISBN 0–333–74557–4

First published in the United States of America 2000 by
ST. MARTIN'S PRESS, INC.,
Scholarly and Reference Division,
175 Fifth Avenue, New York, N.Y. 10010

ISBN 0–312–22138–X

Library of Congress Cataloging-in-Publication Data
Emig, Rainer, 1964–
W.H. Auden : towards a postmodern poetics / Rainer Emig.
p.   cm.
Includes bibliographical references (p.   ) and index.
ISBN 0–312–22138–X (cloth)
1. Auden, W. H. (Wystan Hugh), 1907–1973—Criticism and
interpretation.   2. Postmodernism (Literature)   3. Modernism
(Literature)   4. Poetics.   I. Title.
PR6001.U4Z67   1999
811'.52—dc21   99–27617
                                                                CIP

This book is printed on paper suitable for recycling and made from fully managed and sustained forest sources.

10   9   8   7   6   5   4   3   2   1
09   08   07   06   05   04   03   02   01   00

Printed and bound in Great Britain by
Antony Rowe Ltd, Chippenham, Wiltshire

For Gerald

'To you simply
From me I mean.'

Contents

Acknowledgements

This book has a long history that dates back to my first endeavours to come to terms with English Literature as an undergraduate at Johann Wolfgang Goethe University in Frankfurt am Main, Germany. There, an undergraduate seminar on the 1930s, taught by Harald Raykowski, gave me a taste of the writers of this period. As is so often the case, my engagement with Auden derived from an initial resistance: I did not like his poetry very much to start with. But it was that very negative initial impression of preposterous cleverness and abstract detachment that kept me fascinated, to the point that I eventually wrote my M.A. dissertation at Warwick University on Auden's early poetry, very kindly supervised by Edward Larrissy. During my time as a doctoral student in Oxford, I had the privilege not only to be supervised by one of the greatest Auden scholars in Britain, John Fuller, but also to be permitted to participate in one of his M.Phil. seminars on Auden. Since then I have learned most about Auden through teaching his works at Frankfurt University and the University of Wales, Cardiff. I am grateful to Cardiff for providing me with an intellectual environment in which the study of literature and debates in Critical and Cultural Theory go hand in hand. This outlook has very much shaped this book. I am also grateful to my students for reminding me that they find Auden's poetry difficult, while at the same time showing a level of interest that has kept me convinced that it might be worthwhile to add to the existing corpus of Auden studies another voice that signals his continuing relevance in the literary and critical debates at the end of the twentieth century.

Editions used in the Text and their Abbreviations

Auden's complete works are in the process of being collected in a complete critical edition at the time of writing this book. Unfortunately, the volume containing Auden's poetry has not been released to date – for reasons that can easily be guessed by anyone familiar with Auden's habit of constant revisions. The present study therefore uses the most easily accessible collection of Auden's poetry throughout, and supplements it with an edition of his early writings when necessary. Auden's verse plays are taken from the first volume of the new complete edition. References to some of his prose writings refer to the first volume of the latter in the critical *Complete Works*.

CP   W. H. Auden, *Collected Poems*, ed. Edward Mendelson (London: Faber & Faber, 1976).

EA   W. H. Auden, *The English Auden: Poems, Essays and Dramatic Writings 1927–1939*, ed. Edward Mendelson (London and Boston: Faber & Faber, 1978).

Pl   W. H. Auden and Christopher Isherwood, *Plays and Other Dramatic Writings by W. H. Auden 1928–1938*, ed. Edward Mendelson, *The Complete Works of W. H. Auden* (Princeton, NJ: Princeton University Press, 1988).

Pr   W. H. Auden, *Prose – Volume 1: 1926–1938*, ed. Edward Mendelson, *The Complete Works of W. H. Auden* (Princeton, NJ: Princeton University Press, 1996).

DH   W. H. Auden, *The Dyer's Hand and Other Essays* (London and Boston: Faber & Faber, 1963).

1

Taming the Monster

'Auden is a monster'. With this neat formula Geoffrey Grigson sums up Auden's position among English poets at the height of his fame in 1937. For Grigson, the dominant feature of Auden's poems is their refusal (or inability) to integrate themselves into established literary patterns:

> Auden does not fit. Auden is no gentleman. Auden does not write, or exist, by any of the codes, by the Bloomsbury rules, by the Hampstead rules, by the Oxford, the Cambridge, or the Russell Square rules.[1]

Auden's poetry denies reverence to contemporary standards, such as free verse, and refuses to accept the great models of its time, Yeats and Eliot. Instead it prefers decidedly unfashionable poetic ancestors, such as Housman and Kipling, and forms as dusty as Icelandic sagas and Anglo-Saxon verse. But just as much as it ignores current norms and fashions, it is eager to create a tradition of its own. Together with the writings of other young authors, such as Stephen Spender, Cecil Day Lewis, Christopher Isherwood, and Edward Upward, Auden's poetry aims to set standards whose benchmark becomes the problematic adjective 'new'. *New Signatures* and *New Country* are the anthologies of these writings, *New Verse* and *New Writing* their periodicals.[2] 'New' always means more than mere artistic innovation – as it does in the various modernist avant-garde movements. It always includes a political stand, usually a left-wing position that occasionally drifts towards doctrinaire Marxism. Unlike Eliot's absurd royalism, Yeats's esoteric flirting with right-wing ideology, and Pound's outspoken, yet equally ineffectual support for Mussolini that derives from an imagined lineage connecting Italian fascism with ancient Chinese emperors, a significant part of the literature of the 1930s is determined to engage with the actualities of its time. More than that, it tries to respond to them actively, often by appropriating styles of propaganda.

This commitment to the political and economic landscape of their time has proved fatal for many writers of the Thirties, and this includes Auden. Today, the former monster occasionally frightens sixth-formers and undergraduates, but he rarely troubles serious academic debates. 'Auden is the foremost poet of the Thirties'; 'Auden's poems depict the industrial decline in England's North'; 'Auden's poems take sides in the political conflicts of the time': these are some of today's standard responses to his works. Equally common is the problem that, even for those who appreciate his poems today, it is difficult to justify their taste. Auden's indisputable technical brilliance very often presents itself in mere witticisms; his descriptions usually defy firm classifications; his ideas are at best difficult to grasp, if not contradictory or encoded in private references. The political convictions of his poetry, if unambiguous, appear dated and boring, if not worrying and opaque.

Moreover, compared to the revolutionary stylistic achievements of the modernism of Eliot and Pound, Auden's poetry seems a mere hiccup, if not a step backwards to traditions already overcome. Unlike Eliot and Pound's writings, Auden's poems have therefore not been firmly placed into the canon of either modernist or 'post-war' English literature. His innovatory phase, common agreement has it, was the 1930s, its violent end the Second World War. Yet while no-one can be blamed when even revolutionary novelty eventually becomes dated, and integration into the established canon – though also a question of chance and fashion – does not spare the most anti-establishment work of art, in the case of Auden's poetry this inclusion has only been possible through a wilful neglect of many of its features. A second look at the main judgements concerning his works (i.e. that they are descriptive of their times and politically motivated)[3] shows that they regard the texts as mere reflections of their context, a sort of transfer of the times in which they were written. A similar, though more subtle approach, which follows the same dubious premise, is the analysis of Auden's poems in psychoanalytic terms. Its results are taken as hints of the psychic disposition of Auden, of the period he wrote in, or both.[4] This is especially problematic as Auden's writings were themselves thoroughly informed by Freudian ideas and other forms of psychoanalysis, which were not always interpreted in orthodox ways and often featured as travesty rather than serious exposition.[5]

This study proposes to take the basic ambiguities of Auden's poems seriously for an assessment of their importance as a contribution to the artistic and cultural debates of the twentieth century. Grigson once more shows remarkable insight when he pinpoints Auden's central aesthetic concept in the same essay in which he declares him to be so monstrous:

> One of the most frequent images used by Auden is the image of the frontier, the line between the known and the feared, the past and the future, and the conscious and everything beyond control, the region of society and the region of trolls and hulders (and Goebbelses). Auden lives very much in this frightening border territory.[6]

This border territory reflects back on the complex cultural and political issues of his time and simultaneously offers the chance as well as challenge of looking ahead into an artistic no man's land. The main argument of the present study will be that the particularly new poetic territory exposed by Auden's writings is that which leads out of modernism into something uncharted, into a region where the only orientation is provided by images of borders, folds and ruptures. Dylan Thomas, when asked to provide one of the 'Sixteen Comments on Auden' in the *New Verse* double issue dedicated to Auden in 1937, came up with a poetic assessment of his colleague which displays perceptive allegories of these underlying tensions:

> I sometimes think of Mr. Auden's poetry as a hygiene, a knowledge and practice, based on a brilliantly prejudiced analysis of contemporary disorders, relating to the preservation and promotion of health, a sanitary science and a flusher of melancholies. I sometimes think of his poetry as a great war, admire intensely the mature, religious, and logical fighter, and deprecate the boy bushranger.[7]

Concerned with knowledge, practice, and sanity – or engaged in a great war, which is often fought with unorthodox and indeed immature means: these contradictions need to be investigated. By closely examining Auden's poems and by linking them to some of the crucial theories of twentieth-century literary and critical theory, this study will try to show that Auden in fact paves the way for a poetics of postmodernism.

This approach will of necessity relegate autobiographical and historical references in Auden's works to the background. This can be justified, I believe, by pointing at the abundance of studies that show Auden's writings as landmarks in history or the development of Auden's personality – and also, sadly enough, by the limited insights that these approaches have procured. Such attempts at integrating Auden's works into pre-existent patterns (of history or personality) generally try to override the obscurities and difficulties exposed by them instead of accepting them as crucial. This study will also refrain from using Auden's many prose writings as clues or guides to the exploration of his poetics. One of the crucial aspect of this poetry, as will become evident in the course of this study, is the question of authority. Granting the author complete authority over the reading of his texts would probably have pleased Auden (one can almost hear him exclaim 'Mother knows best'), but it would do little justice to the complex struggles for mastery that go on in them. At the same time my readings will try to avoid the related temptation to subject Auden's poems to another authority: that of the fashionable, if still vague, concept of postmodernism. They will read his texts through contemporary theoretical lenses, because their aim is an analysis of their issues as relevant for the present day.

If postmodernism has been chosen as a point of orientation, this is because his writing starts at least partly as a response to modernism. A study of Auden's life and times can provide a useful insight into his role, first, as a devotee of the modernisms of Yeats and Eliot, then as their critic and parodist, and finally as their successor. Auden's artistic development begins at a historic junction when a pattern repeats itself that also brought modernism into being. If modernism, as I have claimed elsewhere, is an artistic response to the challenges of late modernity as exposed in the drastic developments and rup-tures of the early twentieth century,[8] then the response to the fur-ther development of this modernity as well as to its initial artistic critiques gains a different status. As Wolfgang Welsch argues con-vincingly, this need not represent an anti-modernism that often amounts to a relapse into pre-modernist patterns of thought and art-istic expression. It might represent postmodernism – not as a false antithesis to modernism, but as its critical continuation.[9] This, I believe, is what Auden's poetic development represents and what justifies the attempt of the present study to link his works with the by now almost embarrassingly ubiquitous, yet still insufficiently explained term 'postmodern'. The 'towards' in the title of the present study is therefore neither coy nor an expression of indecision, but an attempt to signal the complexity of the relationship between postmodernism and poetics as well as the character as process rather than position that marks Auden's aesthetics.

Over the last years studies concentrating on the textual features of Auden's poems have begun to appear.[10] To those this present analysis is indebted. Nevertheless, it has some aims of its own. By an application of formalist, structuralist and post-structuralist concepts and a concentration on some dominant topics, namely the problem of meaning, text and history, identity and community, authority and certainty, it strives to elucidate the complexity of Auden's works, a complexity that is not restricted to themes, poetic modes, or the use of manifold traditions, but affects the bases of poetic structures.[11]

Though not a study of poetic development, Chapter 2 of this study will consequently start its investigation with Auden's earliest properly published poems, the first volume of which formed the 1928 pamphlet *Poems*, privately printed by Stephen Spender in an edition of circa thirty copies. It will examine the images, symbols, and intertextual references of Auden's early poems and demonstrate that they show a struggle with the very concept of truth in signification.

The rarely discussed Auden plays *Paid on Both Sides* and *The Dance of Death* and the results of his collaboration with Christopher Isherwood, *The Dog Beneath the Skin, The Ascent of F6*, and *On the Frontier*, will be analysed in Chapter 3 as sly assessments of Englishness. Yet they will also be shown as attempts to escape from literary and cultural traditions through the introduction of the then fashionable theories of Marxism and Freudianism and the avant-garde techniques of Surrealism and Dada. The results of these wild mixtures are self-relativising and ultimately self-destructive, which has led many critics (including the authors of the works) to dismiss these plays as failures. I will argue that important postmodern concepts *avant la lettre*, such as deconstruction and dialogism, are prefigured in these experiments.

An important climax in Auden's early poetics is reached with *The Orators*, which was first published in 1932 (a second revised edition appeared in 1934).[12] There, the conflicts between poetics, psychology, and politics that are at the forefront of Auden's early writings culminate in a work that is as puzzling as it is fascinating. The text's concern will be shown to be the relation of language to subjectivity and the establishment of authority in language, which – in the shape of rhetoric – encapsulates the problematic link between self and others. Chapter 4 will be devoted to this complex text which is rarely discussed in depth and which Auden himself regarded as a noble failure. The chapter will demonstrate that the apparent self-destruction of *The Orators* paves the way for an aesthetic that breaks out of the solipsistic artistic closure of many modernist texts. It opens up possibilities for political writings that are non-authoritarian, because it incorporates its own dangers of manipulation and as a consequence highlights choice and resistance.

In the short period of only six years Auden appears to discover a unique position for his writings after his contact with modernism, especially Eliot's *The Waste Land*. Yet the period also sees his struggle against Eliot as a limiting model and eventually its final abandonment and – I would argue – supersession. Compared to the radicalism of *The Orators*, Auden's subsequent poetry may at first glance appear to retreat to safer poetic ground. Yet a closer look at the poems written during the remaining years before the Second World War reveals that they, too, abound with problematic positionings, of voices, political convictions, and historic evaluations. Chapter 5 of this study will focus on the intrusion of concerns about history into Auden's writings. It will show how Auden's poems criticise his earlier strategies and fixations – especially those with leader figures and symbolism of power – as inadequate, hollow, and dangerous.

The long poem '1929' will be analysed in depth as a subtle registering of the clash between private myths and historic events (here the collapse of the Weimar Republic in inter-war Germany). *Night Mail* and related 'documentary' verse will be discussed as attempts to combine an awareness of social reality with Auden's style. That Auden's development concerning history is by no means straightforward will be shown in examination of his relapses into heroic poses, as in his infamous poem 'Spain 1937'. Two interesting pieces of travel writing produced in the 1930s, *Letters from Iceland* (with Louis MacNeice) and *Journey to a War* (with Christopher Isherwood), will again demonstrate an almost narcissistic concern with Englishness and attempts to turn away from history. Yet by 1939 and after Auden's decision to leave Britain for the United States, this earlier posturing will be shown to give way to a humility that downgrades artistic experiment in favour of the problematic registration of facts. This does not lead to a turn towards more realistic forms of writing, but instead to endeavours to link subjectivity with objective questions of power and war in a new poetics.

Auden's post-war writings will be analysed in Chapter 6 in terms of their difficult positioning in American as well as European (Italian, English, and Austrian) contexts. Rather than merely tracing back the location of voices and styles to Auden's repeated personal relocations, the chapter will link questions of displaced subjectivity with issues of nationality and identity in an attempt to examine the sometimes irritating changes of style and tone of Auden's 'middle career'. The main argument will concern the farewell to authenticity of origin that this stylistic variation signals, and will outline Auden's attempts to locate his artistic roots in a wider cultural context.

Rather than again pursuing a biographical path that links ageing with the renunciation of sexuality, Chapter 7 will claim that in Auden's later poems a thorough reassessment of his earlier concerns takes place. This takes the form of three inquiries that Auden himself named in a review of Kierkegaard's *Either/Or* in *The New Republic* in 1941.[13] The first concerns the self's relation to its past, with Freud as its starting-point. The second examines the self's relation to the present (and has Marx at the basis of its inquiry). The third one eventually investigates the relation of self and future or transcendental goals. Kierkegaard is one of the guides in this inquiry. Out of an essential pessimism (noticeable, for instance, in *The Age of Anxiety*), Auden manages to generate a paradoxical optimism. This positive outlook derives from the acceptance of human imperfection and joy in artistic production, which must also be regarded as forever unfinished and in process. This chapter will again employ poststructuralist theory, but will also refer to some contemporary philosophical and theological ideas in order to make sense of Auden's appreciation of the limit – noticeable, for instance, in his famous poem 'In Praise of Limestone'.

Auden's last works will be analysed in Chapter 8 for their seemingly objective concern with everyday objects (visible in the collections *About the House* and *Thank you, Fog*). The chapter will argue that behind this apparent objectivity there still lurks a sly and playful attempt at transcendence, yet one that refrains from ultimate certainties, orientation, and goals. As in the preceding chapter, religious impulses in Auden's works will be shown as linked with artistic playfulness and the pleasure of use and change rather than the belief in certainty. In the emphasis on the superiority of the object world over the creations of fiction – and the joy of expressing this exactly in a writing that manages to make itself 'disappear' – Auden's last works will be shown to pave the way for a large number of post-war poems whose strategies wholly rely on an analytical objectivity behind which lurks a self-limiting and often ironic artistic mastery of writing.

Chapter 9 of this study, in conclusion, will sum up the detected strategies of Auden's long and varied career. In terms of Auden's achievements, the approach of this study hopes to overcome the 'taming of the monster'. By this I mean the common integration of Auden into a pattern that is as well-trodden as it is generally useless: the young poet attempts certain artistic innovations, some of which are interesting and fertile, others of which go over the top and prove counterproductive and dangerous. In his middle age the poet calms down and accepts the complexity of existence, while in his later years he philosophises about the meaning of life and the approach of death. In Auden's case, this pattern is often employed as a polite way of disguising the conviction that the early Auden wrote interesting and controversial, if flawed, poems and plays, the mature one became more balanced, while the old poet was little more than a stylistically capable conversationalist and bore.

In contrast to the above (un)critical routine, I would like to demonstrate that there is a structural and theoretical challenge and paradoxical coherence, at least of problems, in Auden's writings. This leads from the farewell to transcendental symbolism via the struggle between writing and reality to a playful armistice in which writing relativises itself while continuing to question the reliance on even its own fascinations, such as subjectivity, reality, and finalities. It is to be hoped that the attempt to describe the dominant features of Auden's works by means of a series of theoretically informed close readings will not only lead to a re-evaluation of this sometimes difficult author, but also to a renewed readability of his works. Especially in the light of many current philosophical and political problems, his poems provide interesting insights and points of departure. In connection with the ongoing debate about the validity of the concept of postmodernism, they offer positive arguments in favour of the abandonment of modernism and its radical supersession by a related, but more radical and 'open' aesthetics. 'A serious being/Cries out for a gap', argues 'Mountains' in Auden's late cycle 'Bucolics' (CP 428). While I have tried to fill what I perceived to be a gap in the critical literature available on Auden, I am convinced, and indeed hope, that after my engagement with his works many of these challenging and productive gaps will still remain.

2
Early Auden: Farewell to the Signified

Although the basic images in Auden's early poems seem fairly easy to comprehend, the texts prove remarkably evasive when it comes to questions of meaning. The beginning of Justin Replogle's *Auden's Poetry* is a typical example of the confusion they tend to create:

> The pattern of Auden's ideas, though often talked about, has never been very clear. His earliest poetry was vigorous, energetic, and on the surface at least original, untraditional, and obscure. Readers could sense vast energies pouring forth without quite knowing what the commotion was about. Yet at first the energy itself seemed meaningful. To a young generation at odds with society, energy suggests rebellion.[1]

The passage displays a puzzling array of terms for 'meaning': there are underlying structures, there are ideas, and there is a pattern created out of them. Replogle also mentions a discrepancy in lucidity between the different layers. The basic features of Auden's poems seem easily perceptible. His ideas, however, remain obscure, and a pattern or meaning can hardly be constructed out of them. Rather, the texts create an 'energy', which, however, remains unspecific and hardly signals permanence.

A passage like Replogle's tells us that a more organised approach to the problem of meaning is required. What this chapter will attempt is a rather formal analysis of the images in Auden's early verse and the ways in which they are linked, both on the syntactic level of word order and the paradigmatic level of symbols and metaphors. It will then ask if and how 'meaning' is created by the strategies and patterns in these poems. The analysis will show that Auden's strategies are analogous to a crucial claim of twentieth-century linguistics, Ferdinand de Saussure's influential insistence on the arbitrariness of the sign. More than that, Auden's poetic practice will be shown to be more radical than lingustic theory, to an extent that links his writings with much later postmodern theoretical radicalisations of the signifier–signified debate, especially the ideas of Jacques Derrida.

IMAGES

In the privately printed *Poems* of 1928 Auden's images already display a transition from an imitation of Eliot to the characteristics which have become famous as the so-called 'Audenesque' style. The poem beginning 'We saw in Spring' illustrates this contrast between model and 'imitation' (*EA* 437). It describes a surreal scene in which an unspecified 'We' perceive strange and seemingly symbolic objects, such as the 'frozen buzzard' floating down a weir towards the sea. Trees are presented as throwing shadows in challenge, before autumn arrives unexpectedly and – in a typically technical Audenesque phrase – focuses stars more sharply in the sky. Returning to spring, the poem merges images of a 'bulb pillow', a skull, a crocus, and clenched teeth.

These images are clearly related to the first part of Eliot's *The Waste Land*, 'The Burial of the Dead'. The daring metaphor which fuses 'bulb', 'pillow', 'skull', and 'teeth' echoes Eliot's technique of placing meaning in the gaps between the associations of terms. But 'We saw in Spring' also exhibits many features of Auden's own emerging style. The problematic presentation of the speaker(s) in the faceless plural 'We' is one of them. Another is the energetic activity implied in most of the verbs ('flipped', 'threw', 'thrusting', 'clenched'): activity which, surprisingly, is not attached to the observer but to objects or unnamed forces. Apart from the image of the crocus bulb, all nouns are clear-cut images with limited connotations; the majority are accompanied by a definite article, as if to give them even more unambiguous shapes.

None the less, the 'frozen buzzard' gains a near-symbolic quality through this very article, even though its eventual significance remains opaque. The midges are equally ambiguous. The adjective 'snoring' activates their near-homonym 'midgets', 'dwarfs', and thus subtly introduces one of the fairy tale characters that populate many of Auden's poems. Together with the strangely animated trees and the crocus, they contrast strongly with the neutral, almost scientific language which reaches its climax in the line 'To focus stars more sharply in the sky'. The latter is a good example of what became known as Auden's 'clinical style': any probable Romanticism inherent in the image is undercut by the forced – and consciously 'unpoetic' – technical expression. Without going much deeper into this poem of rather dubious quality, it is possible to state with some plausibility that it describes a tension between passive observers registering loss, death, and aggression, and a world which is both real and mystical, and altogether animated by a force that is invisible and beyond human control

A more radical poem in a similar vein in the same collection begins 'Consider if you will how lovers stand' (*EA* 438). Again there are obvious allusions to Eliot, but this time the model is outspokenly rejected and even ridiculed. The sequence 'others,/Less clinically-minded, will admire/An evening like a coloured photograph' mimics the famous simile in the first lines of 'Prufrock' which shows the evening as an etherised patient. 'A music stultified across the water' parodies the quotation from *The Tempest* in *The Waste Land*. The parody also introduces the new poetic ideal explicitly: clinical-mindedness. The effect on the imagery of the poem is remarkable. Except for the parodying sections, it hardly contains any concrete images, but deals with abstractions. But these abstractions are treated as if they were real objects through their coupling with concrete nouns and verbs: 'the suction of good-bye', 'ligatured the ends of a farewell'. The concrete images, however, are again either animated, like the 'finishing blade of grass' that threatens the amorous relationship, or they invoke a symbolism that is not so much subjective, immediate, and potentially transcendental as objective, detached, and intertextual.

The 'dazzling cities of the plain where lust/Threatened a sinister rod' are connected with a desert and show desire as a mere *fata morgana*, yet one which endangers the Christian doctrine embodied in the 'sinister rod'. The hovering of the images between the abstract and the concrete successfully mirrors the poem's discussion of the irreconcilability of love and intellect. Both love and intellectual exercise are depicted in an unfavourable light: love has no insight, but the 'study of stones' no life. It splits Eve's apple rather than eating it. Since the speaker places himself (again in the faceless plural 'we') on the side of the intellectuals, though unwillingly and constantly nostalgic for lost love, this tension is maintained throughout the poem. Solomon and Sheba's fault, the poem concludes, was not their love, but their belief that love and intellect could go hand in hand.

What becomes evident in these early poems is a tendency to link private and personal concerns with larger impersonal issues. At the same time the texts refuse to present a coherent self embodied in a singular speaker. Nor do they commit themselves to firm and identifiable settings, much less to transcendental symbolic certainties. The effect is unsettling and often unconvincing. None the less, these first poetic exercises already hint at a farewell both to a simple realism (no matter whether it is a psychological or a social one) and modernist attempts to employ symbols in order to transcend contemporary reality in the direction of a vague 'human condition' (Yeats and Eliot are representatives of this strategy). When they use traditional reference points, such as the Bible, they do so in a self-exposing fashion, and interpret or even criticise their models.

A poem frequently cited as typical of Auden's early style is the third poem in *Poems* of 1930, 'Who stands, the crux left of the watershed', later simply called 'The Watershed' (*CP* 41). In it we find the West Midlands, the declining mining country of Auden's schoolboy poetry.[2] But how realistic is its description? The introductory 'Who stands' could be interrogative or declarative – and thus shows the overview as a mere possibility. The 'crux' could mean a crossroads or a dilemma; 'left of' may be a verb or a direction. Even 'watershed' is ambiguous.[3] Already the setting of the poem oscillates between the realistic and the symbolic.

'At Cashwell', however, at least pretends to place the poem on the map of Britain. But its description of the industry and especially an engine is anthropomorphic again, and prepares the poem's eventual shift into the mythic mist of the final lines of its first section. In spite of its apparent obscurities, the final image of these lines confronts the reader with an archaic drama, the death of the doomed hero, perhaps as the result of a mining accident. Characteristically, it is related in the plainest terms possible: 'in wooden shape' he 'nosed his way' 'Through long abandoned levels' 'And in his final valley went to ground'. There are no descriptive adjectives except 'wooden', which belongs to an opaque subclause. Even the nouns are as neutral as possible. The protagonist remains as abstract as the addresser or addressee ('Who'). What starts like a tale of the dangers of mining ends up in a mythic landscape which prefigures those of Tolkien.[4]

The second paragraph of the poem is even more clearly split between concrete realistic imagery and abstractions. It addresses a 'stranger' directly and asks him to turn back. The land of the poem will not communicate with him. Cut off, it cannot be accessed by someone '[a]imless for faces rather there than here'. The traditional prerequisite of narratives, the crossing into new and unknown territory, is here rejected as futile. The reason for this failure is located in communication and therefore ultimately in language. The first part of the section contains only nondescript nouns, 'stranger', 'young stock', 'land', 'content', and 'faces'. Its verbs and adjectives describe the rejection of this stranger (most probably the 'Who' of the first stanza) by the semi-mythical waste land. At the same time, however, the images are illustrations of the effect of the poem on the reader. The refusal of communication, indeed, becomes even more pertinent when also linked with the text itself.

The paragraph is concerned with the loss of contact between the self and reality. The latter is introduced in its second part by a number of mundane images which show intrusions into an everyday world without consequences. Beams of light from a car may cross bedroom walls, but 'They wake no sleeper'. The same failure or refusal to communicate applies to the wind that can be heard 'Arriving driven from the ignorant sea', but which merely 'hurt[s] itself on pane'. Although these images blame the unresponsive reality for the failure of communication, the earlier description of the stranger as aimless and only interested in new experiences shows that the fault is mutual. If reality shows no response, then the stranger lacks any real interest in it. It is clear that the Romantic communion of nature and man has ceased to function. The speaker's position is indeed precarious: when he is denied entry into the land that lies before him, the directive 'Go home' offers no help either, because there is no home in the poem. 'There' remains as empty as 'here' is vague.

The poem introduces explicitly the concept of the border which becomes so prominent in Auden's early poetry. This border is the dividing line between generations, political convictions, and countries. But it is also the barrier between the poem's message and the reader. More often than not it proves an unbridgeable gap – as in the above poem. Those that approach it are endangered and dangerous at the same time. The hare that is alluded to in the poem's last line rightly scents danger, but the threat could derive as much from the stranger as from something in his surroundings. The close relation between landscape and observer, state of mind and reality, will reappear again and again in the analysis of Auden's early poems, and so will the doomed hero who moves along borderlines: the airman, the secret agent, and the stranger.

It would be misleading, however, to see Auden's colourless images –
which constantly verge on abstractions and hardly seem to deserve
to be called 'images' – exclusively as effectively employed devices
illustrating the division between intellect and reality, a division
which seems to produce most of the conflicts in his early poems.
Often vague images are ostensibly used for the very sake of obscurity.

A poem written in 1930, 'Who will endure', later entitled significantly 'No Change of Place', shows the beginnings of this addiction
(*CP* 42). It not only starts with a construction similar to 'Who stands,
the crux left of the watershed', but also ends with a denial of entry.
This time, a 'gaitered gamekeeper with dog and gun/Will shout
"Turn back"'. The anonymous protagonist, however, has now more
clearly turned into a soldier or secret agent. He is once again balancing on a borderline. None the less, the constructions which are
meant to describe his hardships are either meaningless and obscure
or tautological. What does, for instance, the 'winter danger' lurking
in this poem signify? Tautological are its images of a 'Journey from
one place to another' (is there any other way of travelling?) and
'headland over bay/Between the land and sea'. The expression 'hour
of food' eventually gives the constructions away as inflated artifices
which cover sheer banality. Their none the less impressive effect is
often created by the absence of articles (Auden is always radical with
them) which lends an archaic appearance to them, as if the stanza
dealt with eternal truths.

Indulgence in poetic artifice which couples signifiers with only
seemingly meaningful images can also be noticed in a poem written
in 1929 that starts with the lines, 'Will you turn a deaf ear/To what
they said on the shore' and was later entitled 'The Questioner Who
Sits So Sly' (*CP* 47–8). Apart from the fact that the setting of the
poem is far from clear (who are 'they', and which shore is meant?),
the list of persons introduced in the second stanza to illustrate the
empty 'they' does not help the reader at all. One always senses possible explanations of terms, but is left defeated when it actually
comes to pinning them down. It is not even very helpful to be told
that the 'stork-legged heaven-reachers' is Auden's private joke on
the tall Stephen Spender.[5] All it tells the reader is that much of the
obscurity of the poem derives from its massive use of private references and schoolboy codes.

Yet even the deliberate obscurities observed above have a specific
poetic function, and so do the original metaphors used in the

poems, such as 'bombs of conspiracy'. Like the daring metaphors in Eliot's poems, they gain their particular value by the impossibility of scrutinising them fully. In Auden's poems, they are often created by the problematic use of the conjunction 'of'. It tends to combine terms that have no logical relation. Sometimes it suggests a connection that is much more complex than the economical 'of' can express. William Logan calls this device the *vignette*.[6] It is used to dramatise abstractions, but it can also compress a complete narrative into an image. An example is the 'wooden shape' that is perhaps a coffin in 'The Watershed', where a simple metaphor conjures up an entire drama.

The significance of the obscure images derives from the absence of identifiable signifieds. Both obscurities and daring metaphors become prominent in Auden's early poems. 'Which of you waking early and watching daybreak', for example, a poem imitating the style of Gerard Manley Hopkins, contains 'a leader of movement', 'the dawn of common day', 'growth of movement', 'The entire record of change', and 'truth's assurance of life' (*EA* 41–2). 'Get there if you can and see the land you were once proud to own', which can be read as a shorthand for the malaise of the 1930s, presents an entire stanza which shamelessly mixes famous persons with entirely private references (*EA* 18–9). It lists Cardinal Newman, Plato, Pascal, Baudelaire, Bowdler (the prudish nineteenth-century editor of Shakespeare's works), Freud, and Flaubert side by side with 'Ciddy', 'Fronny', 'Doctor Frommer', 'Mrs. Allom' and 'the Baron'. Some of these obscure figures can be identified as personal acquaintances of Auden, yet even this ascription of meaning only leads to the already evident insight that the poem sets up a relation between public figures and private ones. In this way it functions like many of Auden's early poems which equate public concerns with private anxieties.

Structurally, the difficulties of Auden's early poems are the effect of a number of techniques. The lack of clear signifieds can be caused by overlapping signifiers to create ambiguity. Another cause of obscure images can be the missing context of signifiers.[7] Yet neither strategy automatically produces meaningless texts. The absence of a definable meaning can also be interpreted as a calculated strategy which fulfils a function of its own in Auden's early poems. Auden's poetic technique thereby puts into practice what Ferdinand de Saussure formulates theoretically as the arbitrariness of the sign. Saussure is eager to point out that the link between that which signifies, the *signifier* or signal, and that which it signifies, the *signified* (which he sees as a mental image), is governed by convention and not by a natural relation. 'A linguistic sign is not a link between a thing and a name, but between a concept and a sound pattern' is his summary.[8] The choice of particular signifiers for certain signifieds is arbitrary, according to Saussure, and its establishment in a linguistic system, that is, a language, is achieved through the conventions of a linguistic community.[9]

Auden's early works go further than that and actually multiply the absence of natural relations and identification while simultaneously stressing the problematic entanglement of language and community. What they achieve are self-relativising and often surreal scenarios in which seemingly clear and even clinical language competes with complete obscurity and anarchic flux. They reverse the traditional hierarchies of realism and mimesis according to which texts use certain mechanisms to mirror an external reality.

Yet they also go beyond the aesthetics of modernist poetry. Roland Barthes characterises the modernist use of poetic language as follows:

[Modern] poets give to their speech the status of a closed Nature, which covers both the function and the structure of language. Poetry is then no longer a Prose either ornamental or shorn of liberties. It is a quality *sui generis* and without antecedents. It is no longer an attribute, but a substance, and therefore it can very well renounce signs, since it carries its own nature within itself, and does not need to signal its identity outwardly: poetic language and prosaic language are sufficiently separate to be able to dispense with the very signs of their difference.[10]

It is precisely this naturalising of language that Auden's early poems refuse. By making it unpoetic and clinical, they actually problematise the status of their material. By producing obscurity and ambiguity, they question the notion that poetic language might have a substance. When Barthes continues his description of modernist poetry's attitude towards language, in *Writing Degree Zero* p. 53, with the shorthand formula 'the word in poetry can never be untrue, because it is a whole', the differences between this poetics and Auden's become strikingly evident. Auden's poems deny their material wholeness. Yet that does not mean that they devalue language. In fact, one could argue that the modernist procedure is the real devaluation, since it turns language into a mere appendix of metaphysical concepts, such as Nature, Reality, and Truth.

Jean-François Lyotard's description of postmodernism, on the other hand, corresponds much more closely to the features of Auden's early writings. In an essay provocatively entitled 'Answering the Question: What is Postmodernism?', he states:

> The postmodern would be that which, in the modern, puts forward the unpresentable in presentation itself; that which denies itself the solace of good forms, the consensus of a taste which would make it possible to share collectively the nostalgia for the unattainable; that which searches for new presentations, not in order to enjoy them but in order to impart a stronger sense of the unpresentable.[11]

In the subsequent analysis of the mechanisms and models of Auden's early poetry the rejection of 'good forms' and consensual taste as the nostalgia for unattainable metaphysical goals will be demonstrated. The search that Lyotard includes in a seemingly contradictory way in his above description will be encountered as a dominant theme of Auden's early works.

MECHANISMS

The dominant mode of arranging images in Auden's early poems is the list.[12] Mechanical parataxis can be observed in many instances, and the listing of items can be either completely playful or slyly meaningful. The second stanza of 'Half Way' (*CP* 67–8), a poem that shows the surreal instruction of a spy by what might be a collaborator as well as a mad person, for example, lists an annual camp for the Tutbury glass workers, the spy's bird-photography phase, his dream at the Hook, a winter in Prague, as well as his public refusal of a compass.

An example of vague symbolism is found in the following lines from 'The Question' (*CP* 58): 'Afraid/To remember what the fish ignored,/ How the bird escaped, or if the sheep obeyed'. One senses a possible symbolic significance, for instance, in the escape of the bird or the submissive sheep. Yet at the same time the complex (and indeed Freudian) thought experiment of 'Afraid/To remember' and the clearly nonsensical ignorance of the fish add an air of inscrutability

to the text. One also suspects a possible influence of Old English rid-
dles, a link reinforced by the poem's title. Yet as a question it has no
obvious answer. What a question without an answer does, however,
is attract attention to the power of language – not as an expression of
something, reality or a higher truth , but as an entity in its own right.

This claim of autonomy for language is the poem's ultimate stance
when it parodies the old schoolboy riddle 'What is black and white
and re(a)d all over?' The answer to the riddle is a page of writing or
a book. Writing is that which stresses the non-immediacy of language. It cannot establish a direct link with the world of things,
because it is itself part of this world. In its failure to establish a stable
connection between thought and reality, language reminds the
human being of the isolation and alienation that are the price of consciousness. This is what Auden's poem 'The Question' signals
through its very lack of an answer.

After calling the asking of the hard question simple, because it
represents the 'simple act of the confused will' (itself a rather confusing claim), the poem states that the answer is even harder and also
hard to remember. The reasons for this are elaborated in images –
strikingly enough – of words, which are listened to, yet which have
no definite meaning and might easily be forgotten. These are linked
with eyes and hands that are taught something whose significance
remains equally unclear. What this insecurity produces is regression
and nostalgia. Auden's version of the above schoolboy pun yearns
for 'What has been dark and rich and warm all over', and although
the poem names love as a possibility of recovering this almost pre-
natal wholeness and shelter, it presents the power of love not as a
certainty, but as a question, that of its title. It also shows its own nostalgia as dangerously coupled with ghosts, cowardice, and the
yearning for obedience and a master.[13] The alienation that Auden's
early poems describe not merely through but as a consequence of
language is never a mere personal anxiety: it also has clear ideological and political implications.

The list as a means of stressing the power of language and its alienating effect can take over entire poems, as in the already mentioned 'Get there if you can'. In 'Venus Will Now Say a Few Words'
(CP 49–50), it forms a very odd collection of advice for a prospective
lover. The central section of the poem embarks on an investigation
which is indeed not so much connected with love but again with
language. It discusses naming, writing, and the connection of language with culture and history. 'You in the town now call the exile

fool' introduces instantly the problems of adequate reference as well
as of the historicity of language. What the exile does (and what perhaps makes him a fool) is exactly writing, writing 'home once a year
as last leaves fall'. We have encountered the problem of a missing
'home' earlier in 'The Watershed'. Here the absence of this important reference point is coupled with the futility of establishing a connection with it, a link that is symbolised by writing.

Yet language is also that which guarantees identity and establishes
cultures. 'Think – Romans had a language in their day', the poem
continues and asks its addressee to acknowledge the importance of
language doubly: by referring to history and to the memory of it,
which is acquired by learning. Yet even though the Romans ordered
roads with their language, it eventually had to die – although not
quite: what history does to language is remind its users of the pri-
macy not of the spoken but the written word. What survives of the
language of the Romans is written Latin, as a dead and yet paradoxically influential language. The place-names that Auden's poem
mentions function in the same way, as a further argument together
with, significantly, jotttings for stories and references in letters. Not
unimportantly, it concludes its argument with the image of equip
ment, and although the connection of this line is unclear, it might
very well refer to the paradoxical autonomy of language as a tool. In
The Orators the list is eventually transformed to utmost abstraction
with encyclopaedic arrangements which are hardly identifiable as
poetry and compete with other 'unpoetic' devices, such as graphics and
prose sections. We will encounter these in more detail in Chapter 4.

Commenting on Auden's use of the list, William Logan identifies
certain characteristic features: precision, shading into a prissiness
which can amount to tyranny; a preference for *bon mots* instead of
the bon mot; and a cumulative rather than an integrative model of
imagination which notes with clerkly precision the inventory of experience in order to make it not only nameable, but an acquisition.[14]
But unlike Eliot's extended images which derive from an unspeak-
able centre of meaning, or Pound's layers of translation which illustrate the search for the correct expression and thus a distrust of
language, Auden's verbal acrobatics are not the expression of a
struggle against language, but rather an assault on the concept of a
firm reality underneath it. His early poems attack the belief in referents with that unlimited ammunition of language, signifiers.

In the poem 'No Change of Place' mentioned above, the second
stanza starts with the lines 'Metals run/Burnished or rusty in the

sun/From town to town' (*CP* 42). 'Metals' are, of course, rails; the *mot juste* is there, the signified is easily identifiable and not at all a difficult abstraction or a transcendental concept, but related to a concrete referent. The reluctance to use the proper term is the very foundation of poetry, but that explains Auden's transgression of the linguistic rules as little as blaming it on his intellectual ingenuousness which sometimes verges on flippancy. The much more serious motif underlying the excesses of his vocabulary (which in his later poetry leads to a menacing use of the *Oxford English Dictionary*)[15] has been described above as a stress on the autonomy of language and its potential as a tool rather than a link between concepts and reality.

One can be more precise and claim that Auden's early poems put their entire trust in signifiers. They exercise an important shift in language in modernity: the concept of the sign eventually ceases to function as the binary concept of the sign (the signifier/signified dichotomy as developed by Saussure). As an outcome of modernity, but also relativising many of its main assumptions, the signifier eventually becomes privileged over the signified. The signal achieves predominance, while concepts related to it are increasingly questioned and often abandoned. Jacques Derrida is the theorist whose works describe this shift most fully. In his seminal essay 'Structure, Sign and Play in the Discourse of the Human Sciences' he first historicises and then conceptualises human beliefs in origins and presence. Structure, he claims,

> or rather the structurality of structure – although it has always been at work, has always been neutralized or reduced, and this by a process of giving it a centre or of referring it to a point of presence, a fixed origin.[16]

The concept of centre and presence, Derrida claims, serves to fight the anxiety over what he calls the 'play' of the structure. This often-misunderstood term does not simply set up a binary opposition between order and anarchy; but refers to the transformations and creations of the material – themselves organised – out of which concepts are formed: language, in short. One of these transformations is, of course, the poetic function of language. When traditional views of poetry speak about poems creating a world of their own, we find in them the problem in a pre-theoretical nutshell. When this alternative world seriously questions the existence of a 'real' world or problematises its relation to it, we are faced with a poetics that privileges the signifier, questions the givenness of signifieds, and denies the simplistic belief in a link with objective referents. Derrida formulates this as an 'event' in the history of the concept of structure: 'The absence of the transcendental signified extends the domain and the play of signification indefinitely.'[17] This shift of emphasis on signification is one of the benchmarks of the concept of postmodernity.

Referents are indeed regarded with suspicion in Auden's early writings. Reality is at best a vague notion; often it completely gives way to surreal flux. This explains the constant vacillation of Auden's imagery between the abstract and the concrete, and the resulting difficulties of pinning down the meaning of his compound signifiers whose individual parts seem so easy to grasp at first sight. This farewell to a firm concept of a reality of origins and presences is by no means a voluntary or easy step. It entails the loss of traditions and securities, and its consequence is a lasting longing for replacements of this security, which is enacted in painful rituals and can easily be manipulated. One possible consequence, the craving for authority, has already been mentioned.

Closely connected with a distrust of reality is the second prominent mode of Auden's early works, the question. 'Who stands, the crux left of the watershed', 'Under boughs, between our tentative endearments, how should we hear', 'Will you turn a deaf ear', 'Which of you waking early and watching daybreak', 'Who will endure', and 'What's in your mind, my dove, my coney' are first lines of poems written before *The Orators*. There are many more questions, either explicit or rhetorical, to be found within the poems.

These initial questions shift the poems at once into the realm of the intellect. What they create is an explicitly anti-sensual, anti-Romantic and clinical imagination. Reality is constantly shown to be the playing-field of the mind, and this dominance of the intellect is as arrogant as it is painful in its solipsistic isolation. Even pseudo-naturalistic descriptions, such as the derelict mines in 'The Watershed', are depicted as mental landscapes, not so much those of a meditation, but of ruthless analysis. Intellect swallows all experience and transforms it into words, into signifiers. Any other grasp of reality seems impossible.

Time is the agent of this intellectual imagination. It distances event and perception, as in the early poem 'Under boughs between our tentative endearments' (*EA* 29), which couples a limited and un-romantic sensuality with unsettling images of 'drums distant over difficult country'. The events it alludes to as a threat to erotic fulfilment are labelled 'Events not actual/In time's unlenient will'. This apparently confusing explanation fits perfectly and, indeed, only makes sense as a further elaboration of the inextricable link of time and intellect – which now becomes so all-powerful as to dominate reality completely. It is even hostile towards the individual itself. The suffering that this all-powerful intellect causes the self is therefore self-inflicted.

This self-inflicted loss depicted in the text parallels that of Auden's texts as a whole. As has been explained above, on the level of textuality it is writing itself that creates distance between event and its representation.[18] Auden's poems are consequently the very cause of the loss they lament, creating the frontier from which they glance into a country they are forbidden to enter: reality. They are very well capable of seeing their dilemma and thematising it. Yet they cannot solve it. A poem later called 'The Secret Agent' (CP 41) talks about 'Control of the passes' leading to a 'new district', but cannot say who will get it. Its protagonist, 'the trained spy', is already caught in a trap, that of 'the old tricks'. Training and tricks are once more intimately linked with communication, conventions, and language.

As we have already noticed, there is no satisfaction to be found in the textuality of the poems either, since they are devoid of stable signifieds. Auden's early poems do not attempt to settle down in the imagination (as, for instance, Yeats's early poems attempt to do in their fairy-tale imagery). The uncomfortable borderline position is compulsory. A poem written in 1929 in which the enemy eventually turns out to be the lover or the self, or both, illustrates this predicament in images of 'Sentries against inner and outer' and an equally confusing, desperate question of 'how shall enemy on these/Make sudden raid or lasting peace?' (EA 33).

The vocabulary of Auden's early poems turns increasingly martial. The conflict within them is indeed a violent one, that between being and not-being, reality and fiction. The effect of the liminal position on the identity of the speakers in the poems will be analysed below; but some of the more obvious consequences are easily pointed out: an ever increasing feeling of meaninglessness is created and a growing conviction that action is necessary to fight it – albeit without any firm ideas about where to start and what to do. The refrain of one of Auden's early imitations of music hall songs, 'It's no use raising a shout', summarises these impasses neatly: 'But what does it all mean? What are we going to do?' (EA 42–3).

The feeling that action is urgently required is unquestionably related to the many imperatives which seem to address the reader as directly as the questions in Auden's early poems. 'Watch any day his nonchalant pauses, see' (*CP* 46), 'Consider this and in our time' (*CP* 61), 'Get there if you can and see the land you were once proud to own' (*EA* 48), and 'Look there! The sunk road winding' (*CP* 53) are typical first lines. But with the exception of the ironic short poem which begins with 'Pick a quarrel, go to war' (*EA* 50), all these directives do not really encourage action, but rather again observation and reflection. Once more, though trying to break out of their textuality by a direct appeal to the external entity of the reader, the poems end up trapped in their own imagery and therefore also in language. Directives as well as questions remind the reader of the power of language. Consequently, the imperatives can be taken, even at this early stage, as symptoms of a susceptibility to authoritarianism, especially the schoolboy discipline and routines which can be detected in so many of Auden's early poems.

MODELS

The virtuosity of Auden's poetry, its use of many distinct traditions and allusions to a plethora of poetic models, is closely linked with the desperation over the suspicion that meaning and reality as firm reference points have vanished. It becomes possible to say things in so many different ways, because there is really nothing to be said. Auden's celebrated 'spongelike nature of imagination'[19] has kept critics busy trying to find possible influences. Edward Mendelson lists Wordsworth, Walter de la Mare, W. H. Davies, and A. E. [George William Russell] as models for Auden's earliest writings, then Thomas Hardy and Edward Lear, Housman, Robert Frost, and Emily Dickinson, until all of these were eclipsed by Auden's discovery of Eliot in 1926.[20] The summary is, of course, far from complete and should also include Hopkins and Yeats for Auden's early stages, while it is almost impossibile to compile for his later works.

Despite this long list (Auden would probably have enjoyed turning it into a poem), his poetry is not at all derivative. When a model is employed, it is generally used consciously and in most cases with an obvious critical or parodistic intention. Auden's extraordinary versatility lends itself easily to parody, but even when no identifiable model is in the background and the poems merely use traditional techniques, such as the alliterations and kennings of Old English poetry, the sonnet, or even the naughty schoolboy two- and four-liners, there is always a distance between form and imagery. This creates a permanent tension in the poems which can ultimately be referred back to the distrust of meaning. The very formal variety thereby helps to relativise or even discredit the messages that are apparently conveyed.

The schoolboy ditties, for example, are always much more serious and ambiguous under their obscene disguise than the form can easily tolerate. 'Schoolboy making lonely maps:/Better do it with some chaps', for instance, puns on the ambiguous 'it' and enjoys its sheer naughtiness (*EA* 50). None the less, a more serious note is struck by the rather curious 'lonely maps', one of Auden's evasive images. In the context of those of Auden's early poems which deal with land-scapes and their overview by an isolated observer, the silly two-liner becomes a self-reflection of Auden's poetry, a hint at the aims and impasses concealed under surface frivolity. Once more, this discovery of a lack is coupled with the paradoxical imperative: act!

The unrhymed sonnet 'The Secret Agent' previously mentioned is equally awkward (*CP* 41). While conforming to the conventions of setting up a situation or argument in the two quartets, the final sestet is anything but a solution. More like a vision, it hovers between two entirely opposed settings ('The street music' and 'the desert'/ 'the dark') and themes, namely the desired lover and the expected death.[21] Auden's 'Anglo-Saxon' poems introduce concepts whose challenging modernity contrasts strangely with the heavily form-alised language of their historic models. 'Doom is dark and deeper than any sea-dingle', later named after its model 'The Wanderer', for instance, contains the line 'Of new men making another love' (*CP* 62).

One of Auden's early poems that foregrounds the problem of poetic form in a particularly obvious manner is another sonnet, an imitation of Gerard Manley Hopkins's 'Thou art indeed just, Lord': 'Sir, no man's enemy, forgiving all' (*EA* 36). Hopkins's poem is an anxious appeal to God to change the barrenness in the life of the speaker, though it also conveys overtones of a rather aggressive complaint, even an accusation. Its form is the prayer. God – addressed as 'Lord', 'lord of life', and, astonishingly, 'Sir' – remains nondescript; the text carefully avoids familiarity while anxiously trying to reach intimacy.

Auden's poem adopts the characteristic address 'Sir' and the prayer form, but this is already the end of the apparent similarities.

In Auden's poem the addressee is already clearly defined in the first two lines: 'Sir, no man's enemy, forgiving all/But will his negative inversion, be prodigal'. The description is so limiting and directive that it sets the tone for the rest of the poem, which therefore becomes not so much an appeal as an order. Since the addressed force is sympathetic or at least not hostile to all men, all-forgiving except for the negative inversion of the will (whatever that may be), it can hardly deny the request anyway.

The curiously inverted syntax of the second line, which makes understanding the poem quite difficult, might be another echo of Hopkins' style. It perhaps also signals the influence of German on Auden's writing (Auden lived in Berlin at the time of the poem's composition; the grammatical construction is common in colloquial German). The appeal 'be prodigal', with its connotations of guilt, supports the impression that the 'Sir' of the poem is obliged to the speaker anyway. His desired response is almost a recompense. The demands, however, are rather odd. The speaker demands 'power and light' as well as 'a sovereign touch/Curing the intolerable neural itch'. Modern terminology and a characteristically clinical 'neural itch' meet archaic beliefs and their vocabulary.

Power and light are, of course, the traditional requisites of strength and illumination. In connection with the technical terms of the second line, the 'negative inversion', they appear in an almost futuristic light, as if the archaic aims had found their current representation in electricity.[22] The 'sovereign touch' then shifts the image back into the past, when this very touch was supposed to cure scrofula.[23] The 'intolerable neural itch' which takes the place of the disease in Auden's poem is a circumscription of sexual desire. Unlike Hopkins' poem, which asks to be freed from it, Auden's remains highly ambiguous. Taken as a pun, the 'sovereign touch' could well mean sexual activity, the two lines then forming a request for satisfaction. Together with the subsequent line featuring 'the distortions of ingrown virginity', and in the context of the whole of Auden's works, in which sex is usually regarded as a positive force, this appears more likely than a wish to be redeemed from desire.

The first lines of the poem contain several examples of a dominant mode of imagery in Auden's poems, images in which a psychological state is projected onto the body in the form of a psychosomatic illness ('the intolerable neural itch', 'The exhaustion of weaning', 'the liar's quinsy', 'the distortions of ingrown virginity'). The psychological state, however, is itself a symbol of a more general situation. All the illnesses which appear in the poem are preceded by a definite article, but are attached to no particular person, not even the speaker: 'The exhaustion of weaning', for instance, showing that the state that needs altering applies to an entire generation, the younger generation as opposed to that of the mothers. The poem operates in Freudian terms by indicating that the necessary emancipation from the mother lies at the heart of the problem.

The 'liar's quinsy' pushes the equation between psychological disposition and physical health even further. To understand this apparently nonsensical term correctly one has to know that in the late 1920s Auden was strongly influenced by the psychological doctrines of John Layard, who taught a very simplistic theory of psychosomatic illnesses which for example, related lying with sore throats and repressed creativity with cancer. Layard's theories in turn derived from Homer Lane, whose ideas can be traced back to Freud and Groddeck.[24] It is rather futile to discuss the extent of Auden's allegiance to these teachings. Undoubtedly, they procured images that suited his clinical perception; but, like all his other models, they are not spared criticism and ridicule. In the above poem, the idea that a clinging to virginity can produce distortions seems plausible. Its description as ingrown like a toenail, however, is both sordid and incongruous. Despite its serious form, the poem manages to undermine its own gravity constantly.

The subsequent four lines then display a significant change of tone. The merciful healer of the first six lines is transformed into an authority (the strict schoolmaster is once more not far away) who prohibits and corrects. He is asked to forbid 'the rehearsed response' and to 'correct the coward's stance' gradually. Eventually he appears in the shape of a searchlight from a watchtower that discovers cowards and forces them to emerge and fight. Edward Mendelson rightly hints at the discrepancy between the idea of healing through overcoming one's repressions and the desire for a restrictive authority expressed in the central part of the poem.[25] Even more important is the dilemma displayed in the lines 'Prohibit sharply the rehearsed response/And gradually correct the coward's stance'. The poem, itself an exercise in undermining and discrediting a traditional form, argues against all forms of rehearsed response. Yet by asking for prohibition, it introduces its own distinction between right and wrong, legal and illegal. The problem is highlighted in the correction of 'the coward's stance'. In order to correct, there must be a norm. But norms are exactly what the poem abhors.

Consequently, the rest of the poem hovers rather uneasily between pathos and meaninglessness, this time not consciously employed and thus paradoxically meaningful, but rather a sign of a badly digested intellectual concept that has backfired and left a seriously tumbling poem. Already the heroic action demanded by those in retreat has a hollow ring, because it lacks direction and goal. The last four lines of the poem mix obscure private references with slogans. They are the textual equivalent of aimlessly attacking soldiers spotted when already in retreat, and indicate a poem defeated by its own lack of logic.

In a kind of infantile regression, the poem then refers to its own origin. The great healer has now become a publisher; his power is required to support an unspecified number of healers, miniature versions of the addressed authority who emerge from him like Russian dolls via their books or pamphlets. The power that is addressed is once more the power of the written word; but this time it is this very force which fails in the poem. The description of the abode of the healers is perhaps a private reference; undoubtedly it is so unspecified as to be meaningless. The poem lapses back into a private code after having started as a universal analysis. The final lines exhibit an even more serious lapse: traditional religious language crops up again, this time not in ironic shape, but as an attempt at a serious culmination of the poem's argument: 'Harrow the house of the dead; look shining at/New styles of architecture, a change of heart'.

This pretended argumentative climax remains hollow, though. Although the biblical 'house of the dead' is also very likely an allusion to the world of the older generation from which the healer is asked to rescue the younger ones in the same way as Christ rescues the souls from death, it is not at all evident why there should be a difference between the young and the old. They are shown as equally passive and dead. This passivity contradicts the poem's energetic tone. Who is the speaker who claims authority for the requests that he makes in the name of an entire generation? Is he not part of it, and if he is, where does his energy come from, when the rest of his generation is so utterly passive?

The answers to these discrepancies remain as open as the images of the poem's finale are empty. Though a rhetorically pleasant contrast between modern term and religious phrase, the juxtaposition does not quite work. There are many very different new styles of architecture. 'New' does not signify anything in itself. Neither does 'a change of heart', if there is only a contradictory and collapsing ideal available as a replacement for the old.

Auden's early poems set themselves a goal that is impossible to reach. In their questioning and constant undermining of certainties, they grant language an autonomy that frees it from the metaphysical enslavement to concepts of the Real and the True. At the same time, this radicalism threatens to make Auden's early works impotent when it comes to tackling questions which are generated by the very prominence of these metaphysical concepts in everyday life. It also reinforces the alienation that spawns the poetic detachment in the first place, and, by making language independent from the Real, also separates the self from traditional attachments. This is not experienced as a liberation, but rather as a loss, and the curious responses that it produces are nostalgia, regression, and the desire for authority. We will re-encounter this conflict between an aesthetic stance that I would call postmodern *avant la lettre*, and psychological and ideological positions in dramatic form in Auden and Isherwood's early dramatic works, in the next chapter.

3
Libidinous Charades: The Auden-Isherwood Plays

PAID AND BOUGHT BY BOTH SIDES

When Auden's first properly published collection, *Poems*, appeared in 1930, it was prefaced by a short verse play called *Paid on Both Sides*. The piece had previously appeared in *The Criterion* in January of the same year, through T. S. Eliot's enthusiastic patronage. John Fuller calls the play 'a major influence on English poetic drama of the 'thirties', and places it alongside Eliot's *Sweeney Agonistes*. Yet at the same time he acknowledges that it owes little to Eliot, and concedes that the play has rarely been performed.[1]

The play has indeed little to offer to entice readers and possible producers. It is both annoyingly simplistic in its use of the most traditional of plots, the tragic love story between two members of hostile families à la *Romeo and Juliet*, and exaggeratedly complex when it heaps onto this clichéd structure elements of Icelandic sagas, Old English poetry (its title is already a reference to *Beowulf*: *Pl* p. xvi), Marxism, and Freudianism. Its dramatic elements include echoes of the music hall, Christmas pantomimes and mummers' play as well as the dream sequences beloved by German Expressionism and French Surrealism. Consequently, critics have tended to either give the text short shrift or attempted to hijack one of its features for a one-sided interpretation, most commonly a Marxist or psychoanalytic one.

Yet the central position as a preface to Auden's early works should attract attention to the elements that *Paid on Both Sides* shares with Auden's early poems. Its very title introduces the borderline that divides factions, generations, and also lovers: here, the ancient feud between the Nowers and the Shaws, whose origins are as obscure as its cause.[2] Yet it also problematises the division at the same time: there is no one side or another, but the split doubles everyone and everything (the play explicitly asks for some parts to be doubled, too). It undermines positions as well as identities, and makes both equally inauthentic and treacherous. This is clearly the dramatic equivalent of the figures of spy and secret agent in so many of Auden's early poems, who are themselves the dark mirror-images of heroes, leaders, and airmen.

The 'Paid' of the title adds a further aspect to the divisive doubling: it signals that this is not a Romantic conflict or a metaphysical struggle of good against evil. On the contrary, the materialistic implications of 'Paid' alert the reader to the fact that the division is based on economic principles. In fact, there is no obvious paid traitor in the play at all; the term refers to the entire cast of characters, who are shown as equally entangled in a setting from which they profit, but which eventually controls them rather than being mastered by them.

The charade that forms the subtitle of the play is therefore an appropriate label for the play as well as a further complication. It seemingly removes the epic issues of the play onto the familiar domestic plane of a house party. Yet it also alerts to duplicity and internal strife as inherent features of middle-class existence. The symbolically charged setting of the play on Christmas Eve doubles this effect cunningly, Christmas being the time when charades are traditionally enacted, but also the time of Christ's birth as the saviour of mankind and the beginning of something new. Once again, a metaphysical concept of origin and presence becomes subjected to a play. But this play is hardly without rules, since it happens inside the conventions of both Englishness and the middle class. The 'new' that is so much a fetish in the writings of the 1930s as well as in Auden's early works is radically subjected to the deadening influence of tradition in Paid on Both Sides. The play begins and ends not with a rebirth, but with a death. John, born prematurely after his mother receives news of the murder of her husband, consequently inherits the family feud between the Nowers and the Shaws unwittingly. In fact, he becomes a travesty of Christ, 'an infirm king' (Pl 16).

There are no authentic positions in the play. Every personality is already predetermined by an epic plot that is beyond anyone's control. Self clearly becomes text, and a text that is not original, but the intertextual derivative of a pre-existing one. The Shaws and Nowers are primarily members of a clan whose identities are indicated as well as constituted by 'different coloured arm-bands' (Pl 14). In symbolic terms, they are ghosts from the start, since the play merely re-enacts the same tragedy over and over again: 'Dangerous new ghosts; new ghosts learn from many' (*Pl* 15). Learning in the play is mere initiation. It does not lead to individuality, but to conformity; a pattern that we will re-encounter in *The Orators*.

Consequently, it does not matter whether the plot of *Paid on Both Sides* concerns itself with strategies of outwitting the other party or discusses rugby teams and Christmas presents. In the surrealist equation that it sets up, war is the guiding metaphor, and it can be found in the microcosms of family and public school as well as in partisan warfare. All three have rules to which individuals are subjected, but which also guarantee individuality in a perverse double bind. Indeed, every individual of the play is 'paid' and 'bought' at the same time.

In a vague symbolism, names also determine personality. While the Nowers enlist Germanic-sounding characters (Walter, Kurt, Zeppel), some members of the Shaw clan have Jewish-sounding names (Aaron and Seth). When Auden wrote the play in Berlin in 1928, the increasing display of anti-Semitism must have provided plenty of material for such symbolic distinctions. The surnames, too, smack of symbolism. While the archaic meaning of 'shaw', thicket or copse, might not be too far-fetched for a faction that specialises in ambush and represents the static forces in the play, John Nower, the tragic hero who wants to break out of the vicious circle of killing and revenge, literally has 'nowhere' to go. Already the name of John's mother, 'Joan', which sounds uncannily similar to that of her son, indicates that there are links that are unbreakable, if deadly. Since identities are predetermined by inheritance, and learning only reinforces tradition, any attempt to break out of both must end in the loss of self and place. Far from presenting a free play of signification, the play sets up a deadly play of tradition, yet, paradoxically, through an emphasis on signifiers.

When John Nower reflects on his predicament, he sees that 'Always the following wind of history/Of others' wisdom makes a buoyant air' (*Pl* 21). History both persecutes the individual, and elevates it to the plane of established sense, 'others' wisdom'. The loss of this second-hand wisdom (Derrida's concept of origin) creates a vacuum: 'Till we come suddenly on pockets where/Is nothing loud but us; where voices seem/Abrupt, untrained, competing with no lie' (*Pl* 21). Far from opening up the space for the creation of something new and original, as apparently achieved in the undoing of tradition in Romanticism and also in modernism with its emphasis on avant-garde and *tabula rasa*, here the loss of the old lie takes away any point of orientation and comparison.

This is the predicament of the 'new' and the dilemma of a new aesthetic, one that consciously rejects holistic ideals and refrains from setting itself up as autonomous, but which instead emphasises its entanglement in many previous narratives. In short, it is the dilemma of a budding postmodernist aesthetics and poetics, which sheds overarching master narratives (including that of its own unlimited authority) at the expense of acknowledging its debt to many reduced narratives.[3] It remains historically aware by refusing to write its own history as truth. Instead it writes stories, even though the price it pays is the obvious loss of totalising control over its many strands of plot. The loss of mastery of existence throws the individual into a crisis: 'O how shall man live/Whose thought is born, child of one farcical night,/To find him old?' (*Pl* 22), asks the Chorus. Indeed, the awareness of this predicament makes the individual unfit for life, as the eventual killing of John Nower demonstrates. But halfway through the play, the surreal trial and eventual execution of a spy who has no other name or identity but that of being Seth Shaw's brother (again, traditional family ties override individuality) already provide an arena for the debate of the dilemma.

First Father Christmas enters the play as an unlikely judge. Already his introduction to the audience sheds light on the double position of inclusion and exclusion in the surreal use that *Paid on Both Sides* makes of tradition: after a conventional address to his audience, he asks them to tell their friends about what is to follow and even 'bring the kiddies', yet at the same time urges them to keep it secret. His little speech attracts further attention to the double nature of the war in the play, both intimate and public, and places the audience as well as its characters on 'both sides'. The aim is to achieve Auden's dramatic ideal: 'Ideally there should be no spectators. In practice every member of the audience should feel like an understudy.'[4] This is hardly a comfortable position in a play in which the two sides are inseparable and engaged in a bloody feud.

In a manner that prefigures Beckett's plays, the trial introduces two witnesses, Bo and Po, whose names already signal that they are as faceless as they are interchangeable. None the less, they argue two contradicting positions. First Bo talks in favour of abandoning the past; yet the means he suggests for this are difficult and even frightening: 'By loss of memory we are reborn,/For memory is death'

(*Pl* 22). A little later he advocates the use of a 'strange tongue'. The suggested separation from the past is only possible through an abandoning of identity which rests once more on signification. Yet the 'strange tongue' that acts as a self-reflection on Auden's poetic technique is a highly dubious concept. Language is itself established through tradition and learning, the two elements of the deadening past that the play actively seeks to reject. We will re-encounter the problem of the 'truly new' in the chapter on history below.

Po, on the other hand, speaks in the tongue of this very tradition. 'Past victory is honour' (*Pl* 23) is his introductory statement, and quite predictably his speech leads via images of an 'island governor-ship' and 'estates/Explored as a child' to the word 'son', which en-capsulates the intrinsic problem of tradition as both private and public. In an obviously Freudian way, this son is '*her* loving son' [my emphasis]. It is the mothers who provide identity, but who also keep the war of the play – which is the implicit war within family and society – alive. As a consequence, the identity that tradition promises in Po's speech is that of a soft burial in snowflakes.[5] Po's vision of belonging is as unproductive and eventually lethal as Bo's ideas of departure and rejection are illusory.

The spy, who has already been threatened with a symbolic feed-ing bottle, consequently groans under these impossible alternatives as if under torture. When a truly surreal figure, that of the Man-Woman, appears 'as a prisoner of war behind barbed wire', his pains increase. The Man-Woman is an inheritance from the folk tradition of the Mummers' Play; but s/he also represents the androgyny and bisexuality featured in many of the psychoanalytic theories that fas-cinated Auden. The merger of feminine and masculine was the linchpin of many theories of homosexuality and sexual deviance advocated in the early twentieth century (Magnus Hirschfeld's con-cept of the 'third sex' is perhaps the most prominent of these). S/he further corresponds to Freud's concept of the phallic mother, the fantasy that helps the child overcome castration anxiety. But just as much as symbolic castration is the prerequisite for identity in Freud's Oedipal model, the Man-Woman in *Paid on Both Sides* can neither heal nor stand outside the feud (this is what his/her status as prisoner indicates). 'Because I'm come it does not mean to hold/An anniversary, think illness healed' (*Pl* 23) are his/her introductory remarks.

The healing s/he fails to achieve is desired and feared at the same time. The Man-Woman appears because s/he is 'Hearing you call for what you did not want'. The healing s/he could offer leads through acting ('Lastly I tried/To teach you acting'), which accepts self and possibly gender as performance in a way that prefigures Judith Butler's ideas, but also reflects back on the charade of which this utterance is part, and to the play with its own rules.[6] But the eventual wholeness that might be achieved in this way is one that neither knows joy nor tolerates an utterance: 'No, you, if you come,/Will not enjoy yourself, for where I am/All talking is forbidden' (*Pl* 24). Lack of fulfilment is indeed shown in these cryptic remarks as the very starting-point of language – and thus of identity. In the same way as self and deadening tradition cannot be disentangled, writing is triggered by the very lack it laments and tries to overcome. 'I can't bear it,' exclaims John Nower as a consequence, and shoots the spy. Yet by shooting him, he also propels forward both the plot of *Paid on Both Sides* and his own end.

In the same way as the characters of the play cannot break out of the feud that guarantees their identities, their self-analyses remain entangled in the tautologies and repetitive loops of its epic plot. The Doctor is another surreal figure in *Paid on Both Sides* whose presence is desired as much as it is feared. 'Ten pounds for a doctor./Ten pounds to keep him away' shouts a chorus of unidentified voices after the spy's wounding (*Pl* 24). After a surreal declaration that lists as the diseases that he can cure serious as well as ridiculous-sounding ones that are none the less symbolic of middle-class existence, namely 'Tennis elbow, Graves' Disease, Derbyshire neck and Housemaid's knees' (*Pl* 24), the Doctor comes up with the strangest illness of all, when he claims that he has discovered the origin of life.

Life itself turns out to be the cause of the conflicts of existence; escape becomes impossible. This is emphasised once more when the Doctor 'treats' the wounded spy. The treatment consists of the removal of an enormous tooth. 'This tooth,' the Doctor declares, 'was growing ninety-nine years before his great grandmother was born. If it hadn't been taken out to-day he would have died yesterday' (*Pl* 25). The problems of existence are part and parcel of life itself – and escape is only possible in death, and perhaps not even there, since even then it takes a further absurd operation to remove the past from the individual, a past that kills even before death.

In *Paid on Both Sides* it is the mothers who win, as the text itself declares. While Anne Shaw urges her lover John Nower to leave, he decides to stay. One could see this as a repetition of the positions outlined earlier by Bo and Po: Anne would then follow Bo's ideal of starting afresh and migrating, yet John would not merely replicate Po's acceptance of tradition, but seek to work out something new inside the old. Reform rather than rupture would be his ideal. Yet this is undermined by the mothers: Anne's mother urges her son Seth to avenge the death of her other son, and the wedding consequently turns into a bloodbath that leaves Anne in the same position as John Nower's mother at the start of the play. The scene is set for a further round of repetition.

Paid on Both Sides presents no viable concept of how to reconcile tradition and self, past and present, in order to design a future that is more than a repetition of the past. Yet while its complex 'message' is indeed the same as that of many circular modernist plays, its techniques of reflecting back on its enclosure, and its use of contradictory and indeed anarchic means, undermine its coherence significantly. A play in which Father Christmas acts as a prison guard, and in which a doctor who specialises in the healing of middle-class symptoms declares death to be the effect of tradition, sits uneasily with a pretended genteel setting as a Christmas charade. In a similar vein, its gory plot is punctuated by classist remarks, such as those of the Chief Guest, 'Will any lady be so kind as to oblige us with a dance?' (*Pl* 32), when it is exactly the 'ladies' who trigger brutal action. The simultaneously immature and serious character of *Paid on Both Sides* make it an irritating, but also challenging play to present-day audiences and readers.

DANCES WITH MARXISM

After the experimental start of Auden's career as a playwright (due to the fact that performing *Paid on Both Sides* could hardly have been considered outside a private circle of friends), he faced a more pragmatic challenge when he was commissioned to write a play for Rupert Doone's recently founded Group Theatre in 1932. *The Dance of Death* once again mixes genres freely. As its title indicates, it contains elements of ballet – but it also refers to the music-hall tradition, signalled by a jazz band on stage and actors planted as hecklers in the audience. The dancer of the play is clearly an embodiment of the death-wish of the middle class, a sentiment whose complexity and overwhelming power had been ably if complexly demonstrated by *Paid on Both Sides*. It is also evoked, albeit more implicitly, by the title's allusion to one of August Strindberg's

plays, where this struggle is manifest in the private sphere of an
unhappy marriage.

Unlike *Paid on Both Sides*, however, *The Dance of Death* seems to
refrain from multi-dimensional and self-contradicting messages. In
fact, it verges on sermonising and propaganda in many sections. Its
beginning already seems to give the game away, when the Announcer's very first declaration is 'We present you this evening a picture
of the decline of a class', and the Chorus replies 'Middle class' (*Pl* 83).
In an equally didactic vein, the play then shows typical fads of the
early twentieth century, such as the craze for sunbathing and physical exercise and the cult of youth, as easily exploited by politics,
when the Dancer steals the sunbathers' clothes and replaces them
with uniforms. When the play apparently announces a revolutionary working-class uprising, its sinister Announcer has little trouble
in manipulating the many personal motives for the revolt for his
own openly racist and totalitarian ends. After seeming to speak the
language of socialism ('We must have an English revolution suited
to English conditions, a revolution not to put one class on top but to
abolish class, to ensure not less for some but more for all,' *Pl* 91), he
steers his assertions into nationalist and racist territory ('a revolution
of Englishmen for Englishmen [...] Our duty is to keep the race
pure, and not let those dirty foreigners come in and take our jobs,'
Pl 91).

The crowd he addresses responds by voicing their individual
egotistic interests. The farmer wants higher pices by excluding foreign competition; a girl resents the attraction of foreign countries to
young men; a former Black and Tan misses the violence he is accus-
tomed to; and the unemployed person is willing to follow anyone
who promises money. The first action that follows these declarations
is the beating of the supposedly Jewish theatre manager. Abstract
ideals (and this includes currently fashionable Socialist ones) are
drastically shown as a disguise for petty motifs, and their apparent
achievement happens through the very traditional picking on a
scapegoat.

The play continues with more references to the corruption of the
English class system. When the Dancer collapses, a 'Sir Edward' per-
suades a doctor to give him a strengthening injection rather than
stopping the performance. The analogy used by the doctor is that of
a run-down business, and Sir Edward advises to 'pump in fresh capital' (*Pl* 95). The parable could not be clearer: English middle-class
society is on its last legs, only kept alive through economic injustice.

Its dance is a dance of death. The play eventually concludes with the entrance of the figure of Karl Marx to the tune of Mendelssohn's 'Wedding March'. After being hailed as the great analyst of society who 'know[s] the economic/Reasons for our acts', Marx declares the dancer 'liquidated'. 'The instruments of production have been too much for him' (*Pl* 107).

If the play is ultimately saved from one-dimensional didacticism, it is through the figure of death as a dancer itself. He is presented in a variety of diverging and indeed contradictory roles. He is not merely the embodiment of the bourgeois death-wish, but also combines Auden's favourite figures of leader and heroic saviour, before he eventually becomes a sacrificial scapegoat. If the play aims at describing symbolically the death-throes of the bourgeoisie, then its description is itself deeply immersed in bourgeois traditions, the choice of ballet being one of them. It is also far from clear where the liquidation of bourgeois values will lead. Even though the Dancer leaves the privileges and property of the middle class to the working class in a poetic will that is counterpointed with the history of Western civilization as one of the rise and fall of ruling classes, the Announcer-turned-dictator promises as bleak a future as the Dancer's miraculous turning of civilian clothes into uniforms. Marx's laconic pronouncement of the Dancer's liquidation prepares the way for an equally problematic line in Auden's later poem 'Spain 1937' which talks about a 'necessary murder'. Neither proves convincing, not even to Auden himself, who declares in a remark he scribbled into a friend's copy of *The Dance of Death*, 'The communists never spotted that this was a nihilistic leg-pull' (*Pl* xxi). Contrary to *Paid on Both Sides*, from which Auden lifted what he obviously considered the most successful sections, no parts of *Dance of Death* are reprinted in his *Collected Poems* or his *Collected Shorter Poems*.

The Dog Beneath the Skin, or, Where is Francis?, Auden's second play for the Group Theatre, is more obviously multidimensional than *Dance of Death*, as can already be glimpsed from its rather confusing title – which alludes to a line about 'the skull beneath the skin' in Eliot's poem 'Whispers of Immortality'. The plot of the play matches its surrealism: in the imaginary English village of Pressan Ambo the heir of a local squire has disappeared. Alan Norman (already in name the embodiment of Englishness) is chosen to search for him. A large dog joins him and at the end of the play turns out to be the heir, Sir Francis Crewe, in disguise.

The obvious joke of the play is its juggling with concepts of class: the upper-class heir literally becomes the underdog, and he learns a number of things about society in the process. The action shifts from one allegorical scene to another. Accompanied by two cynical journalists, Alan and the dog visit the corrupt monarchy of Ostnia. There the king himself executes revolutionaries, as part of a genteel ritual during which he declares (similar to the Announcer in *The Dance of Death*): 'Believe me, I sympathise with your aims from the bottom of my heart. Are we not all socialists nowadays?' (*Pl* 214). After a visit to the Red Light District of the Ostnian capital with gratuitous glimpses at hetero- and homosexual prostitution and sly nods in the direction of the seedier side of Berlin that Auden knew personally, the search party enters the totalitarian state of Westland. There, Alan finds himself locked in a lunatic asylum. The world of the lunatics, however, does not differ much from the totalitarian regime outside, controlled by a figure called 'Our Leader'. On the contrary, it merely magnifies the mechanisms and effects of totalitarianism by demonstrating that the effects of ideological manipulation on its patients are exactly the same as the responses of the so-called 'normal' majority outside the institution. Once again, psychology becomes the symbol of politics.

After being freed by the journalists and the dog, the group travels back to England, where Alan first resists material temptation embodied by a financier and then learns to be critical of more personal forms of temptation, such as the solipsism of a young poet and two lovers whom he encounters in the tellingly named 'Paradise Park', a mixture of park and hospital garden. There he also meets an earlier quester for the lost heir, who eventually loses his life at the hands of a surgeon, when the dog dons the mask of a probationer doctor and makes the nurse administer poison instead of life-saving adrenalin. This scene is followed by another symbolic interlude, in which Alan's feet enact a debate about the British class structure, the Right Foot assuming the cultured voice of the middle class, the Left Foot speaking in a cockney accent.

The scene is one of Isherwood's contributions.[7] Isherwood also prevented the play from becoming even more chaotic than it now appears by insisting on cutting a sub-plot involving escaped Reformatory boys dressed in dogskin and drag, which featured in the version called *The Chase* in which the play first reached Faber & Faber (*Pl* 109–87). Although straightened, *The Dog Beneath the Skin* still presents a wild intertextual and contextual mixture which merges recycled elements from Auden's earlier works (and those of others) with contemporary politics, such as the rumour that the wife of the Austrian chancellor Dollfuss took cakes to the widows of executed Socialists.[8] As such it is none the less strangely appropriate as a play about the confusions of identities and an assessment of contemporary British culture – both from the inside of its traditional emblem, the village, and its not-so-different 'outside' of thinly disguised European politics.

The last station of the quest consequently takes Alan and the dog to the aptly named Nineveh Hotel, a place with all the trappings of a Babylonian society on the brink of collapse. A cabaret is performed, in which a nationalistic anthem (cunningly entitled 'Rhondda Moon' and thereby evoking industrial decline rather than patriotic pride) is followed by a self-critical song and dance act, the Nineveh Girls, that stresses the objectification of women in entertainment. To complement the picture of a culture about to die of oversaturation, a figure called 'Destructive Desmond' then ruins a Rembrandt painting for the cheering audience. Eventually, Miss Lou Vipond, 'The star of whom the world is fond!' (*Pl* 266), appears and effortlessly seduces Alan. Even though Lou is nothing but a shop-window dummy given speech by Alan himself, he sacrifices his mission and a great deal of money for his vision of love. In the same way as culture (in the image of the destroyed painting), the individual ultimately brings about his own downfall. Tellingly enough, the only remedies also derive from 'within' – and they take the twin shapes of the old: authority and tradition. It takes the threat of prison (following the discovery that he is unable to pay his bills) and the dog identifying itself as the lost heir to bring Alan back to reality.

Yet before the dog decides to give up his disguise, another crucial symbolic scene is enacted. The skin of the dog has a long and detailed monologue in which it describes its history. It used to belong to a famous author of 'virile' poetry who suffered from indigestion and guilt at the sacrifice of young men during the First World War while 'the sedentary and learned [...] are the assassins' (*Pl* 273). What posed a crucial ethical challenge for much modernist writing (Pound's *Hugh Selwyn Mauberley* is a telling example) and, of course, the War Poets, of whom Auden admired Owen in particular,[9] now becomes a mere ridiculous cliché. Ostensibly talking to the clock, Auden's author describes human beings as tied up in images and ideas: 'pictures mean more to him than people'. 'Too many ideas in their heads!' (*Pl* 274). This is an attack directed towards art as escapism, here from social and political responsibility. Yet the choice of the skin as a transitional object also shows once more the influence of psychoanalysis on Auden's thinking. The skin is another symbol on which the problems of society, culture, and politics are inscribed. The only subtle difference to the psychosomatic symbolic bodies of Auden's earlier poetry is that the skin is already detached and dead – and can perhaps be shed, just like outdated literary conventions.

That things are not so simple, and that a binary opposition of new and old in literature and the arts as well as society and politics is questionable, becomes clear when Francis, the heir, eventually returns to the village. There he encounters what amounts to a domestic version of a fascist demonstration, complete with youth groups, uniforms, and banners. Another opposition crumbles: that between the safe conservatism of rural England and dangerous European politics. Without knowing the background of the movement, the first journalist none the less manages to summarise its underlying ideology: 'Standing outside all political parties and factions, for Church, King and State, against communism, terrorism, pacifism and other forms of international anarchy, to protect Religion and succour England in time of national crisis', because, as the second journalist adds: 'It's the usual, er . . . programme' (Pl 574).

Francis responds with a speech in which he describes his personal observations of the master–slave relationship between social superiors and inferiors that is only thinly disguised in their everyday relations. He reminds the villagers of existing social divisions and tells them that they are part of an ongoing struggle, the class struggle. But surprisingly enough, he decides to fight on the side of his traditional class enemies, that of communism. The villagers and the pinnacles of their community, the General and his wife, the Vicar, and Miss Iris Crewe, Francis' sister, suddenly appear in animal masks, thus prefiguring the later allegory of Orwell's Animal Farm.

That this finale was a little too simplistic to be convincing was proved by the impossibility of staging it successfully. While the class-struggle version was the one printed by Faber in 1935, the concluding scene was rewritten for the Group Theatre production of January 1936 (Pl 566). In the revised finale the heir is killed by a hysterical woman, Mildred Luce, after uncovering that her pathological hatred of Germans for killing her two sons is based on a lie. She never had sons, but was briefly engaged to a German who then left her. In an interesting move, a political ending is abandoned in favour of a psychological one, even though the echoes of class conflict and international tensions remain. Some parts of *The Dog Beneath the Skin* were eventually salvaged by Auden for his *Collected Poems* where they appear under the significant title 'The Witnesses'.

PARODY OR PATHOS: *THE ASCENT OF F6*

The frontier that provided an implicit allegory in the above plays gains concrete shapes in the two plays that Auden co-wrote with Christopher Isherwood in the late 1930s, *The Ascent of F6* and *On the Frontier*. The imaginary mountain F6 in the first play is situated on the borderline between a fictional British colony, 'British Sudoland', and a competing colonial power, 'Ostnian Sudoland'. The plot is driven by the race for domination of the whole of Sudoland, for which the Ostnians employ a local myth: whoever reaches the peak of the F6 first will rule Sudoland for 1,000 years.

The British side is represented by Sir James Ransom, a colonial officer, Lady Isabel Welwyn, the upper-class product of the Empire who cherishes fond memories of submissive natives, General Dellaby Couch, and the newspaper magnate, Lord Stagmantle. They conspire to enlist the services of Sir James's twin brother, Michael, a passionate mountaineer. In the same way that the above figures present an allegory of power in the Britain of the 1930s, Michael Ransom is another symbolic character in the mould of John Nower. Literally held ransom by several forces – his own will, the forces of the British Empire, and, most strongly, his mother – he remains entangled in contradictory impulses and eventually loses himself in a quest whose goal is never completely clear to him or anyone around him.

In a manner already encountered several times in Auden's early poems, the realms of private and public are shown as interlinked. The play emphasises this further by adding to the scenes on stage some in the boxes to the left and right. In the right box Mr and Mrs A, representatives of lower-middle-class Englishness, enact their dreary daily routines, into which eventually the story of the ascent of F6 enters via the mass media. The story is further mediated by the public voices situated in the box on the left. From there, an announcer first provides the public view of events; eventually Lord Stagmantle and Lady Isabel add their Establishment voices. As a consequence the character of Michael Ransom is torn in two directions and his actions are subjected to the scrutiny of both private and public opinion – which eventually converge in a frightening chorus of frenzy. This technique is later radicalised and emphasised in *The Orators*.

After first resisting the colonialists' entreaties, Michael is eventually persuaded when his mother is brought into play. He is determined to resist established authority by refusing to cooperate. We encounter him first in a long poetic monologue in which he refutes classical learning (represented by Dante) as a disguise for power, and does not want to become 'party to the general fiasco'. But already in his introductory words he cannot but link general political ideas concerning mastery with private ones relating back to the most symbolically potent of all figures in early Auden, the mother: 'O, happy the foetus that miscarries and the frozen idiot that cannot cry "Mama"!' (*Pl* 296).

Michael Ransom tries to find refuge from the powers he abhors in the company of his bohemian friends: Doctor Williams; the botanist Lamp; Shawcross, a fellow mountaineer; and the womanizer Gunn. Yet even in the idyllic location of a pub in the Lake District they are found by the representatives of colonialism and Englishness. At first Michael manages to resist his brother's proposition – which Michael characterises as 'concerned with prestige, tactics, money and the privately arranged meaning of familiar words' (*Pl* 310). Once again, signifiers are ultimately the most potent weapons of power, and in the same way as Auden's early poetry, the play sees concepts as intimately connected with signification and discourse rather than as essential and substantial.

Michael then resists Isabel's appeal to his masculinity in a similarly brusque manner. He does not want to make her – and all English-women – proud. Eventually Stagmantle proves to be the most down-to-earth character. Already in the Colonial Office where the scheme to use Michael was plotted, he responds to Isabel's ostensible patriotism with the weak 'Oh, England – yes, quite so, of course' (*Pl* 303).[10] He, too, sees through the constructedess of nationalism and other ideals. Now he takes Michael aside and asks him to ignore abstract propositions and concentrate unashamedly on the commercial possibilities of an expedition. Economy diplays the closest parallels to the play of signification and power, and after the historic experience of economic collapse and inflation in the late 1920s and early 1930s, this equation is not difficult to understand. Michael therefore responds to Stagmantle's suggestions with some sympathy, but eventually still refuses to cooperate.

As a secret weapon Sir James now produces Mrs Ransom, his and Michael's mother. A strange dialogue between Michael and his mother follows, in which she first declares her pride and understanding of Michael's decisions – including the refusal to climb F6. But she soon touches a sore spot when she starts comparing his actions to those of his twin brother. This seems to stir up memories of infantile competition and anxieties about being loved less. To this Michael's mother responds that she wanted to turn him into a truly strong man by the very withholding of her love: 'You were to be unlike your father and your brother/You were to have the power to stand alone;/And to withhold from loving must be all my love' (*Pl* 313).

The theme of the truly strong man is a continuing thread in Auden's early works. Like the whole of his early poetics, it is a split and doubled concept, in which the greatest possible strength is also the greatest weakness. In order not to become like one's father, one has to follow the wishes of one's mother. Breaking out of one form of authority does not lead to self-determination, but to another Oedipal bind. Indeed, in Freudian terms the self-divided, truly strong man is the one who internalises the Oedipus complex so completely that he embodies and lives it. The overwhelming power of this will (which is ultimately a sensual urge for withheld love rather than intellectual determination) eventually leads to blindness and self-destruction. But, as becomes evident during the eventual ascent of the mountain, it also produces the problematic charisma of leadership.

Michael eventually succumbs to his mother's wishes, and the expedition gets under way. Accompanied by the public voices of the announcer, Lady Isabel and the newpaper baron – which deliver the sanitised, public version of the trip to the public – the party arrives in a Sudoland monastery. There, a strange ritual reminds them of the local belief in the existence of a monster on the mountain. They also enounter a symbolic blue crystal that enables them to get a glimpse of their deepest desires. The Doctor sees himself in the comfort of his club, the botanist spots the rare plant he aims to discover, and Gunn sees a sports car and a woman. Shawcross, the realist, refuses to look into the crystal. Michael, the doomed hero, pretends to see nothing. Yet he is merely embarrassed by the fact that what he glimpses in the crystal are masses appealing to be saved by him, as if he was a second Christ. His vocation as truly strong man, however, makes him unable to love the masses. His elevation and isolation are completely overpowering. 'Was it to me they turned their rodent faces, those ragged denizens of the waterfronts, and squealed so piteously: "Restore us! Restore us to our uniqueness and our human condition"' (*Pl* 325). This is just what a leader, according to the concept of Auden's truly strong man, will never do, because to him the masses are indeed less than human – they are mere vermin.[11] Despite the sometimes precarious oscillation between Marxist and fascist ideas in Auden's early works, here already is evidence that he regards overcoming alienation, as demanded on an individual level by Freudian theory and on a political level by Marxism, as irreconcilable with the totalitarianism of personalised leadership.

Hurried on by the news that an Ostnian mountaineering party is threatening their triumph, Michael and his team eventually rush their ascent. As a consequence, they lose first Lamp and then Shawcross, who commits suicide when he discovers that Michael has chosen Gunn to accompany him to the summit. Shawcross, although superficially strong, cannot deal with rejection. As he declares himself, he had been a narcissist all along, and narcissism is weakness rather than strength. On a personal level, narcissism is the failure to take up the challenge of the Oedipus complex, the refusal to enter object-cathexes.[12] On a social and political level it can be seen as the equivalent of blindness towards the historicity of power and its structure as a relation of oppression and resistance. Shawcross therefore resembles the ridiculed constipated author of *The Dog Beneath the Skin* as much as he does the unreconstructed 'heirs' of power in the plays.

After leaving the doctor behind, Michael and Gunn eventually approach the summit. But before they reach it, Gunn dies in a blizzard. The scene is set for Michael's lonely encounter with the mountain demon, and structurally for a bracketing scene that brings together the drama's beginning and end. Somewhat unsurprisingly, he first meets his hated brother James in the shape of a dragon, who recites a clichéd speech reminiscent of a politician's defence. James and Michael then play a surreal game of chess, in which all the other characters of *The Ascent of F6* form the pieces. Michael eventually loses the game, when the mountain demon appears – who turns out to be none other than his mother. Michael buries his head in her lap, and accompanied by a duet between Mrs Ransom and the chorus which features fairy tales and family ghosts, he dies.

The play can easily be criticised for drifting from a multifaceted perspective which posits personal anxiety and social reality in interconnected positions to a mere psychological drama – which is often enacted in vulgar Freudian terms. Yet one must not overlook the overkill effect of the theatrical devices, such as choral chants and endless repetitions, and the sly finale. In it the chorus first stresses that the only way in which the truly strong man can become a fulfilled individual is through death. Then it condemns the forces of history for producing truly strong men in the first place. Those who 'have their power exerted', the very last lines of the play exclaim, 'to dissolution go'. There is no eternal law in this play, not even the Oedipal one. Eventually the play refrains from positing even psychological disposition as origin. It subjects it to history and thus turns history and self into interdependent and equally doomed entities.

After having moved from Britain to the United States, Auden and Isherwood wrote a different ending for *The Ascent of F6*, in which they tried to solve the problem of the irreconcilability of private desires and anxieties and the demands of society. In Edward Mendelson's words: 'They transformed Ransom's death into his triumph. In his dying vision after he attains the summit, Ransom sheds his pride, overcomes his fear of love, and acknowledges at last his common humanity. His political ambitions and personal longings fade. The division in himself between the public and the private worlds dissolves in his final lines' (*Pl* xxviii-xxix).

A close look at these final lines, however, reveals that their solution is more wishful thinking. Ransom first invokes nature in order to achieve separation from history, 'Now storm and distance hide me from those valleys/Where history is manufactured every day', before switching to a rather problematic version of forgiveness: 'Valleys and men, forgive me. Oh, we all/Stand much in need of our forgiveness' (*Pl* 643). Even the revised version cannot decide where the redemptive power lies, outside the individual, inside it, or in its communion with others. We will re-encounter the eventual proposition of this revised ending of *The Ascent of F6* repeatedly in Auden's writings: 'Man is an animal/That has to love or perish' (*Pl* 643). It is both tautological (being human means to perish eventually) and contradictory (asking whether animals are capable of love). Rather than resolving the conflict between individual and society, the play once more emphasises it.

ON THE FRONTIER

As its title implies, *On the Frontier: A Melodrama in Three Acts* takes the theme of partings, boundaries, and divisions furthest by turning it into the dominant image of the play, even determining its title. This time the theme has gained greatest urgency, and what seemed to brew ominously in the background of earlier plays – hostilities between rival factions or nations and the emergence of dubious leader figures – now achieves a drastic topicality.

The play reintroduces the Ostnians, already encountered as the enemy in *The Ascent of F6*, and sets them against the Westlanders, who are not so much the British in disguise as Teutonic fascists. Already their names locate them firmly on the ideological map of the late 1930s: the Westlanders have Nordic ones (the Thorvald family are the main protagonists), while the Ostnians are Slavs (the Vrodny family dominates the scene here). While the Ostnians live in a monarchy, the Westlanders are governed by a histrionic Leader whose power depends on powerful industrialists and his storm troopers. Although the stage instructions are cagey concerning the Westlanders' Leader figure – 'Try to avoid resemblances to living personages' (*Pl* 359) – it is clear that Hitler provides the model.

In the same way as in *Paid on Both Sides*, a spy is used to set off the action, but this time it is made even more evident that spying is an integral element in the interaction of the two states. Valerian, the industrialist, knows that Lessep, his personal secretary, is providing information for the other side, but accepts this as part of an implicitly agreed business relation. What is ostensibly opposed is actually interacting – and therefore hardly different. As in some of Auden's early poems, the spy – who transgresses the borderline between 'them and us' – is marked as homosexual in *On the Frontier* by his description as 'In dress and manner slightly pansy' (*Pl* 359). Once again borderlines are not simply political or geographic, but extend from public sphere into that of the individual, and are determined by codes, here of clothing, but more commonly of language. The double code used by spies reappears in *On the Frontier* in the speech of every character, whether the 'private' characters of the Thorvald and Vrodny families or the 'public' ones of Leader and industrialists.

The plot follows the escalation of what appear to be traditional hostilities between the Westlanders and Ostnians, via a possibly staged terrorist attack on a bridge, to their culmination in full-scale warfare. In a similar way as *The Ascent of F6*, the play depicts this development in a dialogic way, by showing its effect on the two sides in an almost exaggerated symbolism. It brings together the hostile parties in an imaginary shared living room, the so-called 'Ostnia-Westland Room'. The hostile parties are apparently invisible to each other – with the noticeable exception of the son of the Thorvalds, Eric, and the daughter of the Vronskys, Anna, between whom a tender love affair blossoms. In the same way as the fascist demonstration in *The Dog Beneath the Skin*, this trick signals the entanglement of personal and political, but also home and foreign politics.

The older family members are representatives of the 'old guard'. They merely reproduce accepted slogans and stereotypes about the other side. They are out of touch and incapable of responding flexibly to the situation. Dr Oliver Thorvald, Eric's father, is a lecturer at a Westland university. He is first introduced insulting the research of an Ostnian academic as narrow, outdated, and ideologically biased, without realising that his criticism shows him in exactly the same light. On the side of the Vronskys, Colonel Hussek, Mrs Vronsky's father, revels in his past military grandeur and dreams of the times when Ostnian pride put the Westlanders firmly in their place.

It is, surprisingly, the part of the otherwise unsympathetically drawn Leader and the seemingly corrupt industrialists as well as the almost anachronistic king of the Ostnians to show signs of agility and adaptation to the pressures of the times. They wish to prevent an escalation of the crisis, and the Leader of the Westlanders – despite his martial public rhetoric – is actually willing to sign a pact of non-aggression with the Ostnians. He is prevented from doing so when their (supposed?) violation of the border sets off the military machinery.

The two young people, Eric and Anna, who form a similar 'Romeo and Juliet' couple to Anne Shaw and John Nower in *Paid on Both Sides*, are free from the entrenched rhetoric of the older generation, but only at the cost of appearing as dysfunctional dreamers. They are neither powerful figures nor particularly attractive. Eric is described as 'Untidy, angular. About twenty', while Anna 'Must not be played as a mouse. She has character, but has hardly realized it' (*Pl* 358). Once more the play is engaged in a debate about strength. Its 'truly strong man', however, is hard to locate. While the surprising U-turn of the Leader seems to indicate that he might be a candidate, he is eventually completely swept aside by the events. At the end of the play he is assassinated by storm-trooper Grimm (perhaps a grim echo of the Brothers Grimm?) who thus avenges, as he believes, the death of his parents and betrayal by the Leader. They went bankrupt when their shop failed to compete with a big department store, owned by Valerian, the industrialist. Contrary to his promises to support small shop owners, the Leader teamed up with big industry after being elected.

Grimm is no candidate for the truly strong man either, since he is driven by narrow-minded and eventually misguided revenge – which is, moreover, directed backwards to his parents. The industrialist, Valerian, is indeed the one who cynically sees through events. In his very first scenes we see him cleverly manipulating the Westland Leader, and when the director of one of his steel works (whose name 'Stahl' actually signifies 'steel') calls the Leader and his men 'common gangsters', Valerian responds sagely:

> 'After all, there is a good deal to be said for gangsters. One's dealings with them are so charmingly simple. They understand two things: money and the whip. They know where their bread and butter comes from. The Leader is much safer with these boys than with a pack of crooked politicians.' (Pl 370)

Eventually, Valerian reaches a level of insight into himself that by far surpasses any other character in *On the Frontier*, when he recognises in the storm-trooper his own inevitable death. At their first meeting he immediately realises a familiarity, even though Grimm declares never to have met Valerian (Pl 370). When Valerian eventually fails to bribe Grimm, he declares:

> 'How very curious this is! It is quite true. You are actually able to kill me! And you will! [...] When I said that I recognized you, I meant, perhaps, that I recognized that look. I recognized Death. We all know him by sight.' (Pl 411–12)

If Valerian stands for the corrupt old system that has to be eradicated, he also demonstrates that insight, knowledge, and power are tied up with it. The problem is similar to that exposed by *The Dance of Death*, in which death stands for change while itself becoming, rather contradictorily, a stable ideological and artistic concept. This concept is dangerously close to the classical modernist *tabula rasa*, which also presents the other side of modernism's insistence on circular mythical systems, in which change is merely part of a universal (and stable) pattern.[13] The farewell to master narratives can easily lead to the welcoming of new ones. What Derrida calls the 'event of losing faith in origins and presences' need not be an irreversible one. Indeed, in the emphasis on signification there lurks always a threat that the play sets itself up as a new presence and origin. If it did not attempt a new authority, it would indeed be less than a play, because it would lack rules. Linda Hutcheon calls this feature the challenges of postmodernism. In her words, 'These challenges characteristically operate in clearly paradoxical terms, knowing that to claim epistemological authority is to be caught up in what they seek to replace.'[14] This was symbolised by the skin in *The Dog Beneath the Skin*, and is present as the problem of change in *On the Frontier*.

The character of Valerian reiterates the crucial problem of Auden's early works, a problem that eventually culminates in *The Orators*: that although power is always corrupting and problematic, leading eventually to a reassertion of old values, without it change and development become impossible. The pacifistic Eric and Anna in *On the Frontier* remain painfully ineffective. Even though they dream about the survival of their love after their deaths in their final speeches, this seems a rather fragile and unconvincing hope in a play that sees two societies disappearing and fails to present a single character who manages to be both righteous and active. When Anna inquires in a surreal scene that sees her and Eric united as ghosts, 'Will people never stop killing each other?', her own conclusion is a further statement of defeat: 'There is no place in the world/For people who love' (*Pl* 416). This sounds trite, yet condenses the same problem that John Nower embodied in *Paid on Both Sides* even in his surname. For certain positions (be they political, ethical, or merely subjective), there is no ideological and geographic, but also no personal space, because the rules of the play do not permit it. Lyotard calls these rules – in an allusion to Wittgenstein – those of 'language games'. Yet he adds, in a way that illustrates the predicament of the dreamy players Anna and Eric in *On the Frontier*, 'But undoubtedly even this pleasure depends on a feeling of success won at the expense of an adversary – at least one adversary, and a formidable one: the accepted language, or connotation.'[15]

The quest for the good place, a space that is more than a traditional *locus amoenus*, but combines personal fulfilment with political and moral righteousness, is the underlying theme of the many quest plots in Auden's early works. Reducing them to psychological parables or ideological morality tales fails to see that their tragedy is their very insight into the entanglement of the two. The borders that have to be mastered, and that tend to prove so overpowering, cut through individual and society alike, because both are linked by the problem of signification and its rules. Solutions cannot therefore be found on one side alone. Knowing what is right, and combining this knowledge with action, emerges as the most urgent problem in Auden's early writings, a problem for which his texts find no solution – save in apocalyptic scenarios.

Even though the war in *On the Frontier* is a man-made one, what eventually kills everyone is a plague. Auden, intrigued as usual by medical images, once more uses the theme of illness in a psychosomatic vein. Eric's final speech deals with this interiority of the problem. 'Believing it was wrong to kill,/I went to prison/As the sane and innocent student/Aloof among practical and violent madmen.' He begins by trying to divide the world into sanity and innocence (which remains, however, distant and ineffective) and madness and violence (which he calls 'practical', that is, active and effective). Yet he too has to see that he is at fault: 'But I was wrong. We cannot choose our world,/Our time, our class. None are innocent, none./ Causes of violence lie so deep in all our lives/It touches every act' (*Pl* 416). It is difficult to tell how this conviction differs from the fatalistic predeterminism of some radical forms of Protestantism – or indeed, the essentialist theories underlying fascist ideology, with their assumption of inherent cultural and biological greatness or depravity.

The plague in *On the Frontier* is an allegory of the deep-seated illness that affects Westlanders and Ostnians alike. Its exact cause is the frontier on which they situate themselves: it engenders their illness, yet they also depend on it for their self-definition and legitimation. The price that has to be paid for this frontier existence is the impossibility of developing fully fledged personalities capable of individual actions and development. Although it may have appeared as a suitable allegory of the Spanish Civil War at the time, as an emblem of the link between personal and ideological challenges the fatal plague is as successful as it is unsatisfactory. A plague is vastly beyond human control. It also does not differentiate. Symbolically it occupies the same status as traditional divine punishment. It can therefore hardly act as an ideological or even moral device, unless one indeed accepts an external and ultimately superhuman power that is capable of punishing the world.[16] The rejection of authority once again leads to the reintroduction of an even more powerful force, yet one that lacks the historicity of a war, the arguments of the manifesto of a political party, or the personal profile of a dangerous leader. It is this history that will concern us in Chapter 5.

If the apocalyptic pessimism of *On the Frontier* offers any hope, this hope is ironically linked with those figures who are not normally regarded as bearers of good tidings. The soldiers who, after the outbreak of hostilities, operate on the frontier of the play are also the ones who prove capable of fraternising over a few cigarettes. They overcome the frontier by reducing it to its simplest materialistic shape: 'Wot's it like, your side?' 'Wet.' 'Same here.' (*Pl* 402). The second group of optimists in the play seem to be prisoners who expect to die, yet who revel in the fact that they can see through the transience of power: 'They boast: "We shall last for a thousand long years,"/But history, it happens, has other ideas'. Their belief is based on the masses: 'For Truth shall flower and Error explode/And the people be free then to choose their own road!' (*Pl* 374).

Yet while the soldiers' attitude shows immediate consequences, albeit small ones (they exchange cigarettes and matches), the traditional political slogans of the prisoners have a hollow ring. Righteous masses are nowhere in sight in *On the Frontier*, certainly not after the plague has eradicated the populations of both Ostnia and Westland. Even in the hope of the oppressed lurks the malady of tradition, even when this tradition is a revolutionary one. It is by no means easy to break out of the discourse of power, and the play is not sure whether it wishes to recommend this path. By participating in whatever ideological concept of historical development one favours, one becomes part of historical events – and therefore subjected to the forces of domination, differentiation, and delineation.[17] The play's uncomfortable message, in short, is this: the only place for the historically, politically, and personally aware is indeed on the frontier.

4

The Orators: A Study of Authority

The Orators, first published in 1932, is certainly Auden's most controversial poem.[1] Critical evaluations range from a rather baffled acknowledgment as 'the most significant and disturbing long poem of its era'[2] to violent rejections whose attitudes Günther Jarfe summarises in the following way:

> The criticism is directed against the lack of a coherent point of view that is registered with bitterness, against the loss of a visibly organising emotional and intellectual centre in the whole of the poem that is regarded as scandalous, against the abstinence from 'illustrative general physiognomic and symbolic cognition'.[3]

Auden eventually distanced himself from the poem: a 'case of the fair notion fatally injured' is his own verdict in the foreword to his *Collected Poems* (CP 15). Worried about its political ambiguities, he states apologetically in the preface to a third edition in 1967: 'My name on the title-page seems a pseudonym for someone else, someone talented but near the border of sanity, who might well, in a year or two, become a Nazi.'[4]

The aim of this chapter is to propose a reading of the poem which uses the difficulties and ambiguities of *The Orators* as indications that its 'flaws' are artistic devices which help the poem outline a new aesthetics. Far from being proto-fascist, it offers an important political challenge which continues to be relevant to the present date and in its final consequences marks a move beyond the modernist tradition.

CHANGING THE CODE

The title and subtitle, *The Orators: An English Study*, already hint at some of its implications: public speeches, addresses to an audience, a

52

'relation between discourse and power'.[5] Orations require a common code, a language understood by the speaker and his audience, fixed positions for both sides in the communication, as well as a predetermined topic. They are formations of authority requiring authority as their basis, and thus mirror the literary text which establishes an understanding between itself and the reader based upon a previous agreement concerning the linguistic code as well as the cultural context.

The Orators, however, does not conform to the rules implied in its title. Already the plural is a hint at the diverging messages that must be expected. The multiple meanings of the subtitle even more clearly indicate the peculiarities of the text: a study of the English language, a study of the English, and a study in English are its connotations. Moreover, the study is the room reserved for the production of literature, a symbol of cultural identity and security.[6] In the same way as the ambiguity of the subtitle undermines the expectations raised by the title, the denial of the entire text to identify itself as one form of discourse, whether lyrical, prose, letter, journal, or other, takes away the common ground between itself and its reader. That *The Orators*, unlike even the most radical texts of classical modernism, not only uses the rules of literary discourse in very extreme ways but actually eliminates them, will be demonstrated below. *The Orators* does not constitute any clear messages, much less one single one. It denies information about its constitution and point of view. Finally, it plays a precarious role as a reader-controlling device by denying authority to itself as well as to the reader. The problematic textuality of *The Orators* is not only foregrounded by the poem, it is actually torn apart until very little is left that resembles the traditional mechanisms of literature.

'Prologue' (*EA* 61), the first poem of *The Orators*, acts as a description of the whole text. Its shows a young man, not so much in an Oedipal attachment to his mother, but, as Günther Jarfe points out, in an emancipated position from his past and now capable of evaluating his personal history as well as the progress he has made to leave it behind. The attraction of the past lies in its unproblematic fulfilment of libidinal wishes.[7] The second stanza shows this prelapsarian stage as located not before the discovery of sexuality, but before its inextricable connection with guilt and power, in a happy, innocent sexual anarchy.

The sexuality of the emancipated stage presents itself in significantly different shape. Threatening are the 'mountain heights' which could be seen as an extension of 'his mother's figure', as her breasts. Yet the young man is also in possession of sexual power, that of the phallus. The 'finest of mapping pens' combines sexual potential and the power of signification. Both of them, however, derive from distinction and difference, and are consequently characterised by an inevitable lack, one which has to be accepted as the price of escape from the sheltered innocence of childhood. The summer bands of the third stanza formulate the seduction of this stage in an illogical advice. 'Dear boy, be brave as these roots' categorises the young man as immature and dependent, and aims at keeping him in this state, for roots are, of course, not so much brave as simply immobile.

Yet the young man does not remain in the treacherous security of passivity ('the summer bands' indicates that the pleasant reality will change with the seasons, i.e. inevitably). He perceives the danger, leaves this security, and is not afraid to contact strangers. Implied in all these metaphors is a radical change of the discursive situation: the formation of a new message ('the good news'), a different context ('a world in danger'), and, eventually and most radically, a new code ('Is ready to argue, he smiles, with any stranger'). Neither of those utopian goals is fully illustrated by the poem. They remain abstract, and make the poem an easy target for criticisms based on its vagueness. But those absences are only the final consequences of the poem's attempt not only to outline a break with tradition, a change of code, the ceasing of communication, but actually to perform it. Its effect is apparently an end of understanding, a separation from the common cultural and linguistic bases, an emancipation and isolation that is hardly tolerable for the forces of tradition.

'Coward, Coward' and 'Deceiver' are the accusations of its representatives, the band and the giantess. The latter is perhaps an inflated caricature of the mother. Yet despite her size she remains as impotent as the band; this is indicated by her fairytale character as well as by the verb 'shuffle' – which hints at the negative consequences of attachment to tradition, to the ground. The strength of the poem lies in its trick of including the reader in this chorus of supporters of the status quo. He, too, feels betrayed by a poem that not only talks about the necessity of putting an end to an exchange of mutually agreed formulas, but actually ceases to communicate. As an introduction to the whole of The Orators, 'Prologue' assumes the paradoxical role of a tempting warning sign that lures the reader into a text that does not want to be understood.[8]

That *The Orators* is indeed concerned with the functioning of its own code, with the alienating effect of literary language, becomes evident at the very beginning of Book I. After the denial of access to the reader in 'Prologue', the heading 'The Initiates' seems ironic at first sight, because it completely contradicts all that has happened before. 'Address for a Prize-Day' (*EA* 61–4), the first part of Book I, supports this heading none the less, for it not only fits the title *The Orators* as the only oration in the strict sense, but also suits the heading 'The Initiates', because it reproduces, at least superficially, an established ritual of British society. It therefore includes the reader in its cultural sphere as an initiate.

By suddenly fulfilling the expectations raised by its title, *The Orators* almost disappoints them again, for it has just prepared its reader to face hermetic closure. In the course of the text notions of conformity and disappointment will become increasingly evasive. Even the concept of alienation will become dubious, because the text disintegrates all notions of the real, the bases of expectations, as well as its own structures, the two elements required for the comparison which is the understanding of the text.

This is the more fascinating as the poem continually employs familiar features. In the case of 'Address for a Prize-Day', these are the well-trodden rhetorical set-pieces of an old boy's speech at a school anniversary. These are cleverly used as a frame for a self-reflection of themes and topics of the whole of Auden's early poems. The first section, an excellent parody of a speech almost entirely devoid of meaning, takes up some dominant Audenesque themes: the drawing of borderlines and the attempts at polarisation without a capacity to distinguish, and/or lacking differentiation of the things that are to be divided. 'Commemoration' (*EA* 61) is a term that implies a definable past, but the missing information about the object of commemoration gives it an absurd status. The repetition of this initial term as well as the following 'What does it mean?' give the introduction away as an empty ritual – or perhaps not entirely empty, for in the world of signifiers which is that of Auden's poems the ritual becomes its own meaning, and the question it generates achieves almost universal significance.

The remaining divisions of the first paragraph function similarly. There is once more the problem of the speaker's identity in 'us, here, now' as opposed to 'them, there, then'. There is also a comparison between absence and presence (the dead versus the living) which inevitably remains vacuous, because the first are a myth, the latter without identity. The allusion probably refers to the lost generation of the Great War, the missing role-models for the young men of the 1930s, and the cause of their difficulties in finding an identity of their own. The resulting questions are the two recurring ones in Auden's early poems, 'Why are we here? What are we going to do?' These are unmistakable signs of a missing ontology and teleology. The final statement of the paragraph which characteristically takes the place of an answer, 'Let's try putting it another way', is much more than just a deferral: it is a self-characterisation of *The Orators*.

The parable that follows re-examines some of the dominant images of Auden's early poems and condenses them to a surrealist story. The view from above, that of the hawk or the airman, returns in a new disguise in the shape of angels, thus giving away many of its implications, especially the wish for metaphysical detachment. Characteristically, these mythical figures possess an objective insight, and are described in Auden's clinical language as 'qualified experts on the human heart', in which faith and psychoanalysis merge. They set out on a quest through an Audenesque Britain of petrol pumps and furnaces. Their goal is familiar, too: the creation of a map.

The determining categories of this map, however, do not fit into the system of Auden's poems at all. What is first described in vaguely religious tones as 'lost persons' (*EA* 62) is then qualified as all those guilty of deficient love according to the distinctions in Dante's *Divine Comedy*: the excessive lovers of self and of their neighbours, the defective lovers towards God, and the perverted lovers. All of them are described in the tone of the amateur psychologist, but not without ironic hints that either add completely unlikely features or advice for therapy that is at best idiosyncratic or ambiguous, but more likely plain useless. Two aspects of this strange system are particularly striking. First, love as a decisive quality is always a dubious phenomenon in Auden's early poems; but now it suddenly becomes the all-important measure. Second, after disqualifying polarisations and norms inherited by tradition, the recourse to the prototype of a hierarchical model of the world, the *Divine Comedy*, is a contradictory move which cannot simply be explained away by taking into account the dubious narrator of the story or its surrealism.

The categories of deficient love in 'Address for a Prize-Day' constitute neither a serious ethical concept nor an ironic dismissal of Christian and humanist ethics. Rather, they are a reassessment of the values and concepts of Auden's earlier poems. First of all there is the striking distinction between the lovers of the self, of the neigh-bours, and of God. Although these can also be found in Dante's epic, they are the representatives of more general principles in *The Orators*: the self, the Other, and the answer to the questions 'Why?' and 'Whither?', the supplement to the missing certainty of origin and direction. In this concept, love becomes a metaphor for the establish-ment of clear relations, the utopian goal and stumbling-block of many of Auden's early poems.

Yet once more the text refuses to give examples of a proper rela-tion between the self, the Other, and metaphysical finalities. By restricting itself to illustrating the undesirable, it undermines its own authority as a guideline – and necessarily so, because, as will become evident below, it includes itself in one of its categories. The excessive lovers of self and their neighbours represent the various forms of distorted identity, either lacking Lacan's mirror-image and thus awareness,[9] or only in possession of a mirror but without anything reflected in it, and consequently solipsistic. The deficient lovers correspond to the characters in Auden's early poems who sense the crumbling certainties and experience the loss of reality and identity, yet react with passivity and paralysis (compare the inhabitants of the sanatorium in '1929' in the next chapter; *EA* 50–3).

Interestingly enough, the perverted lovers remain nondescript, although they are labelled 'worst'. Their lacking features give them an almost universal presence, and the tone of the question 'Is he one? Was she one?' (*EA* 63) is almost paranoid. They could be every-where, but what are they like? 'So convincing at first, so little appar-ent cause for anxiety', they have nevertheless 'lost their nerve'. An example of this attitude is close at hand: *The Orators* is itself an illus-tration of completely distorted and eventually lost relations between interior and exterior, self and reality. In its poetic discourse the text reproduces the corrosion of distinctions, the dissolution of directions and definitions which, as the text itself indicates, are so common as to be hardly noticeable. *The Orators* refers to its own 'madness' by prefiguring some of the motifs which will reappear in the text later. The 'simple geometrical figure' that 'can arouse all the manifesta-tions of extreme alarm' (*EA* 63) will crop up as 'A Sure Test' in 'Journal of an Airman' and culminate in 'it is wiser to shoot at once' (*EA* 74). One of the 'haters of life' who 'end in hospital as incurable cases' (*EA* 63) returns as the writer of 'Letter to a Wound'. The reader, part of the discursive practice of the text, is not only implicitly included in the accusations of its speaker. By a subtle rhetorical mechanism which has already made him part of the audience, one of the boys (notice the implications of submission to authority), he becomes one of those directly attacked, even hunted in the last two paragraphs: 'There you sit' (*EA* 63).

The authority which underlies this reproach remains paradoxical. The descriptions of the deficient forms of love, and especially the suggestions of possible treatment, indicate that the speaker's authority is that of tradition; the excessive and defective lovers are those who violate its rules. Their treatment aims at integration: 'ask if you can come too? Why not go out together next Sunday?' (*EA* 62), 'Try inviting them down in the holidays to a calm house', 'Give them regular but easy tasks and see that they do them properly' (*EA* 63). Even the drastic advice 'Hit them in the face if necessary. If they hit back you will know they are saved' tries to provoke the 'proper' reaction. This impression is supported by the fact that there seems to be no cure for the perverted lovers. Their break with tradition excludes them from its 'healing' powers.

In the last paragraph before the turbulent finale of 'Address for a Prize-Day', the accusations suddenly take the opposite form. The assembly is reproached for its adherence to tradition: 'You're going to have friends, you're going to bring up children. You're going to be like this forever, all the time, more terrible than the bursting of the bolted door or the exhausting adverse wind of dreams' (*EA* 64). Conformity is shown to be worse than revolt or subversion. By this turn, the authority of the speaker becomes seriously flawed. He is unmasked, and shown not so much to be unreliable as impossible to categorise, to locate as either 'us' or 'them'. In terms of textual authority, the reader is left with a vacuum, because all the contextual structures, here that of the British education system, rely on a stable representation of authority. A coherent view of society becomes impossible through this failure, and even opposition becomes an empty phrase – in the same way as the famous line of 'Address for a Prize-Day', 'this country of ours where nobody is well' (*EA* 62), remains useless as an analysis of the social, economic, and political conditions. Without clear positions and their mutual relation, neither authority nor opposition to it can exist.

The final paragraph of 'Address for a Prize-Day' depicts an anarchic chaos. What has started as a hollow sermon about spiritual improvement turns into a surrealist reversal of authority: the schoolboys hunt their headmaster, teachers, and chaplain. Even their

The Orators: A Study of Authority 59

execution is announced, before the scene ends with the suggestion of mere bullying, of putting them into the 'Black Hole': 'New Boys were always put in it' (*EA* 64). Although supposedly subversive, the ritual in fact conforms to tradition again. The final 'ready, steady – go' shifts the scene from actual brutality to a mere game. The adherence to tradition, to a view of the world which polarises, categorises, and organises hierarchically, is shown as no longer viable. Yet the fight against these static norms can easily lead to an equally hypocritical attitude which, despite its forceful or outright brutal appearance, relies on a mere reversal of tradition – and therefore on the same outdated concepts.

One could read these features of the poem as a critique of the attachment of the troubled capitalist society of the early 1930s to the liberal ideas deriving from the Enlightenment. But it is just as much a criticism of the two currently dominant oppositions to traditional capitalism: Italian and German fascism, and the communism of Stalin's Russia, both of which are developments of Enlightenment ideas. What is obvious is the attack on rhetoric in 'Address for a Prize-Day': as long as the discourse is about authority, it remains hypocritical and mere propaganda, a signifying system in which all signifiers are exchangeable, because they all mean the same: power. Lyotard sums up a number of theories of legitimation in terms that illustrate perfectly the 'logic' of the first oration in Auden's long poem. He writes about consensus:

> It has two formulations. In the first, consensus is an agreement between men, defined as knowing intellects and free wills, and is obtained through dialogue. This is the form elaborated by Habermas, but his conception is based on the validity of the narrative of emancipation. In the second, consensus is a component of the system, which manipulates it in order to maintain and improve its performance. It is the object of administrative procedures, in Luhmann's sense. In this case, its only validity is as an instrument to be used towards achieving the real goal, which is what legitimates the system – power.[10]

Every discourse is already a discourse of power[11] – that is the message of 'Address for a Prize-Day'; only it is not a message at all, but its absence. In order to criticise the language of authority, this section of *The Orators* blasts its own authority and becomes a discourse of madness.

UNWRITING THE SELF

The subsequent three parts of Book I of *The Orators*, though of significantly different shape, are almost equally obscure and rivalled in difficulty only by Book II, 'Journal of an Airman', with which they form the centre of the entire poem. Yet in spite of the vagueness of the text, it is apparent that 'Argument', 'Statement', and 'Letter to a Wound' take up the themes of the introductory address and develop them further, to drastic results. All three parts are once more concerned with identity; they repeat the three aspects of its formation exemplified in 'Address for a Prize-Day': the relation of the self to itself, to others, and to metaphysical finalities (for which another symbolic representative is introduced, the hero). In Parts II, III, and IV of Book I, the order introduced in Part I is reversed. 'Argument' is concerned with the relation of the self to the hero, 'Statement' with its interaction with others, and finally 'Letter to a Wound' with its position towards itself.

'Argument' (*EA* 64–69) is an exploration of hero-worship. Three features of this theme are particularly striking: the changing character of the hero; the varying shapes of his admirers; and, last but not least, the self-presentation of the three parts of 'Argument'. Part I starts with the epic 'Lo', a reference to Old English poems,[12] setting the tone for the section's stylistic mixture, which employs the alliterations of Anglo-Saxon poetry and even attempts modernised kennings (such as 'the grassy squares of exercise' for playing-fields), but which also displays Auden's own idiosyncrasies, such as the frequent elimination of articles, and a largely paratactic sentence-order which resembles stream-of-consciousness writing. The stylistic hints at a dead tradition are mirrored in the speaker's self-identification as a skull. The section deals with the projection of hope onto an absent hero-figure whose description (or rather lack of it) as capitalised 'He' has strong religious overtones. He is shown as everything from spiritual redeemer (i.e. Christ) to mythical hero and even lover. Although nondescript, his power is illustrated in the various appeals of the speaker. Yet this indirect illustration is incoherent and even contradictory. The depiction as mythical hero portrays him as vulnerable; his strength and courage are developed in spite of his mortality:

> If it were possible, yes, now certain, To meet Him alone on the narrow path, forcing a question, would show Him our unique

knowledge. Would hide him wounded in a cave, kneeling all night by His bed of bracken, bringing hourly an infusion of bitter herbs; wearing His cloak receive the mistaken stab, deliver His message, fall at His feet, He gripping our moribund hands, smiling. (*EA* 65)

The passage lists clichéd images of the relationship between a hero and his admirer, all of them with evident erotic connotations. Part of the attraction of the relationship lies in its masochistic lack of fulfilment.

Another description shows the hero as a leader of the youth movements so popular in the 1930s.[13] The allusions to physical exercises and the advice for clean and healthy living all refer to this shape of authority:

> On the concrete banks of baths, in the grassy squares of exercise, we are joined, brave in the long body, under His eye. (*EA* 64)

> Girls, it is His will just now that we get up early (*EA* 65)

The third guise of authority is the religious one. The repeated 'His will' is reminiscent of Christian rituals, and like these it is closely attached to language as in 'His word waiting' (*EA* 65). The strongest religious allusion is to the Eucharist: 'Speak the word only with meaning only for us, meaning Him, a call to our clearing' (*EA* 64). The merger of the diverse hero-figures in the spiritual leader unites the various implications of hero-worship. Its rituals (from 'handing round tea' to vegetable offerings and a maternal song) once more depict it as juvenile, as a not entirely successful emancipation from one's past: 'Walking in the mountains we were persons unknown to our parents'. This incomplete breaking free is regarded as a change of reality and achieved via language; thus the allusion to the Eucharist. Language seems capable of liberating without isolating, because it permits new attachments with what was hitherto alien. It becomes an agent of the formation of identity.

A strong identity is the result of this trust in language, yet the newly created identity is a fictional one. 'If it were possible, yes now certain' (*EA* 65) shows secure knowledge as a mere exchange of one word for another. The supportive 'yes' indicates the need to overcome any doubt in the procedure. This is illustrated even more drastically a few sentences below: 'on the north side of the hill, one writes with his penis in a patch of snow "Resurgam"'. Once again, sexuality and the power of the word appear related, but this time it is not the phallus, 'the finest of mapping pens' as in 'Prologue' (*EA* 61), but the limp penis whose writing leads to no real resurrection in either sense of the word.

One of the reasons why the construction of a stable reality and identity through language cannot work is the lack of specificity of the latter. Not only does the meaning of words undergo continual transformations; their use is also not restricted to a limited number of people. Languages and codes can be translated and are thus accessible. If language is the vehicle for the manifestation of power in discourse, it is also the origin of opposition. The Eucharistic formula 'Speak the name only with meaning only for us, meaning Him' (*EA* 64) demands the impossible and describes at the same time the unavailable requirements for an identity that would transcend fiction.

In terms of its authority as a reader-controlling device, the strongest manifestation of the fictional identity in the poem is also the most evident symptom of its problems: 'Stranger who cannot read our letters, you are remembered' (*EA* 64). Although the text plays on the vagueness of 'Stranger' and the ambiguity of 'letters', the implications are evident: the reader is addressed here, and the text boasts its changed code and also its authority, which does not only control, but integrates, dates, and transforms the reader into another sign system: memory. Of course, the text does neither of these things – or only in very indirect ways. The reader is not at all a stranger to the text. The text itself has declared him an initiate. If the poem has the power to change its code, then the reader has the power to translate. It is not the text that shifts the reader into memory, but the reader who – provoked by the archaisms of the poem – declares it dated, and who not so much remembers as disremembers it. Doing this, he nevertheless acts according to the instructions of the text.

A similar self-devaluation can be observed in part II of 'Argument'. Very unlike the seemingly disorganised prose of part I, it is a poem with a regular structure, a parody of the responses in an Anglican service. Like those, it lists people in need of deliverance, the reason for their troubles, and asks for redemption. Yet the list in 'Argument' has nothing in common with the Christian service, but is once more an inventory of 'Auden country', an assembly of sufferers from psychosomatic illnesses, eccentrics, or mere ordinary people who reflect the signs of the time. Still, it is more than a repetition of arguments of earlier poems, but – like 'Address for a Prize-Day' – a reassessment and even dismissal of most of them. The 'death-will of the Jews' (*EA* 66), or Freudian teachings, and 'the wish to instruct', that is, the parabolic approach of Auden's earlier poems, are rejected as much as the fatal influence of the past, 'the immense bat-shadow of home'.

The addressees of those responses are equally strange: they are private detectives and public houses. This is an evident caricature of the concept of the hero. The diversity of the addressees destroys any notion of real power; their fictional character unveils them as myths and devalues the address. Only the final one is directed to an actual historic person, King George V. Generally regarded as a weak monarch and plagued by a stammer (the implied linguistic incapacity is not unimportant, because the hero's power lies in language), he is an utterly useless authority for a general appeal such as 'calm this people' (*EA* 68). The prayer is disqualified as a means of achieving a functioning identity free from the scathing influence of the past because of three obstacles: there is no metaphysical addressee which is not fictional, nor any addresser who is more than a nondescript grammatical 'us'; and most importantly – language itself, the agent of identification, stands in its way. 'Remember not' (*EA* 66) starts the prayer, before acting against its own plea to refrain from clothing its concerns in words.

A disillusionment concerning language, and eventually, the impression of its impotence governs the imagery of Part III of 'Argument'. In a way constituting a return to Part I, with its theme of hero-worship, it supplements the 'arguments' of its predecessor with much less optimistic images. Already the introductory paragraph is concerned with failure: a magician appears to be guilty of a ruined harvest. This might be an autobiographical reference, in which Auden (who used to be called 'Uncle Wiz' by his friends) examines his own convictions and finds them immature ('the schoolroom globe', *EA* 68, hints at the schoolboy world so prominent in his poetry). The trust in language, the major device of magic as well as poetry, is especially attacked. This distrust of language, which is continually developed in *The Orators*, represents a radical departure from the principles of Auden's earlier works. The consequences of the disillusionment are thoroughly negative.

The impression of the hero changes once more in Part III of 'Argument'. The images describing him are now either meaningless or show him as odd. He is not at all free from idiosyncrasies, psychological flaws which undermine the myth of the truly strong man. Eventually he is reduced to the proportions of a schoolboy's idol or an undergraduate's crush: 'Catching sight of Him on the lawn with the gardener' (*EA* 68), 'His insane dislike of birds' (with a pun on 'birds' for 'girls', thus a sly hint at the hero's possible homosexuality[14]), 'His sharing from His own provision after the blizzard's march', 'His refusal to wear anything but silk next to his skin'. His transformation from a Christ-like saviour figure (traces of which are left, for instance, in the biblical allusion to 'Hysterical attempts of two women to reach Him') to a rather dubious character is once again shown as closely connected with his problematic attachment to language: 'His fondness for verbal puzzles. Friendly joking converting itself into a counterplot, the spore of fear'.

The lapse into the dilemmas of language is inevitable; attempts at flights into silence of speech and thought are illusionary ('Shutting the door on the machines, we stood in silence, thinking of nothing'). Disillusionment and doubt cannot be escaped, as the subsequent sentence shows. 'We forgot His will' and 'His words after we had failed Him' eventually connect language explicitly with failure. Ultimately, all heroism finds its expression in an inscription on a memorial or tombstone which indicates failure through death, and worse, an eventual surrender to tradition. It is not even read any more by the boys who play a game on its steps. Its name ridicules the hero's quest for freedom and accurately comments on its eventual outcome: 'prisoner's base' (*EA* 69).

Another illustration of the importance of language shows a representative of the establishment, a priest, whose 'mouth opens in the green graveyard, but the wind is against it'. The true power is not that of the word, but the unintelligible force of nature which can also symbolise history in Auden's poems. Once more the text addresses the stranger, and once more he is very likely the reader who has been led through images of graveyards only to be called 'Loiterer at carved gates, immune stranger, follow. It is nothing, your loss'. The message is sombre, even contradictory. After all the images of death, destruction, and decay, 'follow' can only mean 'die'. 'Immune' seems strangely out of place, but fulfils an interesting double function in the struggle of the text with its own textuality. Undeniably, the reader remains outside the turmoils of the poem in that it is only fiction he is confronted with. His loss is indeed nothing, no *thing*. What the text tries to take away from him is illusion and belief, the language of hope and faith.

After the elaborate deconstruction of ontological and teleological certainties in 'Argument', 'Statement' (*EA* 69–71), another form of expository prose practised in English schools,[15] seems to do the opposite, namely establish securities. It is concerned with a second way of achieving identity, the identity that derives from man's relation to others. The first paragraph shows men in common situations which are, however, once more Audenesque rather than representative, leading to a formula reminiscent of Marx: 'To each an award, suitable to his sex, his class and the power' (*EA* 69).[16] The Marxian allusion is followed by pastiches of Old English poems, 'The Gifts of Men', 'The Fortunes of Men', and 'Maxims', all of them from the *Exeter Book*.[17] Auden's paratactic style is here employed in its most straightforward form, that of the list. The three sections of 'Statement' represent three different examples, the first a list of capacities and features of a number of persons, the second one of the fortunes and misfortunes of people, the third a list of consequences, pieces of advice, and rules. The characters in the lists remain anonymous; they appear as 'One' in the first two (*EA* 69–70), as 'man', 'woman', 'boy', 'girl', and so on, even as 'the muscular' and 'the murderer' in the third one (*EA* 70–1).

Several other features of the lists are equally significant. First of all, they lack an ordering principle. The list of characteristics and capabilities contains everything from physical attributes such as beautiful skin to the talent for organising study circles. In the same manner, the list of fortunes and misfortunes puts death by accident and arrest for indecent exposure side by side. Both lists contain a surprising last entry: the first, 'One does nothing at all but is good', the second 'One is famous after his death for his harrowing diary' (*EA* 70). Unrelated as they appear at first glance, they are indeed statement and commentary. After the confused list of Part I, the adjective 'good' seems welcome because of its connotations of metaphysical certainty, or ethical soundness. Its context, however, brands it as empty and fictional. That is exactly what the last entry of Part II indicates. In the chaos of accidental incidents, the image of the diary evokes a structured existence – which, however, remains exactly as vacuous as the concept of 'good' in Part I. It also prepares for the 'Journal of an Airman', and thus acts as a further self-referential device of *The Orators*.

The implicit self-devaluation of the lists, the unwriting of their order, is emphasised by the short paragraph that follows each of them as a commentary. After the positive features in Part I, the comment on the passing of a curse from father to son seems not only out of place, but almost tasteless. Part II is followed by the obscure image of a 'red bicycle leaning on porches', linked with a reference to complete annihilation. Mendelson explains it as an allusion to 'the telegraph boy who brought death notices of fathers and elder brothers during the Great War'.[18] All knowledge of human lives does not lead to a system of knowledge, because personal features as well as events are accidental; they neither follow an underlying pattern nor create one. In that respect, the juxtaposition of Marxian doctrine and Old English maxims represents a twofold criticism: both of them are shown as inadequate because of their adherence to a horizontal concept of reality that integrates events and personalities into systems based on stable underlying structures, whether God's universal power or the laws of class struggle and the history of capital. Both concepts are idealistic fictions, incapable of explaining, much less of mastering reality.

The third part of 'Statement', though similar in construction, is consequently a collection of wisdom which is dubious from the very beginning. A mixture of influences as diverse as Gertrude Stein, Blake, and – once more – Old English maxims,[19] it starts with a genesis culminating in the insight that nothing new is possible, everything is a mere repetition of the past. This, of course, is the very concept of the reactionary traditionalists. Yet it is also the belief that Auden's earlier poems implicitly expressed in their desperate and eventually futile attempts to create something original.

The discarding of horizontal historicist systems – as exemplified in Parts I and II of 'Statement' – affects the bases of the intellectual concepts in Auden's poems as well. In Part III the reaction to this loss is a plunge into a complete abandonment of values which leaves only paradoxes. D. H. Lawrence's chauvinist maxims of sexuality and procreation as ordering forces of reality serve as a framework for the chaos of images of this part, yet these ideas are not the expression of a sincere belief, but of a general disorientation. Faced with the insight that there is nothing new, but 'Life is many' (EA 71) and directions and structures are nowhere in sight, the conclusion 'That brings forth' is helpless actionism. This is evident in its lack of object. What is produced by this aimless activity? New life, if 'new' were possible? Or perhaps just excrement, as the preceding line 'The belly receives; the back rejects' indicates? At least the contracting system of The Orators has made its own decision: it brings forth language.

After all the syntactic and semantic chaos of 'Argument' and 'Statement', the conventional prose of 'Letter to a Wound' (*EA* 71–3) comes almost as a relief. Its form is that of a rather conventional, not particularly passionate love-letter written by an addresser whom Spears characterises as 'a bourgeois intellectual of sedentary habits'.[20] Its formal coherence is the direct result of its attempt to illustrate a third way of constituting identity. After the recourse to metaphysical finalities in 'Argument' and the development of an identity in relation to others in 'Statement', 'Letter to a Wound' exemplifies the attempted constitution of identity by the recourse of the self to itself. The narcissistic closure of the discourse finds its expression in the intimate tone of the part, the private references so frequent in Auden's early poems – on which 'Letter to a Wound' thus sheds a critical light.

The letter deals with a psychosomatic state (a wound takes the place of a lover) which Spears interprets as the death wish of the bourgeoisie.[21] Yet this death wish is closely connected with the constitution of the 'I', the writer, which is central to the text. Thus it comes as a surprise that the writer actually gives away very little about himself, 'I can't recognize myself' (*EA* 71), he states, but keeps rambling on about his history, the history of his relationship with the wound. Language is the one thing he is in control of ('free to think of you as I choose'), but it is also identified as an obstacle ('As it is, I've still far too many letters'). His attempt to concentrate entirely on his wound, i.e. himself, is troubled by its vagueness, which always also introduces the Other, even when it is only meant to mirror the self. It is striking that in the list of useless things destined for a great clearance 'presentation pocket-mirrors' and 'foreign envelopes' stand side by side, the equivalents of a love-letter to the self and the intruding other.

Even though the intentional alienation of the writer from society, the other(s), is shown as partially successful, it does not lead to clear identifications either of the self or of the wound. This wound remains as nondescript as the writer, although it is shown to be permanent, probably even mortal. It is essentially a lack, an absence, of physical integrity in the Freudian sense. On the textual level it represents the missing congruence of signifier and signified. The verbal representation of the wound is always too close to the 'I' to permit the emerging of a coherent identity, but too much the Other to make a negative definition of identity possible. The text eventually discards the third attempt to define identity, the recourse to the self.

Yet its declaration of an achieved maturity is not ironic: 'knowing you has made me understand' (*EA* 73), the addresser writes. Yet this understanding is the exact opposite of knowledge (of the self, its relation to others, its origin and purpose). It is the insight that no stable knowledge is possible.

READING THE OTHER

The foregrounding of the relation between the reader and the text which was central in the narcissism of 'Letter to a Wound', a section ending with the advice 'Better burn this' (*EA* 73), becomes even more complex in Book II of *The Orators*, 'Journal of an Airman' (*EA* 73–94). The privacy of 'Journal' puts the reader in a voyeuristic position; this journal, however, is not only concerned with the life of an airman, but just as much is an attempt at defining the Other, who appears – as in Auden's earlier poems – as the enemy. The reader, however, is nothing but this Other in terms of the text. At the same time, he quite naturally tends to identify with the speaker of the poem; he is even invited to do so by various textual devices.

'Journal of an Airman' starts with a discussion of the relationship between 'a system' and the enemy which is so open to interpretation as to cover politics as well as the manoeuvres of the text itself. The first statement is also the central one: 'A system organises itself' (*EA* 73). But the system remains vague, and inevitably so, since – as the third paragraph indicates – one has to introduce 'first causes and purposive ends' to understand ordered structures which are the natural result of tensions. Ontological and teleological certainties are not applicable, however, and are unknown to the text, and are therefore not introduced as the necessary supplements of its first statement. Thinking in these categories is labelled as the influence of the enemy. Its victims are 'us'; the plural, again, includes the reader. The distinction between him and the speaker is blurred from the start.

The very desire of the reader for clear distinctions between the textual identity and his own is immediately ridiculed in 'The second law of thermodynamics' (*EA* 73). While self-care and minding one's own business are described as perfectly natural, self-regard is shown as problematic. This time, instead of repeating its accusations against ontology and teleology, the text compares self-regard to the transformation of news into a private poem, the shifting of public discourse into a private language. Yet this is exactly what *The Orators* does. Even its dedication states: '*Private faces in public places/ Are wiser and nicer/Than public faces in private places*' (*EA* 59); and it attempts to construct an identity out of statements, even though this identity clearly remains a fictional one. At the same time the text tries to undo identity and coherence; hence its complexity and self-destructive moves.

'A Sure Test', the next section of 'Journal of an Airman', introduces a strange device for distinguishing friend and enemy, us and them: a graphic test used by psychologists.[22] Thus, it performs exactly what it accuses the enemy of doing: it attempts to introduce a definition of the self against the other, self-regard. The 'Sure Test' is consequently a very dubious affair. The choice of a symmetrical, harmonious form is supposed to disclose the friend, an asymmetrical choice the enemy. The advised reaction to the latter is 'to shoot at once' (*EA* 74). Once more a surrealist reality takes over with terrorism as the common way of survival. The choices of the friend follow the traditional norms of beauty; their resemblance to war medals is perhaps not accidental. One is made to ask if the friend must suddenly be sought on the side of the traditionalists, until the text itself confronts the reader with one of its crucial statements: 'THE ENEMY IS A LEARNED NOT A NAIVE OBSERVER'. Yet learning is exactly what the test forces its reader to do. Again, the text confuses its distinctions.

The chaos of information and disinformation continues in the following notes of the journal, which deal with concepts of sympathy, kindness, and love, and once more with the problem of inheritance and tradition. The airman is now called the agent of the central awareness, a metaphor for the various forms of relations between the interior and the exterior of the self, its super-ego. But it is not at all clear how he is related to the concept of the self (which in Figure 5, *EA* 75, resembles very much an infantile drawing of female breasts). He is probably a double agent, a spy. As the first note states, 'Introspection – spying' (*EA* 74), and introspection is certainly what the discussion of sympathy, kindness, and love tries to achieve. The notes are another form of internal contradiction. The second one (confusingly called 'Note I', *EA* 75), for example, states that the relation between the centres of circles which has just been called love is nothing but ancestor-worship (another hint at the maternal implications of the breast-shape of the diagram). It introduces an illogical distinction between this ancestor-worship and history, and discredits the latter as a myth.

In the same way, the idiosyncratic interpretation of genetic rules tries to convince the reader of the true ancestry of the uncle or the great-grandfather rather than the parental generation. This seemingly absurd move, which shifts the problem of tradition rather than solving it, has autobiographic roots. Auden had a homosexual uncle who was – quite understandably – more supportive to Auden's lifestyle than his mother.[23] Thus the private aside 'My mother's dislike of my uncle' (EA 76) is accompanied by remarks parodying conventional attitudes towards homosexuality with the image of the aviator as a thin disguise: 'If the Lord had intended people to fly He'd have given them wings' or 'You are a man, or haven't you heard/That you keep on trying to be a bird?' The homosexuality of the airman explains his role as a double agent; but the text does not leave uncriticised this symbolic interpretation and the attempt at a solution – no matter how idiosyncratic.[24] The obscure poem crammed between Figures 5 and 6 deals with the fight against established norms: those that challenge the deadening tradition become themselves infected with its disease, corrupted by its mythopoeia, 'Drain out the Dragon's Pond but die from dropsy' (EA 75).

Any attempt to grasp reality by introducing a fictional order must necessarily end up in myth which reproduces tradition even when it is intended to supplant it. 'Journal of an Airman' goes on to reinterpret some of the dominant features of Auden's earlier poems, the drawing of a map and the reliance on private references, and shows them as exactly what they are meant to overcome: restrictive devices of authority. The poem which follows contains various lines resembling those of earlier poems, only they are now the utterances of the enemy. Its very first line, 'We have brought you, they said, a map of the country' (EA 77), is one of them. Control and love are shown to go hand in hand ('We shall watch your future and send our love'). This is a much stronger threat than the suspicion that successful love resembles the establishment of traditional certainties, for instance in the poem later called 'This Loved One' (CP 44).

As in earlier poems, the clock becomes the symbol of the authority of tradition, while the diver (in this poem, in the plural) symbolises distraction from its rules (compare the early poem 'No trenchant parting this', EA 21). But mere distraction does not mean breaking free. The protagonist, an anonymous 'he', eventually comes 'to love/ The moss that grew on the derelict vats' (EA 77). He settles down and accepts the dead tradition. The derelict vats are, of course, another allusion to the imagery of Auden's early poems, to another private tradition.

A more radical violation of this tradition, the poem suggests, is going to the wood, because 'There's a flying trickster in that wood'. Obviously the authority of tradition ceases there ('And we shan't be there to help with our love'). The flying trickster alludes to a paper by John Layard on sorcerers on Malekula, an island in the New Hebrides, who are thought to be able to fly, and whose rite is passed from maternal uncle to nephew.[25] The trickster is the symbol which unites both the subversive qualities of the airman and the paradoxical fact that the attempt to overcome the limits of tradition only ever leads to a new one, another ritual, in the same way as the shifting of ancestry from the parents to the uncle only creates a new form of ancestor-worship. The fictional nature of the counter-tradition is implied in the term 'trickster' itself.

The protagonist of the poem disregards the advice of the forces of tradition, and goes to the wood. This violation of the rules gives him a sense of identity, reality, and satisfaction ('His pulse differing from the clock./Finds consummation in the wood/And sees for the first time the country'; *EA* 77). Yet his discoveries are dangerously close to the abandoned certainties. The final line 'This is your country and the hour of love' is uncannily similar to the words of authority in the first stanza. Transgressing the norm always also means its confirmation. Indeed, power and tradition always require an 'Other', opposition, madness, or crime, in order to constitute themselves. This dilemma of the Other, the double edge of nonconformity, is not only illustrated by *The Orators*, but actually undergone by the poem.

The poem attempts to set up a negative dialectic, one of dissolution, which demonstrates that the achievement of knowledge is not understanding but its very opposite: confusion, chaos, and terror. But there is no relief to be found either in the destruction of certainties, the mere violation of rules. This finds further expressions in the rest of 'Journal of an Airman', and also in Book III of *The Orators*, 'Six Odes'. Their descriptions of the enemy intermingle serious premises of humanist thought and repetitions of the problematic concept of identity with mere jokes. 'A man doing nothing is not a man' (*EA* 78) is one of the claims, but doing nothing does not automatically lead to an identity which is more than a mask: 'The misery of a dispossessed king. Who should know that better than the usurper?' The origin of the dilemma once more is thought, and more specifically, language: 'Their extraordinary idea that man's only glory is to think';

'The enemy's sense of humour – verbal symbolism'. Verbal symbolism, however, is nothing but poetry. *The Orators* gives itself away as
the language of the Other, and demonstrates that the consequences
of its dialectic also apply to its expression, the poem itself.

Perhaps the most successful example of a subversive statement
subverting itself is 'The Airman's Alphabet' (*EA* 79–81). It is certainly
the most radical one, since it demonstrates the effect of the negative
dialectic on letters, the basic element of language. The alphabet represents a dominant ordering mechanism of thought and expression
in Western cultures, standing, therefore, for traditional authority. By
transforming the general alphabet into a private form the code of
authority is undermined. Yet it is strengthened at the same time,
because in form and function the old and the new are similar.

This mixture of traditionalism and its subversion can also be
found in the entries of the alphabet. As in the very first one, 'Ace'
(*EA* 79), tradition, 'Pride of parents', is combined with entries with
erotic overtones, here 'laughter in leather'. Many images in 'The Airman's Alphabet' derive directly from the visual mass media. The
mention of 'photographed person' is the first hint, while 'house of
handshaking' reproduces a typical detail from a newspaper photograph, perhaps even a pilot B-movie of the late 1920s. By this implicit allusion to the mass media, the translation of individual heroism
into public discourse is highlighted; while at the same time public
discourse is re-translated into a private form by the introduction of
erotic ambiguities and innuendoes.

In accordance with a remark that Auden made in a journal he
kept in 1929, 'The sexual act is only a symbol for intimacy',[26] one
could conclude that Auden's early poems treat successful sexual
relations as a mere substitute, similar to poetry which is described as
'verbal symbolism', i.e. enemy language. Love, the connection
between the centres of the two circles in Figure 5 (*EA* 75), is a substitute for the impossible. Eroticism, however, is the perfect translator
of the deficient into the undefinable and vice versa. Auden foregrounds its role as mediator between private and public, and hints
at its propaganda potential and – interlinked – its double role as
revolutionary and reactionary similar to that of its embodiments: the
spy, the secret agent, and the airman.

A very different discussion of the relations between private and
public can be found in the polemical attack against two newspaper
barons, the Lords Rothermere and Beaverbrook, who become
'Beethameer, Beethameer, bully of Britain' (*EA* 86). Beethameer is

accused of forcing his private opinions on the public, 'We should learn from your lips the laws to spell/Of Art, of Religion, of Science, of Sex' (*EA* 87; note the importance of spelling in relation to indoctrination). At the same time he is merely the representative of the collective opinion of the bourgeoisie, whose members appear as the talented contributors (most probably to the letters page) in the fourth stanza, the prophet of the public discourse which intrudes into the privacy of the individual: 'In kitchen, in cupboard, in club-room, in mews,/In palace, in privy, your paper we meet' (*EA* 86). Divisions into private and public are no longer valid, neither in the world depicted in *The Orators* nor for the text itself. It eventually joins Beethameer's propaganda game: the line that follows the polemical outburst is '10,000 Cyclostyle copies of this for aerial distribution' (*EA* 87).

The Orators is aware of the implications of the loss of distinctions and the dissolution of rules. The consequences for the individual are attempts to keep an identity intact that has no chance of achieving coherence; and the symptoms of this struggle are masturbation and kleptomania, both of them transgressions of the norm and symbolic equivalents of the attempts to establish a relation between the self and itself, and the self and the Other. The tools of the symbolic violations of the norm are the hands, strikingly enough also the means of the production of writing. It is obvious that the central protagonist of *The Orators*, the airman, suffers from the symptoms of the disease which appears to be that of the times: the dissolution of identity. At the same time the text discovers, names, and criticises these symptoms in its own structure.[27] The use and simultaneous disqualification of obscurity and private references as the textual equivalent of masturbation (the worship of the lack) and kleptomania (the manic raid of the Other) are indications of this.[28]

The effect of the dissolution of identity and certainties is anarchy; and the final sections of 'Journal of an Airman' depict an ever-increasing chaos, war between the enemy and the party of the airman, whose cause is as unexplained as its outcome is unpredictable. Yet from its first explicit introduction the battle is declared to be lost, its inevitable consequence the death of the speaker. The first vision, 'Dream Last Night' (*EA* 85), includes the archetypal image of the ferryman, the conveyor of the dead. The detailed description of the death of a fellow pilot, Derek, brought about by the sabotage of the enemy (the moss on the cap of the mechanic is seen as a giveaway, *EA* 88–9) prefigures the airman's own. Although thoughts of victory occur, they are labelled daydreams from the start (*EA* 90). The hopes connected with such a victory include the healing of the wound, or the final establishment of a stable identity; but the plans for such an event prove that the speaker is still immature, involving the distribution of the country among his friends (once more private references without context) and culminating in the childish 'Monthly firework displays' (*EA* 91).

On the level of imagery, chaos is illustrated by a mixture of military terms with grotesque images, such as 'At the prearranged zero hour the widow bent into a hoop with arthritis gives the signal for attack by unbending on the steps of St. Philip's' (*EA* 92). Surrealism is the reaction of the text to the dissolution of the distinction between the self, that is, itself, and the Other: between stable tradition and its mirror-image, madness. The crazy world of the end of the journal, in which the effects of the obscure war include ceasing menstruation, vampires, and epidemics of superfluous hair (*EA* 93), is therefore simultaneously hilarious and deadly serious. The loss of direction leads first to a turning of the speaker's utterances against themselves ('What have I written? Thoughts suitable to a sanatorium', *EA* 94) and eventually to another attempt at an already discarded form, the prayer. This time it is addressed to the uncle – who has slyly become capitalised, and thus deified, in the course of 'Journal of an Airman', for the first time in 'Fourteenth anniversary of my Uncle's death' (*EA* 84).

That the poem's lapse into surrealism is not arbitrary but the consequence of its discoveries is symbolically highlighted by the impossible task given to the 'candidates' on the first day of mobilisation: 'Candidates must write on three sides of the paper' (*EA* 92). The text returns to the 'English Study' of its subtitle only to unveil this form as no longer possible: the only way for the text to achieve its aim, resistance against tradition, is, as pointed out in the 'three elementary truths' on the 25th [day], 'self-destruction, the sacrifice of all resistance, reducing him [the enemy] to the state of a man trying to walk on a frictionless surface' (*EA* 93). This can only be achieved if the text ceases to be one, if it gives up its textuality in such a radical way that it even ceases to be translatable. Such a radical transformation is beyond imagination. The only choice left to 'Journal of an Airman' is to disrupt communication, to become silent. After a pronouncedly objective statement of the airman's condition (a modern form of prayer, and obviously useless, since the notions of objective reality have long disappeared) which culminates in the crucial

'Hands in perfect order' (*EA* 94) – that is, the seeming triumph over his deficiencies and that of the text over its pitfalls – the airman's voice ceases. Another hero has been lost – or got rid of.

The dramatic disorder of 'Journal of an Airman' is followed by the conventional shape of 'Six Odes' (*EA* 94–110) which form Book III of *The Orators*. In spite of their form, they are not only adequate as reiterations of the dominant ideas of the entire poem in a more orderly form than could be expected from stream of consciousness or the radical stylistic experiments of the journal; but their shape is even consequent, if one dares apply this term to a text which tries to overcome notions of cause and result.

The ode as lyric in the form of an address is usually directed towards a person or an object worthy of the exercise. The addressees in Auden's odes, however, are very dubious in that respect. The first ode acts as a summary of the themes of *The Orators*: the attempt at introducing an order, here a temporal one; the motif of the wound; the enemy maxims ('Man is a spirit'; *EA* 95); power; tradition; the healer/hero/saviour. It is an ode to self-regard. The second, a parody of Gerard Manley Hopkins and – like its model – an exercise in the Pindaric ode, is a caricature of hero-worship that celebrates, of all things, a rugby team, and foregrounds its immature eroticism in hilarious form.

The third ode is a personal poem addressed to Edward Upward, who at the time shared Auden's fate of being a teacher at a school he did not like. But more than that, it is the critical analysis of being an outsider, the equivalent of the airman. The detached position is shown as ultimately lifeless, dead as the reality from which it tries to distance itself.

Another exercise in discrediting the leader principle is the longest of the odes, number IV. It praises the son of Auden's friend, Rex Warner, as a new leader, while simultaneously discrediting the real leaders Mussolini, Pilsudski, and Hitler as 'the ninny, the mawmet and the false alarm' (*EA* 102). Yet John Warner's leadership potential is more than dubious, since he is still a baby at the time. The crucial quality, youth, only ironically present in him, is elevated to the universal solution of all problems and is even accepted as such by the representatives of the old system, the *Sunday Express*, the teacher, the bishop, and the bumslapper. 'Strewth,' says the speaker, and rejects one of the prominent concepts both of Auden's early poems and the 1920s not only as empty, but ultimately reactionary ('Sooner or later it'll come to the pater'; *EA* 103).

The fifth ode, dedicated to Auden's pupils, was later called 'Which Side Am I Supposed to Be On'.[29] It deals with the consequences of authority and its reproductive device, education. The question that the poem's eventual title highlights is a mere rhetorical one. Infected by the disease of tradition (represented as the Seven Deadly Sins) from the start, the heroic rebellion of the young is futile. Its result, predictably, is the eventual return to the established norm.

This pessimistic tone finds its climax in the final ode, an imitation of the Metrical Psalms,[30] but also similar to Hopkins' desperate poems. It is another prayer, yet a very unusual one, because it asks for defeat:

> Not, Father, further do prolong
>   Our necessary defeat;
> Spare us the numbing zero-hour,
>   The desert-long retreat. (*EA* 109)

In spite of its traditional form, this short piece must be regarded as one of the most radical parts of *The Orators*, an exercise in unwriting the poem while completing it. Indeed, it is a return to everything that has been rejected in the course of the long poem, the eventual surrender to authority and tradition as representatives of universal truths. All those find their symbolic expression in one word: 'Father'. Against this force all the trickery of the text proves useless:

> Against your accusations
>   Though ready wit devise,
> Nor magic countersign prevail
>   Nor airy sacrifice. (*EA* 109)

The consequence of this acceptance of defeat is complete submission.

But *The Orators* would not be *The Orators* if it permitted such an unambiguous conclusion. As it rightly describes itself, 'stubborn and oblique', its sets its maddened foot against any attempt to straighten the notion of reality. In the very traditionalism of the form of the last ode it discovers the means of subverting it. The inverted syntax which is the inheritance of its model(s) is used for the creation of its own ritual, 'Our maddened set we foot', which reverses, makes ambiguous, and contradicts. The very beginning which places 'Not' before the all-powerful addressee already has the effect of a rejection.

The technique of this ode is indeed that of a 'magic countersign': language is employed for the transformation of the discourse of power into that of rebellion. The ode is strongly reminiscent of the belief that a reversed prayer, especially the Lord's Prayer, establishes contact with the forces of evil. Yet this reversal of discourse can never be complete. The last ode of *The Orators* conforms to the long poem's overall dialectic and remains in a suspense of meaning like a pack of cards spread out on a table which – reversed by a quick sleight of hand – suddenly reveals a very different image.

WRITING DIFFERENCE

Taking into account the fact that *The Orators* frequently asks for its own destruction ('Better burn this' in 'Letter to a Wound' is the most obvious example of its request), it may be permissible to use its final part, 'Epilogue', as an angle from which one tries to shed some critical light on the whole text. Or, to remain within the vocabulary of Auden's poem, if one employs it as a basis from which one coordinates its 'necessary defeat' (*EA* 109), it becomes a defeat which is also its final, paradoxical victory.

As Günther Jarfe points out, the poem is one of the examples in Auden's *oeuvre* in which rhetorical finesse is the device of the tradition which tries to paralyse those who attempt to break free from it. 'Reader', 'fearer', and 'horror' are its representatives; their questions aim at keeping their counterparts 'rider', 'farer', and 'hearer' from going on a quest with a nondescript goal.[31] The dangers they try to paint so vividly are manifold, including mythical or fairy-tale elements such as the maddening odours, the dangerous cave, the hostile bird, and the silently approaching figure, as well as real dangers, such as increasing darkness and psychosomatic illnesses. The transgression of the norm is shown to have many unpleasant consequences.

Yet despite its excellence, the rhetoric of prevention fails. The questioners, 'orators' in the best (or worst) sense of the word, get their answers, and they are unexpected ones. Not only do 'rider', 'farer', and 'hearer' – who turn out to be one person, 'he', in the last stanza – refuse to be frightened by the rhetorical threats; their responses question the authority of the questioners. The intimidations are turned against the threateners ('They're looking for you'), the blindness is shown to be theirs, and the rider leaves 'this house'

(*EA* 110), that is, the common reality that has united him with the reader. The poem exercises the shift from the readerly to a writerly perspective *avant la lettre*.[32]

These rejections by the poem's protagonist refuse to give answers in the traditional summarising way ('where are you going?', for instance, usually has a direction as its answer, not a starting-point) and thus attract attention to the lack of connection which underlies the apparent coherence of the questions. The stanzas are, indeed, no real semantic units, but paratactic conglomerations whose internal order is arbitrary. The power of tradition does not derive from its internal logic, but its logic is the result of its established power.[33] Jarfe sees as one of the important arguments of the poem the warning that the exchange of communication for rhetoric leads to manipulation, a distortion of reality, a devaluation of the individual, and a dubious aura of authority and authenticity in the discursive interaction.[34]

This observation, correct as it is, nevertheless requires a wider context, one that the poem itself hints at: the relationship between the text and its reader. The pun of the very first line of 'Epilogue' refers once more to the game the text plays by taking the reader's words out of his mouth and caricaturing his helpless reaction to a text like *The Orators*: '"O where are you going?" said reader to rider' (*EA* 110). The poem delivers the final *coup de grâce* by placing the reader explicitly in the confines of the tradition which it is about to leave. He is not even granted a personality, but only appears in the plural 'them', immobile, threatened, and eventually left behind.

Yet by acting as such a forceful reader-controlling mechanism, one that even boasts the power of quitting the relation which is the reading process, the poem places itself on the side of the 'orators' it has been so busy to disqualify. It is indeed a criticism of rhetoric, but also an indication that every discourse is rhetorical. Even the most distorted form of utterance enters the discourse of power as a statement.

The Orators is indeed concerned with meaning, history, identity, and authority, but it refrains from providing answers to any of the questions arising from those issues. More than that, it denies the very possibility of arriving at secure knowledge. The effect of its continual deconstruction of the mechanisms of literary discourse is an emphasis on the discursive practice which governs our entire existence, the continual process of the mutual creation of reality out of statements and statements out of reality. Auden's poems not only discuss these topics, they actually mirror their discoveries in their own structures. This self-reflection is, of course, the inheritance of modernism. The abandonment of the attempt to create their own model of reality, the eventual disqualification of the endeavour even, distinguishes Auden's poems from the modernist tradition.

A farewell to the established notion that Auden's early poems are brilliant rhetorical propaganda pieces intermingled with schoolboy fantasies seems inevitable. Yet the discarding of their more-than-ambiguous surface politics should not deceive us about their status as eminently political works which question the bases of political convictions and direct attention to the fictional premises of the latter. Their acceptance of missing certainties does not lead to a nihilistic resignation: this would have been as fatal in the 1930s as it is today. Auden's poems go on asking 'What are we going to do?'; they demand action continually. But they do not pamper their reader with the certainty of an authority that justifies action, or with promises of metaphysical goals that can be achieved. The responsibility to live is left to the individual alone (no matter how fragmented), and cannot be projected onto objective certainties. In order to become capable of dealing with this radically changed perspective, a process of learning has to be undergone. Indeed, *The Orators*, as a summary and critical evaluation of the whole of Auden's early poems, can be described as the manifestation of an educational enterprise which is very unlike the common initiation into orthodox certainties, but which is a trial and error course in which even established notions of identity have to be left behind.

5

The Challenge of History

Even though Auden's early poems try hard to expose the forces of tradition, politics, and history as language games, one must not be misled into thinking that the texts thereby counter the challenge of external events and time, of history, once and for all. Indeed, as pointed out above, games are serious issues, and they also always subject the players to their rules. History as a force composed of undeniable and threatening external events that cannot be deflected by 'magic countersigns' enters Auden's poetry gradually, at first almost unnoticeably, until it becomes a dominant topic which eventually determines the title of the largest of the pre-*Orators* poems, 'It was Easter as I walked in the public gardens', which becomes '1929' in later collections (*CP* 50–3).

In the 1928 *Poems* time already makes an appearance. At first it is only metaphorically present, as in 'Spring' and 'Autumn' in 'We saw in Spring' (*EA* 437), discussed above. Yet even there it contains tensions, and they soon develop into a general insecurity punctuated with implicit hints at violence. A typical line from a poem entitled 'I chose this lean country' (*EA* 439–40), 'From angles unforeseen/The drumming of a snipe', disrupts the bucolic bird image by joining it to unforeseen angles. They evoke its near-homonym 'sniper', that then enters a martial association with 'drumming'.

In the 1930 volume, time already sets the tone for entire poems: 'No trenchant parting this/Of future from the past' starts the second poem of the collection (*EA* 21–2). The poem's attempt to define the present as yet another borderline, between past and future, is troubled by the same defect that we have already encountered in 'Sir, no man's enemy': there is no noticeable difference between the two. The destruction of old values, even their reversal (scaring the bogey man instead of being scared by him), is obviously considered necessary to prepare for the future. This reversal, however, has yet to be achieved. There seem to be manifestations of something new, but the failure to overcome established ways of thinking, the old values, prevents their explanation and thus their effectiveness. From the security of their past achievements (both spiritual and material – as expressed in the description 'Buttressed expensively'), the older generation scrutinises the convictions of the young and tries to prove their deficiency: 'The pointed hand would trace/Error in you and me'. The rhetorical trick of the line includes the reader in the young generation thus attacked. Even though the speaker appears in the singular, he is once more the representative of a greater cause. And he is also apparently willing to use means bordering on propaganda to advance it.

The straightforward transcription of the poem given so far betrays its essential difficulty, though. There is, for instance, the inverted syntax of the first lines; there is also a suspicious absence of articles. Throughout the poem, definite articles are restricted to nouns connected with the past and its representatives. Those linked with the present and the future remain without any article, except for the unrealised possibilities of justification and escape, 'an explanation' and 'a way', which are granted an indefinite one. This can be taken to correspond to the problem of the already-defined past ('this finite space') which threatens to eclipse the still unmapped future. The adjective 'unmapped' is deliberate. What are so many of Auden's poems concerned with? Making maps. The difficulties of the text remain unsolved. They derive to a large extent from the terms it employs. All of them are abstract, except once more two which belong to the past, the time gone or passing, 'the pointed hand' (which is ambiguously both accusingly pointed finger and the hand of a clock) and, later, 'the pendulum'.

The remaining six lines of the first stanza of 'No trenchant parting this' are equally opaque. They talk about mitigating 'the stare' and about finding an 'argument too bare'. But frighteningly enough, what resolves the poem's anxiety is once again a pendulum. Time's unlenient will, already encountered as the destroyer of happiness in 'Under boughs between our tentative endearments' (*EA* 29), 'Restore[s] the gravamen'. If 'argument' means dispute then the ambiguity remains indeed unresolved, for the line could then either indicate that the old get tired of their own accusations for a while, until the 'pendulum' renews the attack, or, alternatively, that the young get tired of constantly having to defend themselves. If 'argument' stands for proposition, however, 'argument too bare' could very well be one of Auden's puns on sex. As a defence against the old this makes some sense, because sexuality is conventionally associated with vitality. The young would then claim possession of life through the bare fact that they are sexually active, and the final two lines of the stanza would indicate that the defence of the young is only a temporary one, because sex is a short-lived activity. Instead of defying the attack of the old, the attempted defence only focuses it more sharply.

The 'trenchant parting' that was negatively evoked in the very first line of the poem eventually appears typographically as the gap between its two stanzas. The meaning of this split becomes apparent when one compares their tone. In contrast to the obscurities and ambiguities of the first, the second one is impressively straightforward. It describes the speaker observing a 'diver's brilliant bow' and admiring how he flicks back the hair from his forehead 'With one trained movement'. This leads to a reflection on the joy of observing beauty, but also to the darker notion that 'that which we create/We also may destroy'.

Although still slightly inverted, the syntax is now unambiguous. The nouns are all concrete, except for the 'joy' engendered by the observation, and their meaning is clear. The very first line of the stanza already shows what it is about and why it must of necessity contrast with the poem's beginning. 'But standing now I see' may appear to be nothing but an introduction to the things which follow, but it is indeed highly charged with meaning. 'But' deepens the trench between the two stanzas by its rejecting tone; but it remains none the less connected with the first stanza by indicating a defence against the accusations of the 'pointed hand', signalling that it is the missing argument necessary for the assertion of the young. '[S]tanding' not only fixes the speaker in a firm position after the flux of the poem's first part, but also shows strength through its connotation of resistance. '[N]ow' is perhaps the most direct clue for what has been constituted in the stanza: a sense of the present, the certainty desperately missed in the first stanza. Consequently, the speaker now appears for the first time explicitly as 'I', his characteristic activity once more perception.

What he sees is the diver who is capable of easily transgressing the limitations of the elements. He can ignore 'trenchant partings', and becomes indeed (once more the definite article is an indication) the symbol of the present – and perhaps the future as well. The worship of the beautiful body is common in the 1920s and 1930s. The adjective 'brilliant', which contrasts strangely with the neutral terms of the description, hints at the emotional significance of the scene.

But it is common knowledge that this cult of the body was exploited by the Left as well as by fascism. The diver in the above poem is indeed a rather ambiguous ideal. The attractive gesture of throwing back his hair is described as a 'trained movement'. He does not represent untamed nature but, on the contrary, the rigidity of discipline.

The symbol of the diver, seductive and necessary as it may be, none the less fails in its task. The speaker's verdict on the spectacle modifies its impact by stating rather dryly that he is stung by the same sun that makes the diver's bow appear so brilliant. Symbol and poetic identity are irreconcilable, as the remaining lines of the stanza indicate by paring down the seductive vision. 'The eye' (the I?) 'deliberate/May qualify the joy' discusses the transformation of a sensual impression into signifiers, into mere intellectual categories. It is noteworthy that the enraptured observer is now presented as in control by the adjective 'deliberate' and the genteel modifier 'May' – rather than overwhelmed; while the diver is reduced from quasi-mythical figure to mere spectacle.

The effect of this transformation can hardly satisfy. The adjective 'semi-satisfied' that is employed as its description is indeed an oxy-moron. The symbol, both static simplification and arbitrary concept, does not provide the poem with the sense of the present demanded since its very first line. 'And that which we create/We also may destroy' could be an epithet on the theme of making the present last into the future. It would then be banal and also rather unmotivated, since there is no trace of creation in the poem. None, except for the creation of the diver symbol. Indeed, it seems that the final lines of 'No trenchant parting this' refer to the poem's own fictional construction of a present – as well as to its eventual dismissal. They both accept the impossibility of defining the present, and define it, at the same time, as the empty space created by the deconstruction of the symbol. This links the poem's attempt to write its own (admittedly basic) version of history with the attempts to redefine symbols in non-transcendental ways in Auden's earliest poems as discussed in Chapter 2. The locus of the meaning of 'present' is indeed merely the gap between the two stanzas of the poem. The setting of this present – since both past and future are fictional concepts – must be the intellectual imagination.

Paul de Man employs this temporal impasse as a characterisation of modernist texts. In his essay 'Literary History and Literary Modernity' he describes it (with reference to Baudelaire) as 'the compulsion to return to a literary mode of being, as a form of language that knows itself to be mere repetition, mere fiction and allegory, forever unable to participate in the spontaneity of action or modernity'.[1] Yet while modernist texts merely display this tension and make it part of their aesthetics of failure, Auden's poem actively shows that it considers a mere imaginary solution – such as the one offered by the poem's imagery – to be unsatisfactory. The poem may appear to assert its own identity by foregrounding its control over its concepts, yet this identity is far from stable – and the poem actively participates in undermining it. It thereby radicalises some features of modernist poetry (its hovering between fragmented voices and impersonality), but it also adds a further critical framework by contrasting them with the demands of factual reality. This will be demonstrated in greater depth in Chapter 5.

Poetic identity is always determined by the imagery that surrounds it and which it tries to arrange (as a map, for instance), transform, or – in the case of the 'trenchant parting' – even to overcome. In Auden's early poetry the settings produce unstable and unreliable speakers who are crippled by a past that continues to lurk threateningly in the background. A 1929 poem that was later called 'Family Ghosts' starts with a typical representation of this threat: 'The strings' excitement, the applauding drum/Are but the initiating ceremony/That out of cloud the ancestral face may come' (CP 47). The frighteningly pervasive power of the past (once more, the personal experience is itself a symbol of the general malaise) can appear in Freudian shape, as in the surface banality of the second stanza of 'It's no use raising a shout': 'A long time ago I told my mother/I was leaving home to find another:/I never answered her letter/But I never found a better' (EA 42–3). 'There is no change of place', claims the poem with the subsequent title 'No Change of Place' (CP 42), and many of Auden's early poems indeed describe a paralysis in the face of a danger which grows out of the confusions of the past.

One of the possible reactions against the growing helplessness is the formation of escapist fantasies. They find their expression in various images which are either deliberately ridiculous, as in 'Half Way' (CP 67–8), where a submarine and a false beard are employed as means of escape, or more serious, as in Auden's many quest fantasies. Of course it is unfair to categorise as 'escapist' and therefore as naive, irresponsible, and illusory a concept that is not only very prominent in Auden's early poems, but also – as will be shown below – among the dominant modes of constituting identity. At this point, however, the label is meant to indicate rather neutrally the urge to escape from 'the fatal necessities of the omnipotent apparatus of modern, highly-industrialised societies'[2] which is the inheritance and also the expression of the despised older generation. It seems vital to flee from this threat in order to achieve individual freedom, to leave the old behind to start something new.

The defence against the limiting threat of a historicist perspective which regards everything new as a mere development of preceding states is the cause of much of the energy spent in Auden's early poems. This is one of its links with modernist avant-garde movements and their continual battle cry, 'Death to Whatever Happened Before'. But the crucial new insight of Auden's poems is the suspicion that the real enemy is located *inside*. On the imaginary level, this is expressed in protagonists who are traitors or spies; on the logical level it gains shape in the (partly Freudian) conviction that life is inevitably threatened by the ancestral inheritance. On the textual level, this leads to poems that openly display their logical flaws or whose arguments turn on themselves. The political implication of this dilemma is the desire for personal liberty coupled with a denial of liberalism. The characters of Auden's early poems strive to be free – and also good (doing the right thing is always part of the problem), but they are aware that man is neither born free nor good. On the textual level, the expression of the impasse is once more 'history', this time the history of words and terms, their connotations, the layers of meaning that are always part and parcel of signifiers.

'Always afraid to say more than it meant', the final line of a poem concerned with the new life which starts with the lines 'From the very first coming down/Into a new valley with a frown/Because of the sun and a lost way' (CP 39), could easily act as the epitome for the whole of Auden's early works. Significantly enough, under its later title 'The Letter', it became the first poem in Auden's *Collected Poems* as well as in his *Collected Shorter Poems*. Various strategies are employed to get rid of the surplus of meaning which is always also the discourse of the rejected older generation. Clinical language which reduces the number of possible connotations is one of these devices, but remains an insufficient remedy, since there are no signifiers with limited or stable signifieds. Focusing on one form of discourse does not eliminate the general system of transformation which is the nature of language. Nor does it stop the transformation of statements, the archive which always attests the historicity of all discourses.[3] The travesty or the more subtle subversion of inherited

traditions does not do away with them either: the attempted deconstruction only enforces the underlying subtext, the traditional inheritance, what Hutcheon calls 'epistemological authority'.

Another device employed to fight the paralysing influence of the
past which has already been encountered is the symbol. Auden, of
course, is hardly the first poet to use it in order to define history;
Yeats is the foremost example of this approach among his modernist
predecessors. But even in Yeats's poems the strategy is rarely successful (as the problematic bird symbol in the 'Byzantium' poems
shows). When symbols convince as images of history, they owe their
persuasive power to an underlying symbolic system. Such a system
cannot be found in Auden's early poetry. Although there are recurring metaphors with symbolic qualities (such as 'war' or 'the house'),
these are characterised by the absence of stable underlying signifieds: a coherent system which either integrates them or develops
out of them is nowhere in sight. In Lyotard's terms, Auden's poetry
lacks underlying narratives of legitimation,[4] and as a consequence
gives the impression of dislocation. Within a flux of rhetoric, it contains philosophical and political set-pieces looking for an order they
cannot attain.

An equally serious reason for the insufficiency of the symbol is its
foregrounding of the ordering structure that brings it into being in
the first place: identity. Yet this identity, as Auden's poems demonstrate openly, is no virgin territory or *tabula rasa*, but is tainted by
and indeed is the product of its historic becoming. It cannot therefore be employed to escape the impact of the past either.

Still, there remains a device that seems to lend itself ideally to the
purpose of transcending history and identity at the same time, a
device which is massively employed by classical modernism: myth.
As Roland Barthes claims, myth functions as a secondary sign system,
a meta-language that composes a new sign out of already existing
ones. This fusion deprives the pre-existent signs of their 'history',
because the complex relations between their signifiers and signifieds
are eclipsed by the new structure, and signs are reduced to the status of mere signifiers.[5] The ideological effect of this merger is the
transformation of history into nature.[6] There are obvious links
between this theoretical description of myth and the tendency to
portray historic states as nature in Auden's poems – as the symptoms of diseases, for example. Mythical elements can indeed be
detected in many of Auden's early poems. Often their settings are in
a vague 'somewhere' without definable historic attachment. The

observers and doomed heroes who appear out of nowhere and apparently lack any trace of a personal past are further hints at the device. Even the idea of a tragic inheritance is general and ahistorical, and locates historical problems in a problematic 'nature' of human beings.

The dominant perspective of Auden's early poems is that of an overview by an impersonal observer. Once more, a mythical strategy is employed. Myth is truly omniscient, because it only knows itself. A fine example of the technique is the beginning of a 1929 poem: 'From scars where kestrels hover,/The leader looking over/ Into the happy valley' (*CP* 40). Yet already this early text shows an awareness of the dangers of myths and leader figures. The poem culminates in the deaths of the men who accompany the leader, while he remains unharmed. The later title of the poem, 'Missing', invokes the fate of a great many soldiers of the First World War. This, together with its claim 'bravery is now,/Not in the dying breath/But resisting the temptations/To skyline operations' shows that myth is handled with scepticism in Auden's early writings, being simultaneously attractive and dangerous. Yet Auden's poems do not always steer clear of it.

A rather less obvious and indeed uncritical use of the absolutist perspective of myth are the many private references in Auden's writings, which are employed as if they were universally meaningful. This becomes particularly obvious when his acquaintances and friends appear as characters in his poems, where they represent not only historic persons, but universal principles. The tenth stanza of 'Get there if you can', which liberally mixes private references and famous public persons, has already been quoted as an example. An early 1927 poem, 'I chose this lean country' (*EA* 439–40), contains the characters 'Margaret the brazen leech,/And that severe Christopher'. 'Christopher' is Christopher Isherwood, 'Margaret' Margaret Marshall, a psychiatrist who later married Auden's brother John ('leech' is here used in the sense of doctor).[7] Yet even this information does not help the reader who is not initiated into 'the myth of themselves'.[8] One of the inevitable effects of private myths is élitism.

It is precisely this inherent élitism, however, that also prevents myth from becoming the dominant mode in Auden's early poems. Despite their attempt at analysing general states and the conditions of society, Auden's poems take recourse to images of distinctly private origin and – in a way – must do so, because the general situation is always seen as the cumulative expression of private concerns and vice versa. But even though the poems try to distance themselves from historicism and the limitations of a contradictory personality, they do not want to abandon history altogether, and refuse to exchange the individual consciousness for an impersonal one. This is one of the effects of myth. Indeed, myth's paradoxical effect is the strengthening of the conventional concept of identity as well as coherent concepts of history – exactly those structures that Auden's early poems struggle with and eventually strive to transform or overcome.

Not surprisingly, therefore, Auden's early poems – with the exception of a few very early ones that are perhaps too concerned with establishing their own voice to be aware of their own techniques – are not only busy erecting mythopoeic structures, but are equally busy undermining them.[9] The destruction of a mythical *locus amoenus* or beautiful place, the 'happy valley', has been observed in the poem 'Missing' above. Unlike classical modernist poems, Auden's early texts do not use the destruction of myths for the creation of even larger integrative meta-myths,[10] but retain an openness through the evocation of danger from nowhere, a symbolic reminder of essential uncertainty, thus refraining from becoming harmonically closed – and in traditional terms 'successful' – works.

PARABLES

The largest of the pre-*Orators* poems, '1929' introduces most explicitly the device that was already evident in *Paid on Both Sides* and which achieves prominence in the whole of Auden's early works: the parable. Parables, like myths, consist of two sets of signs. Unlike myths, however, they do not merge those units, but relate them in the same way that similes relate individual signs. Parables do not strive for an eventual union of connected meanings, but rather for a depiction of their similarity (which always includes their distinction as well). In this way the parable always foregrounds its own construction. Its purpose is didactic: it invites scrutiny and interpretation. Scrutiny, on the other hand, is the very end of myth.[11] The parable calls for a narrative structure, as is evident in the most important source of parables in Western civilization, the Bible. In Auden's poetry, it is the device which permits a clearer definition of the connection of two issues already encountered: the character of reality and the disposition of the individual, both of which are connected by (as well as being the source of) history. The analysis of '1929' (*CP* 50–3), will illustrate this relation as well as its problems.

The opening line of its first stanza introduces Easter, with its connotations of resurrection, new beginnings, and liberation from sin. It also introduces the speaker. A possible redemption from the past is clothed in Christian terms. Novelty and change become recurring topics of this part of the poem: a new language, new names, a new hand, and new power. But this euphoric potential is already countered by the mundane setting of this epiphany: the public gardens. What could become victory over the old rules and norms is already situated within their structures. The image of exhaling frogs in the poem's second line even verges on ridicule, while the stanza as a whole carefully combines images of nature with a city setting and thus once more avoids Romantic allusions. A subtle example is 'Watching traffic of magnificent cloud', which merges the cloud as a symbol of overwhelming nature with traffic, the index of civilization, and thus evokes nature only in already domesticated form. Reality offers no open spaces, as in Romanticism; like the individual, it is the victim of oppressive structures – and therefore hardly represents a foil for change.

After the dash which marks the end of the description of the urban setting, there is some real enthusiasm none the less. Lovers and writers appear united in what seems at first to be a slightly ambiguous, because incomplete, statement ('do lovers and writers find one other?'), until the succeeding line ends the ambiguity created by the enjambment. All they find is language! However, the importance of this possible union should not be underestimated. In the context of the constant theme of the longing of the doomed individual for a partner, even a short glimpse at the possibility of achieving this aim sets an entirely new and optimistic tone. The apparently anticlimactic revelation that all that is achieved is a new language must be given due consideration, too. The power of the paralysing past is manifested in language as well. Secret agents and spies use this established language for their own means, by transmitting and subverting it (in secret codes, for example). So far the dilemma has seemed that of the impossibility of escaping the traditional impact of language, no matter how it is used. Language has been regarded as both subversive and reactionary, and its power to alter reality remains highly questionable. In this context 'An altering speech for altering things' is hardly a disappointment, but almost a revolutionary achievement – or at least its prerequisite. A change of reality must be accompanied by a change of language.

None the less, the line is not a pragmatic or even propagandistic statement. The causes of the change remain unclear (does language change reality or vice versa?). Its attachment to 'lovers and writers' shows that the change is not so much a general as a private one. The 'emphasis on new names' supports the stress on language, but could also mean new characters, new people. A hint at this is the succeeding clause 'on the arm/A fresh hand with fresh power', which combines the motifs of author and lover once more by not stating whether the hand belongs to the speaker himself or to another person. Power could here once more be Auden's personal code for sexuality. In spite of its ambiguity, the poem clearly signals that its speaker is a writer.

All the enthusiasm of the first eight lines of the stanza is countered abruptly by the 'But' which starts the succeeding line: 'But thinking so I came at once/Where solitary man sat weeping on a bench'. Everything stated before is now characterised as purely fictional ('But thinking so'). The negative final image of the stanza is in extreme contrast to the optimistic ones of its beginning. The presentation of the crying man without an article renders him an allegory of suffering; his description counters all positive connotations of the preceding lines: his drooping head is the opposite of the speaker's hopeful look at the sky; his fixed position is the antithesis of the speaker's leisurely walk. The man's distorted mouth is the travesty of finding a new language. 'Helpless and ugly', he appears in total contrast to the magnificent scenery and fresh power.

Eventually the comparison to an embryo chicken destroys even the pleasant connotations of Easter, one of whose popular symbols is chicks. The poem provides an example of textual deconstruction, here exercised on the level of images, more precisely that of the connotations of its signs, their signifieds. Once again, the attempt to create a stable representation of the present is deliberately blasted by the introduction of signifiers with contradictory signifieds, which seduce the reader who searches for coherent meaning, and then leave him or her with absences. Rather than the possible redemption and new start that the beginning of the poem announced implicitly, the end of its first stanza confronts the reader with a stillbirth. The retroactive reading initiated by the final line also questions the reader's interpretative skills by demonstrating how easily he or she can be led by the nose.

The rather dim view that the poem takes not only of the present, but of the very possibility to grasp its essence, is taken up in the sombre tone of the second stanza. In contrast to the looking forward of the first, it looks back: memory becomes the dominant mode. Death is the condition for development: this is the stanza's most important message. The clinical language and rather scientific approach avoid the emotional potential of the topic, although this attempt is undermined somewhat by the stanza's intimate beginning and its subtle link with the pathetic final image of the preceding stanza through the preposition 'So'. The discrepancy between clinical analysis and sentiment is not the only problem of this second stanza. The speaker remembers in it, but also attacks those who live in their private memories. They are doomed to die; the images associated with them are those of winter – in contrast to the images of spring in the first stanza. The speaker juxtaposes memories of success and failure by using private references. Once more failure is shown as disease (here, cancer) or as a psychological disposition which is subjected to analysis. Success, on the other hand, is linked with figures of Auden's private mythology and his specific symbol of the 'truly strong man'. Mendelson summarises the concept as 'an idea that brings into focus Auden's divided wish for private satisfaction and public responsibility' and locates its origin in the case studies of the psychologist Eugen Bleuler.[12]

The last stanza of the first part of '1929' returns from the interior monologue of the speaker to the realistic scenery of the first stanza: 'A bus ran home then, on the public ground/Lay fallen bicycles like huddled corpses'. The 'public ground' echoes 'the public gardens', and by its emphasis on 'public' distinguishes between the privacy of thought and the public world. The imagery of the final stanza once more mixes optimistic and pessimistic signals. The fallen bicycles which – in connection with the Easter setting of the first stanza – evoke the impression of a biking trip (very popular in the 1920s and 1930s, and associated with vigorous youth culture) are compared to corpses.

The three central lines of the stanza are even more obscure than the above juxtaposition: 'No chattering valves of laughter emphasised/Nor the swept gown ends of a gesture stirred/The sessile hush'. The motionless silence which has already become an organic state can be broken neither by laughter nor by a non-verbal gesture (the gown ends could refer to the public school and university experience which features in some of Auden's texts, and would then be an emblem of authority, as opposed to the playful and undisciplined laughter). Speechlessness has become the universal condition. This is an interesting turn of argument after the stress on speech in the first stanza. Rain as a natural phenomenon must take over the task of communication and bring the day to its close, so giving form to life. Language seems necessary for the establishment of meaning and order in reality; its absence is equalled with death.

The order that language creates in reality is not real, however, but fictional. What has been implied in the second stanza – which was also concerned with the fictional order of memory – is once more emphasised in the perplexing final line of the third stanza: 'Making choice seem a necessary error'. Choice is only a fiction, or even worse, an error. The adjective 'necessary' is strongly reminiscent of political slogans of the time, which abounded with necessity, from Lenin's 'necessary idiots' to the 'necessary murder' that Auden himself advocated in the early version of 'Spain 1937', a poem that will be discussed below. In '1929', however, the term 'necessary error' is not altogether pessimistic in the context of the declaration of the fictitiousness of systems which try to structure reality. On the contrary, it is almost apologetic. The old certainties have disappeared; every move must consequently be a false one, because there are no longer valid norms of right and wrong.

Reality as depicted in the poems analysed so far shows striking similarities to Michel Foucault's concept of the archive. In *The Archaeology of Knowledge*, Foucault describes this basis of human identity, knowledge, culture, and history in terms which fit perfectly as descriptions of the first part of '1929':

[...] its threshold of existence is established by the discontinuity that separates us from what we can no longer say, and from that which falls outside our discursive practice.

[...] it deprives us of our continuities; it dissipates that temporal identity in which we are pleased to look at ourselves when we wish to exorcise the discontinuities of history; it breaks the thread of transcendental teleologies; and where anthropological thought once questioned man's being or subjectivity, it now bursts open the other, and the outside.[13]

The very first lines of the second part of the poem summarise the inextricable connection between interior and exterior, the imaginative activity of clothing experience in signifiers – which offer the only reality available: that of the discursive practice. They link living and thinking, thinking and changing, and eventually changing and living with the self in very intimate terms. When they speak of living as 'Coming out' of the speaker in connection with the seemingly closed circle of living, thinking, and changing, this is not necessarily contradictory. In this complicated image, they describe both the formation of discourse, its utterance, and the constitution of identity through this utterance, so that they become a self-reflective characterisation of the poem itself.

The third line of the stanza indicates that the unity of perception and transformation has reached the intensity of a feeling: 'Am feeling as it was seeing'. It is syntactically mutilated in a very telling way: the subject of the utterance has vanished, and it seems that perception (or rather, its transformation into discursive practice) has taken over. This decisive shift will be discussed in detail in the succeeding chapter of the present study, but it should be obvious that it corresponds to the second condition (or consequence) of the discovery of the archive pointed out by Foucault: the destruction of our familiar concept of identity.[14]

The view is of a group of ducks in a harbour, an almost pastoral image which is contrasted implicitly with the speaker's homesickness and restlessness. Once more the now-familiar dilemma appears: the necessity of action in the face of disorientation. Again, clinical vocabulary is employed for emotional states. The grammatical ellipses and inversions fulfil a double function: they render reading and understanding the poem rather tortuous, and thus mirror the problematic process of self-ascertainment undergone by its speaker. On the other hand, they also create a strange elegance and fluency of the lines, thereby hinting at the artistic potential which can be set free through this painful process.

Concrete historic events appear for the first time in the second stanza of the second part: 'All this time was anxiety at night,/Shooting and barricade in street'. The first line could at first glance be seen to take up the restlessness of the speaker in the first stanza; it would then achieve a smooth transition as well as yet another subtle coupling of interior and exterior states. The possible ambiguity is quickly overcome in the second line. The lack of precision in the description of the events is striking: the poem neither mentions exact time ('at night') nor location ('in street'), so that the event gains universal dimensions.[15]

The stanza takes up the image of the walk of the beginning of the entire poem, yet this time it is undertaken in the company of a friend. Strikingly enough, however, the stanza avoids the impression of intimacy by dividing the verbs 'Walking' and 'Talking' clearly between the speaker and this friend. The friend's narrative is presented in slogan style: 'final war/Of proletariat against police'. None the less it is followed by concrete information about the mutilation of a girl. Yet this girl remains as anonymous as the friend before. After being described as 19 years old in telegraph style (once more by omission of an article), she is then further reduced to 'that one'. An impression of immediacy and urgency is created by this technique, depicting the anxiety of the struggle. Yet it is also telling that 'that one' who is thrown down the stair, that is, the victim, is not at all different from the preceding 'That one' responsible for shooting the girl. Once more the sides in the struggle are hardly as clear-cut as the slogan 'proletariat against police' suggests.

The reactions of the speaker are strangely divided. His outward reaction is positive, but his feeling is that of anger. It remains questionable whether he is angry because of the events or because of their communication by his friend. What becomes evident, however, is that the speaker's approach to historic events happens through fiction. Not only does he transform everything he encounters, but he can hardly be said to encounter reality at all, only ever its transformation into discourse.

A complete change of place happens in the third stanza, which starts with the unexpected line 'Time passes in Hessen, in Gutensberg'. Suddenly, there seems to be precise location and an emphasis on time. But the impression of precision created by the beginning of the stanza is not supported by the subsequent lines. Lyrical imprecision and pastoral cliché abound. Even the apparent clarity of the setting is of little impact. It is not even relevant whether it is fictional or real, since its role is similar to that of Kurt Groote and Gerhart Meyer in the first part of the poem: it is a private myth.[16]

The remaining stanza is a skilful construction full of alliterations, but devoid of concrete information. The speaker appears once more as an observer, small in comparison to the world he is watching. The theme of memory is again dominant, as well as that of vanity, embodied in terms such as 'evening', 'smoke', 'Memory', 'vanishing music', and 'an old use'. The isolated lark is a rather traditional symbol of the artist in his elevated position ('And I above standing'). Here, it paradoxically appears in plural form. Even isolation is not the privilege of an individual any more; it has become a general state.

The direct speech of the fourth stanza – which is characterised as the interior monologue of the speaker – takes a very different shape from the rest of the poem. It is a strange kind of nursery rhyme with nine four-stress lines and *rhymes riches* throughout. Rhyme words are 'mother', 'other', and 'no friend'. The stanza presents a concept of individual development in repetitive rhythmical phrases, even though the object of contemplation, characteristically enough, is not even mentioned. The argument follows the Freudian theme of the development of the self as an emancipation from the mother, and indulges in the contrast between the warmth and cosiness embodied by her and the chilly state of individuality. It is also tempting to see the stress on the 'other' in that process as a prefiguration of Jacques Lacan's already mentioned mirror-stage. The stanza divides this development into three stages: first, the (possibly pre-natal) feeling of being sheltered; second, childhood and youth, with the beginnings of consciousness and resulting suffering; and finally adulthood, characterised by 'wareness', a pun on 'awareness' and 'weariness'. Once more, physical and emotional state are inseparable.

The presentation of this pessimistic vulgar Freudianism as a nursery rhyme is ironic, but it also works in the opposite way and hints at the shelter offered to the consciousness in artistic creations, no matter how primitive. It thus presents the fourth concept of time in the poem. There is the passing of the seasons (which will become more obvious in the subsequent parts), the Christian concept of unredeemed and redeemed time, and furthermore, the empirical noting of actual events. Eventually the poem shows time as the psychological history of each individual.

Although all these concepts have a different perspective and apply to different targets, they are shown as interrelated and, indeed, inseparable. The poem displays a complex construction of parables interlaced almost like overlapping hoops or the parts of a chain. Yet no part of the construction represents a nameable and stable concept in itself. While the common parable consists of one part which uses realistic or at least identifiable images and connects it with another part of a more abstract and general character, all the parts in the hyper-parable of '1929' are characterised by the now-familiar hovering of the images between the concrete and the abstract. Instead of explaining a general concept, Auden's parable explains nothing. It remains empty and only manages to illustrate the insufficiency of the device.

The 'He' that starts off the subsequent fifth stanza is a reference to the self as depicted in the nursery rhyme above. His presentation hints at the unreliability of its message. The central terms of this fifth stanza are 'unforgiving' and 'takes no part'. Both express a failure of which sexuality is merely a symptom: the inability of the individual to overcome its egomania. Clinical language and the equation of the Romantic death-wish (man loves only death, that is, his own self in the climax of its destruction) with the return to the wife at home or the ancestral property in Wales (as emblems of the world of tradition) achieve an irony against tradition as well as against the poem itself. Once more the disjointed syntax of the stanza and its complex structure of rhymes and sounds express the anxiety of the text to construct a particular meaning. Yet this meaning proves far too complex to respect the poem's fixed form.

The sixth stanza is a summary as well as a counterpoint of the preceding ones, as signalled by the 'Yet' of its first line. It discusses the Romantic idea of the unity of man and nature in rather unexpected terms: the futurist admiration of locomotives, the ridiculous image of ducks, and Auden's own symbol of the truly strong man; and not surprisingly, it arrives at ambiguous conclusions. Self-acceptance of the individual is possible, but only by accepting the individual's fragmentation, not by a belief in the myth of a stable identity, no matter whether it finds its expression in the innocent *tabula rasa* of the child or the unconscious natural being, the bird.

Together with the farewell to a firm concept of reality, this acceptance of a fragmented individual and the abandonment of the myth of identity as creator[17] is the cause of mortification. Part Three of the poem describes this painful recognition in terms of a journey towards suffering. Fragmented reality takes control and pushes identity into a remote corner, where it suffers its own discourse running riot (it is telling that an 'I' only appears once in the first stanza, then once more in the fifth one, when it awakes from its trance), while the individual is depicted as deficient and disoriented. The poem hints at venereal disease and homosexuality while contemplating love, and thus once more links illness and psychological disposition before going on to supplement the discussion with economic terms in order to create the dominant trinity of Auden's early poems: body, psyche, and society. The allusion to the biblical parable of the sower is here not employed as an illustration of faith, but of the outcome of personal love – a very dubious one, and thus almost a travesty of Christian teaching. Disappointment, the inevitable result of this deficient love, is clearly perceptible to the sensitive, who are labelled 'mad and ill', a category which the speaker joins. This self-applied label has already been of great importance in the discussion of authority in *The Orators*.

Deficiency and lack of coherence are not, however, regarded in an entirely negative light: the second half of the fourth stanza presents them as creative forces, and a new race and a new language emerge from the transgression of the norms of tradition. The strangers (which now appear in the shape of settlers) symbolise the possibilities engendered by the estrangement of the individual: the transformation of discourse by the introduction of the alien, the strange. This transformation is both the fulfilment of the fragmented individual and its end. 'Moving along the track which is himself', the protagonist of the third part of the poem knows identity only as its fictional representation, the guideline along which he moves, a narrative which is his story as well as history. This guideline is eventually lost in the same way as the settlers lose their cultural and linguistic roots in the strange country by a process which is nothing but survival. This survival is only possible by accepting discrepancies. As a consequence, the 'independent delight' of the stanza's final line ceases to be the contradiction it was when emancipation (from the mother as the representative of tradition) only meant terror.

The fifth and final stanza of the third part of '1929' returns from abstract speculations to a concrete setting. This move is accompanied by the 'violent laugh of a jay', indicating the hilariousness as well as the implicit tragedy of the preceding meditation. Images of the end of summer, the beginning decline within nature, and the dissolution of reality in the perception of the speaker are linked. The focused stars and the frozen buzzard from the early poem 'We saw in Spring' reappear, the elaborate context of the buzzard symbol showing it this time as the farewell to the old and ultimately Romantic myth of identity. The mythical overview of Auden's earlier poems which found its expressions among others in the hawk is discarded as paralysed and dead. The death at the end of the stanza is also the death of this identity. The new conditions are strange and full of opportunities – but also dangers.

None the less, the acceptance of the death of the old identity is not sufficient in itself. The collaboration between thinking and changing is not as simple as the second part of '1929' suggests. To return to Foucault's concept: the myth of identity as creator is overcome by the discovery that the real creator of reality and identity are discursive structures. Yet the discarding of the traditional myth neither changes reality nor its signs. Indeed, if it did, this would prove its creative role. Reality is not overcome, but is destabilised when its constructedness is uncovered. An awareness of the discursive practice which governs its determinants, effects, and limitations changes not so much reality directly as the *perception* of reality. In Foucault's terminology: every statement brings about change.[18]

The slogan 'It is time for the destruction of error', which starts the fourth and last part of the poem, is therefore not entirely absurd (as its lack of context signifies). The destruction of error only becomes meaningful when it also encompasses the destruction of the notion of a stable truth (compare the line 'Making choice seem a necessary error'). This destruction is not only a necessity but an endeavour that requires action. Unlike modernist texts which only know an inside of discourse, a continual integration of reality into the texts, there is a distinct 'outside' in Auden's poems, the discourse of the Other. Yet far from being a benevolent, if demanding presence (as in Emmanuel Levinas's theologically inspired philosophy) or even merely a productive absence (as in Lacan's concept of the subject called into being by the desire of the Other), Auden's Other can be a challenger who tries to silence everything else by claiming possession of the truth. The relation of self and Other in Auden's writings is shown to be a social and political one early on, their link exceeding a mere egotistical concern of self for self or truth. The end of summer as the time of tolerance therefore becomes threatening on many levels.

As communication stops the individual disappears. People only appear in anonymous groups as 'the guests', 'they', 'the children'; or as allegories, such as 'the loud madman' and 'the enemy'. Actions seem to happen by themselves, as the passive constructions of the second and twelfth line and the anthropomorphisms of lines 3 and 8 indicate. Reality is out of control. Its setting is labelled 'savage', and its inhabitants are invalids, madmen, and children, all of which are incapable of taking control. The silence of inactivity is more terrible than the noise of the individual, no matter how dangerous the latter may be. Insight into the situation is only granted to nature and children, both of which are usually regarded as lacking awareness.

The beginning of the first part indicates the danger which accompanies the abandonment of firm truths and a stable notion of identity: passivity. While the stanza employs symbolic and realistic imagery side by side, its tone is symbolist throughout.[19] The dragon is the climax of the apocalyptic images, its labelling as the devourer reminiscent of Eliot's *Gerontion*, where Christ as the tiger assumes this role. Interestingly enough, the dominant theme of Eliot's poem is passivity, too.[20]

The rest of Auden's poem displays a curious change of tone: no longer is there a mixture of the abstract and the concrete, the symbolic and the seemingly realistic. The poem ends up stuffed with Auden's favourite symbols and concepts. The language of its finale is a return to that of Auden's earlier poems (note, for example, the abundance of 'of' combinations). Enemy, spy, and traitor appear in the third stanza, the latter two implicitly. There is a conspiracy as well. Its aim, as usual, is preserving the status quo, the dead conformity depicted in the 'orthodox bone'. Yet the roles of enemy, spy, and traitor are far from clear. Do they support or fight the old? The result of the conspiracy appears to be physical as well as spiritual destruction.

That the poem's change of tone is indeed a lapse back into private mythology, a retreat from the interaction of discourse into a form which knows no exterior, becomes even more evident in the final stanza. Suddenly, there is a second person addressed by the speaker. The theme of the walk from the poem's beginning is taken up once more, but this time its character is very different from a solitary stroll: it is a walk together, linked with erotic touch and secure expectations. This sudden optimistic note is striking. Certainty and knowledge become the dominant themes of the final part of '1929', and although the certainty is that of death, it is the exact replica of the authoritarian discourse despised in the old ('With organized fear, the articulated skeleton'). A biblical parable is once more employed in order to combine the certainty of death with the new life so eagerly advertised and so little formulated: the 'death of the grain' (John 12: 23–5).

The only image which illustrates the promised new life is the homosexual fantasy of a fairy-tale prince waiting (almost like Snow White) in the preserving purity of a lake. His fictional character is obvious, and is thus not distinct from the equally prototypical representatives of 'the old gang': the 'hard bitch and the riding-master'. Already the label 'old gang' indicates the shift of vision from an analysis of a general state, a reflection on society, to the set pieces of a private imagination. None the less, the prince is pronounced real, though still remote: he is 'there'. Real he is indeed, in so far as he is indestructibly embedded in the private discourse of the speaker as a myth. The detailed analysis of this important long poem proves that, eventually, it cannot endure its own discoveries: the end of a coherent concept of history by counter-projection of private onto public discourse and, interrelated with this, the end of a traditional concept of personal identity. The poem's finale shows a return to the old norms, but in a new and seemingly subversive wrapping. The myth of identity as creator is reiterated once again, but displaced from the 'I' to the 'You', and so is a coherent concept of history in its most stable form: that of myth. The empty parables of uncertainty make way for faith, a problematic faith in the healing properties of love.

SYMBOLIC DOCUMENTARIES

After the parabolic approach, the attempt to combine a documentary approach with Auden's style must strike one as a rather odd manoeuvre. Yet throughout the 1930s Auden's poems continually attempt to look at reality objectively as well as linking observation with intellectual concepts. Needless to say, these attempts produce tensions and works that are often uneven and show a tendency to turn observation into symbolism and vice versa. In 'A Bride in the 30's' (CP 111–12), for instance, the very title indicates that an assessment of the time is at least part of the project. (In earlier versions, this title was not used – and, indeed, the addressee of the poem was of indeterminate gender.) Yet the poem starts very much like a conventional love poem. Standard poetic rhetoric, such as 'night's delights', is only very subtly challenged by the mentioning of 'tenements' and the division of Europe into 'sixteen skies'. In its sixth stanza the poem eventually introduces the political figures of Hitler, Mussolini, Churchill, and Roosevelt as well as van der Lubbe, who supposedly set fire to the *Reichstag*, and sets them amid ten thousands desperately marching by (they become ten million in later versions).

But what happens between the personal declaration of love and the seemingly objective assessment of historic reality is worth investigating, because it points towards the structural shifts and difficulties engendered by Auden's attempts to connect private and public, personal and general. 'Looking and loving' are inseparable; this is the implied message of the beginning of the poem's second stanza. It links the scientific term 'behaviour' (which sits uneasily with the theme of love) with emblems of modernity: stone, steel, and polished glass. These images eventually culminate in the love of a railway (characterised as 'pansy' in earlier versions, as 'strategic' in later), in the manner of earlier, almost Futurist praises that Auden's texts had heaped on machinery, but also in images of farms ('sterile' earlier, merely 'run-down' later), and policed cities. Once again the poem sets up the familiar Audenesque scenario, blending society and clan, individual emotional state, and objective lifeworld.

Yet when history exceeds a hazy notion of general doom, and manifests itself in concrete personalities and historic events, this merger becomes increasingly worrying. The poem, indeed, tries to link personal with public themes as well as keep them apart. It discusses a possible relief from historic pressures in love: 'Easy for him to find in your face/A pool of silence or a tower of grace'. At the same time the poem is uncertain whether to believe in those traditional symbols of peace of mind and strength. It attempts a telling trick in its subsequent lines that 'conjure a camera into a wishing rose', and wishes to replace objective perception (of events and history) by a more optimistic, albeit illusory hope.

That it fails in this task is demonstrated by the far from wishful and rosy images that appear a little later, those of invalids (which are sinister mementos of the First World War) and single assassins. Suffering and threatened security are the reality, and love has to operate through these public paradigms: it cannot merely ignore them. Love still appeared as a magical ingredient in '1929', capable of overcoming both personal anxieties and those of history (even though its fairy-tale shape could be seen as a sly disclaimer); but its escapist properties are openly challenged in 'A Bride in the 30's'. The poem sums up its views in a central stanza, which concludes with the statement 'through our private stuff [love] must work/His public spirit'.

Yet the strength of private escapism must not be underestimated. 'Be Lubbe, be Hitler, but be my good,/Daily, nightly', is the scary culmination of the voluntary blindness created by a total privileging of personal emotions. In a stanza deleted from later versions, the poem elaborates on this dubious force of attraction when it talks about the 'power that corrupts, that power to excess/The beautiful quite naturally possess' (*EA* 154). Fathers and children and all those 'who long for their destruction', including particularly the 'arrogant and self-insulted', turn to this force. Against this fatal attraction, the poem sets its proper, because relativised and balanced, view of love: 'Yours the choice to whom the gods awarded/The language of learning, the language of love,/Crooked to move as a money-bug, as a cancer,/Or straight as a dove' (*CP* 112).

This superficially confusing conclusion emphasises choice as well as language. Rather than positioning love outside history, rules and signification are seen as part and parcel of it. And, rather shockingly, positive and negative terms as well as those that oscillate in Auden's vocabulary, such as learning, become possible attributes of this love, depending on individual choice. Neither psychosomatic illness (Auden saw cancer as engendered by the psyche), nor shabby materialism, nor the Christian symbol of the dove are firmly attached to love as its true being or origin. It is language that determines love's properties – a language that is both subject to individual choice and the force that shapes the individual in the first place.

'Night Mail', a poem that Auden produced around the summer of 1935 as the commentary for a film about the British postal service, links him most clearly with the documentary movement that was to gain prominence in the 1930s. The text is renowned for its attempt to depict in its rhythm the train delivering mail to Scotland. 'This is the Night Mail crossing the Border,/Bringing the cheque and the postal order' (*CP* 113) are its first lines. Yet how much of a documentary is the poem? While the film that Auden's text accompanies focuses on the human work that goes into the punctual delivery of mail, Auden's poem uses the heroic couplets of its first part to celebrate a locomotive that is apparently running on its own: 'The gradient's against her, but she's on time'. Not only are the workers totally blotted out in the final version of the poem (earlier drafts still included the driver and 'the fireman's restless arms', *EA* 290), but the machine seems to dominate completely the tiny world of human beings expecting mail, while being ignorant of the efforts that go into its distribution.

'Night Mail' first lists all the various types of mail and the variety of hopes and fears connected with it. The list as a mechanical device corresponds to the overwhelming power of machinery rather than the foundational strokes of human genius. But when its conclusion focuses on the underlying importance of mail for the human psyche, an element of anxiety enters the text: 'And none will hear the postman's knock/Without a quickening of the heart./For who could bear to feel himself forgotten' (*CP* 114). The security of belonging, so central in Auden's poems, is here dependent on mechanistic forces. Even though the machinery is apparently the harmless night train to Scotland, this introduces an inkling of a dehumanised aesthetic that is, indeed, not very different from the superhuman mechanistic images used by classical modernists. Yeats's concept of history as a wheel or as intersecting gyres comes to mind, as well as Eliot's image of the universe as an axle tree in *Four Quartets*. Yet the mundane human anxiety introduced into this aesthetic, together with the specificity of the example, eventually counterbalance any transcendental superhistoricism.

Auden's text seems to attempt to elevate the apparently banal to greater dimensions, while keeping in check general truths. In the same way as the traditionally elevated and sublime, love, for instance, is questioned in his poems and shown as embedded in discourses of power and transformations of signifiers, while the objective world can be invested with symbolic power until it seems to encompass the entire 'human condition'. Yet whenever the partial narrative is in danger of posing as a master narrative, it is cleverly deflated by the use of the mundane and even by clichés: however, this balancing act is not always successful, and occasionally Auden's texts become the victims of their own symbolising powers.

PATHOS

One of the obvious results of investing an attempt at an objective view of history with the nimbus of symbolic meanings and messages is pathos. This pathos can be detected even in seemingly detached and ironic poems. 'As I Walked Out One Evening', a poem written in 1937, is apparently an assessment of the main concerns and obsessions of Auden's early poetry (*CP* 114–15). It mocks the belief in love as exempt from history in a number of amusing images that attempt to reify time in order to make it non-threatening, and appears in the potentially overwhelming images of the movement of continents and stars, all of which are reduced to more manageable proportions. The dried-up ocean becomes a piece of laundry on the line, the stars turn into squawking geese, and eventually the years are shown as running like rabbits.

The poem's speaker, on the other hand, tries to elevate love from a personal affair to the universal 'Flower of the Ages,/And the first love of the world'. In an image that resembles those of Yeats's early love poems, he symbolically declares love the only universal concept, and makes it transcend history by situating it simultaneously at its beginning and end. This is challenged instantly in the text by, interestingly enough, the mechanical image of 'all the clocks in the city'. The text constantly pins potentially Romantic images, usually taken from nature, against anti-Romantic ones of cityscapes and mechanisation. From the challenge of the clocks in stanza 6 onwards, images of nature are actually turned into anthropomorphised allegories that actively interfere with love and try to put an end to it. Time, it seems, cannot be defeated through cute poetic reductions as easily as the poem's beginning signals. Now a glacier is knocking in the cupboard and a desert sighs in the bed. These anti-Romantic nature images are joined by malicious characters, drawn indiscriminately from real life, children's rhymes, and fairy tales. Beggars hoard banknotes, a Giant enchants Jack, while Jill also displays rather loose sexual morals.

Does the relevance of these ostensibly constructed arguments exceed a mere narcissistic concern of Auden's poetry for its own devices? The answer would be 'No' – if the poem did not arrive at some conclusions that are worrying in the context of the attempt to see history as related to choice and determined by the complex interaction of private and public via language. In order to establish what looks like a balanced picture in its final stanza (the lovers are gone, but whether home or into oblivion is unclear; but the accusing clocks have also ceased their chiming), it invokes again an image that it already employed in its second stanza, that of the river. 'And the deep river ran on,' it concludes, after having started its discussion of love 'down by the brimming river'.

If the poem tries to prove that neither eternal metaphysical love nor mechanistic human time rules supreme, then it undermines its own argument by positing the river as eternal. Indeed, the mighty river as a symbol of stability and eternity is both a traditional literary image and a dominant one in classical modernism. Eliot's later 'Dry Salvages' uses the Mississippi as its emblem of time, while the river Thames fulfils a similar function in *The Waste Land*. All the anti-Romantic gestures of Auden's poem lead back into an unquestioned Romantic view of nature as eternal. Realising this, the reader becomes more suspicious concerning images such as the initial one of 'crowds upon the pavement' as 'fields of harvest wheat'. By projecting history onto nature, the poem engages in an act of myth-making. It is no coincidence that totalitarian leaders love to talk about their people in terms of healthy natural growth, even though wheat here also introduces the sinister connotations of eventually being cut down. The recourse to some emblems of stability is understandable in a poetry that tries to balance so many issues at the same time, and that quite consciously borrows from a wide variety of literary traditions also in order to relativise their importance. Yet when this unquestioned recourse to a stability that masquerades as historic while being ahistorical myth appears in texts that directly deal with action rather than reflection, Auden's texts enter a far more dangerous territory.

One of these precarious excursions certainly occurs in his poem 'Spain 1937'. He composed it after an embarrassingly brief journey to Spain during the Civil War, undertaken not, as popular belief has it, to support the anti-fascist cause as an ambulance driver, but as a propagandist. The poem is rhetorically very successful – and continues to be anthologised, surprisingly enough, in the United States, while it has been removed from Auden's *Collected Poems*. But, as the discussion of the importance of language and codes above made abundantly clear, rhetoric is the very device with which authority secures its power. It must therefore be regarded with scepticism. The dominant device of the rhetorical manoeuvres of 'Spain 1937' is the symbol, which transcends objective reality in the direction of the truths, the ideological convictions, that the text wishes to convey. A typical section reads: 'Madrid is the heart. Our moments of tenderness blossom/As the ambulance and the sandbag;/Our hours of friendship into a people's army'.[21]

The structure of 'Spain 1937' already incorporates what was shown as a problematic manoeuvre in '1929' above, and situates concrete historical events inside a universal history of mankind. The poem's first seven stanzas all begin with 'Yesterday' in order to conclude with 'But to-day the struggle'. Not unimportantly, the first element mentioned in the poem's rather idiosyncratic list of cultural developments is language, the 'language of size', without which trade and ritual monuments (represented by counting-frame and cromlech) are unthinkable.

'Yesterday all the past', the poem starts, only to give a rather haphazard rundown of history from the ancient trade routes to China, the invention of the wheel, the trial of heretics, the 'installation of dynamos and turbines' to the 'construction of railways in the colonial desert'. Apparently the past is not all yesterday. If it was, the poem would not be obliged to invoke it for its explanatory setting of the Spanish Civil War. Yet it is obvious even from my description of the poem's summary of history that this sweeping use of history will not suffice. Neither is the poem convincing when it depicts 'the poor in their fireless lodgings, dropping the sheets/Of the evening paper'. Their declaration 'Our day is our loss, O show us/History the operator, the/Organizer, Time the refreshing river' sounds as grandiose as it is hollow.

When applied to concrete historical circumstances, the allegorisation of history fails. It fails because although it may provide an explanation of history, it gives no practical advice for action. This the poem itself acknowledges when it has another related allegorical figure, life, answer the demands of the imagined poor. In it, a voice refuses to be 'the mover'. It calls itself the 'Yes-man, the bar-companion, the easily-duped' and continues to tell them 'I am whatever you do'. It stands for everyday normality, business and marriage, but also supports grandiose plans, such as the one to build the just city, and agrees to participate in a suicide pact: 'I am your choice, your decision. Yes, I am Spain.'

These lines can easily be misread as Auden histrionically declaring his poem to be the voice of Spain. But what they are really about is constructions and concepts which determine individual lives as well as historic struggle. This is what the poem is about and why it needs its sweeping chain of historical developments. It shows history as insubstantial, as subsisting or inherent in the way that Gilles Deleuze sees sense as a human construction and not an essence or a substance.[22] Spain becomes a confluence of discourses, while remaining at the same time a very real field of struggle. Yet through this view of struggle as a contest of ideas, ideals and interests, a view of history is achieved that is not merely one of agencies and protagonists, but one in which long developments, contingent events, and personalities can be seen as linked. It also leads to a poetry that manages to be impersonal without becoming mythical, historical without offering easy traditionalism, and political yet free from cheap convictions.

This open and relativising model can also be found in the poem's most controversial line, which talks of 'The conscious acceptance of guilt in the necessary murder'. It provoked a severe reprimand by George Orwell, who had, after all, actively fought in Spain: 'It could only be written by a person to whom murder is at most a *word*.'[23] Orwell's biting remark substantiates that Auden's early poetry is a poetry of and about language. Auden himself modified the line later to 'the fact of murder' before dropping the poem entirely from his canon. But in a system of thinking that sees history, power, and personality as linked by networks of discourse rather than autonomous mythical entities, consciousness, guilt, necessity, and murder might indeed coexist. The very fact that their coexistence produces the obvious provocation of the original line proves, however, that their self-relativising also introduces an implicit element of self-critique, something that is completely absent both from the Romantic privileging of the self and impersonal and mythical modernist systems. Another controversial line of the poem, 'History to the defeated/ May say alas but cannot help or pardon', also proves this point. It is not, as Stan Smith assumes, history that is speaking in the poem; or if it is, it merely reminds us that *we* make history out of our concerns and convictions.[24]

Auden's eventual rejection of 'Spain 1937', and his poetry's drift away from obvious public concerns, testify that this monadic textual closure became less and less acceptable. After two travelling interludes (which will be of interest in the following chapter), the first of which led him to Iceland, the country of his childhood fantasies, the second to China at the time of the Japanese invasion, Auden decided to settle in New York. The outbreak of the Second World War was imminent, and the decision caused much ill-feeling in Britain, where Auden's move was regarded as an easy escape. Auden gave as his personal reason his fear not so much of the war but of being forced into the role of poet as spokesman. Considering that his fame was by then established, the fear was realistic, and when one takes into account that one of the major works he produced in 1939 is precisely a farewell to one of the last public poets, William Butler Yeats, the fear even manifested itself artistically.

The poem 'In Memory of W. B. Yeats' is a great example of a text that simultaneously manages to honour a writer and to deflate his self-created myth. It is also Auden's reckoning with one of the founding fathers of modernism. The snow that 'disfigured the public statues' in the poem (*CP* 197) is a reminder of the historic vulnerability of the public position. The poem continues with what strikes one as a rather odd attempt to differentiate between Yeats's poems and his person. It starts with the line, 'The death of the poet was kept from his poems', and concludes with 'he became his admirers'. What Auden exercises here is analogous to Roland Barthes' concept of the death of the author: the conviction that the authorial function ceases with the production of the text as artifact, while the text is kept alive and pertinent from that moment onwards by the involvement of the reader.[25] But more than merely prefiguring one of the tenets of poststructuralist theory, Auden's somewhat clinical approach to the death of an established author also mirrors the concerns of his own art. There, the entanglement of personal concerns with public politics proved immensely troublesome, and the idea that responsibility shifts from the author to the reader must have provided some level of relief. The rather complicated fifth stanza of 'In Memory of W. B. Yeats' exercises this new concept explicitly. It talks about 'the importance of noise of to-morrow', and illustrates this noise with images of brokers and the poor, and with individuality as a cell in which freedom is only a dubious conviction. Into this noise the death of the author (in both the literal and the theoretical sense) enters and makes people think.

This may seem little, yet it is all that poetry can achieve. In its act of asserting itself as text and nothing more, it also challenges its readers to make it a text through the act of interpretation. Only in this way can it come to live and indeed survive. In this way, it becomes an event. This is the positive message of the often negatively read, famous line from the second part of this poem: 'For poetry makes nothing happen', a line that in fact continues by asserting 'it survives'. The stanza, then, removes poetry both from the realm of pragmatic interest, by situating it 'In the valley of its making where executives/Would never want to tamper', and from mere personal concerns, when it shows that it 'flows on south/From ranches of isolation and the busy griefs/Raw towns that we believe and die in'. The survival of poetry lies in the very fact of its uneasy position between private and public, in its challenge to the reader to engage with it on its own terms. The 'valley of its making' is not so much the personality of an author as the realm of communication, signification, and discourse that determines both the poetic text and its interpretation. Only by an engagement with poetry on these terms does poetry become 'A way of happening, a mouth'. It remains productive even – or exactly – after the death of its author.

When the poem continues to exercise these ideas in its third part in the metre of Yeats's 'An Irish Airman Foresees His Death', a poem whose emphasis on escapist detachment and near-suicidal solipsism obviously attracted Auden, it challenges us indeed to agree with its (often apparently naive) assertions. By being blunt in form and message, it indeed conforms to its aim. 'Follow, poet, follow right/To the bottom of the night' is as childish as it is accurate when it describes the attempt to write adequately about death and loss. In the same manner, the poem's problematic conclusion, that asks for the start of healing in the 'deserts of the heart' and demands from poetry 'In the prison of his days/Teach the free man how to praise', leaves its reader to figure out the puzzling contradiction of liberty and imprisonment as well as the implied question: who or what are we to praise?

Another iconic figure is honoured (or despatched) in Auden's related poem on the death of Sigmund Freud (*CP* 215–18). There again, the private event of death and loss is set against the public horizon of the awareness of many losses (the Second World War had begun). What Freud leaves behind are 'problems like relatives gathered/puzzled and jealous about our dying'. The poem also acknowledges the possibility of misreading Freud for obvious political purposes: 'Only Hate was happy, hoping to augment/his practice now, and his dirty clientele/who think they can be cured by killing/and covering the gardens with ashes'. The duty to interpret also leaves the survivors with the ethical obligation of deciding on an interpretation. Rightly, the poem therefore compares Freud's own teachings with a poetry lesson: 'He wasn't clever at all: he merely told/the unhappy Present to recite the Past/like a poetry lesson'.

This emphasis on interpretation, its openness and possibilities, must of necessity alarm 'the ancient cultures of conceit', 'the Generalised Life', and 'the monolith of State', all narratives themselves, yet narratives that have successfully obscured their origin in historical agreement and achieved mythical status. Yet the poem is far from a celebration of analysis in its most technical sense. It acknowledges that out of an understanding of existence based on interpretation there also evolves a need for community and exchange. Even the most personal inquiry of Freudian analysis remains bound up with the desire for contact. Auden's poem acknowledges this both in a celebration of maternal love (this time unambiguously positive as 'the mother's richness of feeling') and in unusual praise of the darker aspects of human existence. When the poem claims 'but he would have us remember most of all/to be enthusiastic over the night', it gives as a reason 'it needs our love'. It is exactly the excluded, marginalised, and repressed that requires attention, and more than attention – love. What is excluded in our personal nights is described as 'exiles who long for the future'. Like the tragic exiles of Auden's early poems, they suffer from their past, but point towards the future. History, the poem claims, is not possible without a negoti-ation between past and future, personal night and the light of public day. 'One rational voice is dumb,' it concludes, but without granting the irrational drives of desire complete victory: 'Over his [Freud's] grave/the household of Impulses mourns one dearly loved:/sad is Eros, builder of cities,/and weeping anarchic Aphrodite.'

In the poem that commemorates the start of the war, 'September 1st, 1939', Auden tellingly mixes a now very reduced and personal perspective, that of the speaker sitting in a New York bar, with a general feeling of inevitable disaster. Yet the historic perspective of the poem is not clothed in political or scientific terms, but in per-sonal and, broadly speaking, Christian ones, as will become evident below. Something new apparently claimed prominence in Auden's writings, although he clearly did not feet up to it yet. In 'September 1, 1939' he tackles the Second World War. In a manner not entirely dif-ferent from 'Spain 1937', personal outrage at the German attack on Poland is linked with yet another broadly sweeping view of history and personality disorders. Indeed, the poem connects Luther (who represents the Protestant culture of repression) with Hitler (who appears as a psychopathic god misled by a Jungian imago) and then returns full circle to one of the first historians, Thucydides. 'Exiled Thucydides knew/All that a speech can say/About Democracy,/And what dictators do'.

The poem merges the image of the clients of a New York bar, their private fears, desires, and anxieties, with world history, and merges world history with figures such as Diaghilev and Nijinsky as represent-atives of the conflicts generated by the human need – not for univer-sal love, but for the fulfilment of personal and egotistic desires. None of these aspects, private, political, or historical, is privileged; they are depicted as inextricably connected. The poem even includes itself in this assessment: what can a poetic text say about history? 'All I have is a voice,' it states, 'To undo the folded lie,/The romantic lie in the brain/Of the sensual man-in-the-street/And the lie of Authority.' It associates authority with skyscrapers, but also claims that 'There is no such thing as the State/And no-one exists alone'. If, as it continues, 'Hunger allows no choice/To the citizen or the police', then its own conclusion, 'We must love one another or die', seems somewhat illogical. It is a desperate conclusion; and it is a proof of the seriousness of Auden's concern that he kept chan-ging this line around, first to 'We must love one another and die', a nihilistic version, before deciding to discard the poem altogether for some time.

The contradictory claims of this stanza cease to be so when they are regarded in the context of the non-hierarchical and non-binary concept of history and the self that emerges from Auden's poems. Both the state and rampant individualism are lies, but both of them are operational. There are pragmatic forces, such as hunger, and they do not differentiate between citizen and police, who no longer appear as oppositional as they did in '1929'. The apparently Christian advice of the final line, 'love one another or die', must become ironic in this respect. There seems to be very little love in the rest of the poem. The final stanza of 'September 1, 1939' eventually declares the only possible attitude of poets towards history to be in the shape of 'Ironic points of light'. 'Negation and despair' lead paradoxically to an 'affirming flame'; but what is affirmed is only an insight into the self-destructive relativity of entangled discourses.

HISTORIES OF KNOWLEDGE

W. H. Auden is often perceived as a 1930s poet, a symptom of a time of political upheaval rather than its analyst, a historical artefact rather than an author actively engaging with history. Even the above analysis seemed to uphold this claim implicitly by focusing on the responses of his works to the political upheavals of the late 1920s and 1930s. Yet it is not merely the fact that Auden's career spanned the long period between the publication of his first volume of poems in 1928 and his death in 1973 that should relativise this view. This final section of the investigation into the relation of Auden's writings to history will alert us to the interesting shifts in his poetry that are intrinsically linked with history and which once again situate Auden on the borderline between a classical modernist aesthetics and postmodernism.

Auden himself proves a Foucauldian *avant la lettre* in poems such as 'Makers of History', written in 1955. In it Auden analyses the obsession of traditional historians with artefacts and events, with history as relic, as a dubious substance, rather than a history of ideas: 'Serious historians care for coins and weapons,/Not those re-iterations of one self-importance/By whom they date them' (*CP* 456–7). The message is clear even after the first three lines. Historians who do not question their own underlying assumptions and motivations will remain blind mythmakers who 'could soon compose a model/As manly as any of whom schoolmasters tell/Their yawning pupils'. What is perceived as linear history, as the perfect outcome of enlightened rationality, is in fact nothing but a form of ritual magic that merges legend, daily practice, and contingency into one mythical whole. Retrospective explanations derived from contingent events are unconvincing, as a related poem, 'Secondary Epic', shows. In it, Virgil is reprimanded for his ideologically motivated idea that 'the first of the Romans can learn/His Roman history in the future tense'. History cannot simply be manipulated to create a straightforward story out of chaotic events, and worse than that, one that prefigures the future and therefore prescribes individual action: 'Hindsight as foresight makes no sense' (*CP* 455–6). It is historic contingency itself that undermines history as an explanatory model, as the poem shows when it confronts Virgil's version with the eventual decline and fall of the Roman empire. The 'What next?' that Rome's mythical founder Aeneas asks provokes many stories, but can hardly rely on history as safe ground for an answer. Written in the 1950s, at a time when civilization was desperate for answers to its own history – its collapse into the Second World War and its immediate re-emergence into the Cold War and the threat of nuclear annihilation – Auden's poem warns against history as explanation, instruction, and ultimately exculpation.

Yet it is precisely this retroactive investment of events with sense, with teleology, and their transformation into ideological founding narratives and explanatory models that also gives sense to human existence. As the title 'Secondary Epic' shows, while Auden's poems critically uncover weaknesses by adding a layer of reflection, they also acknowledge that some patterns are inescapable. In 'The History of Truth' of 1958 he not only employs a title that could be Foucault's, but also distinguishes between an empirical model of truth, which is based on apparently unproblematic facts, and a sceptical modern one, which must of necessity remain empty. While archaic truth was simply an attempt to overcome human mortality in fantasies of superhuman power 'The least like mortals, doubted by their deaths', later, in the age of empiricism and materialism, 'Truth was their model as they strove to build/A world of lasting objects to believe in' (*CP* 463). Today, in the age of electricity and the replacement of material by immaterial values, such as communication and transport, we are faced with an anti-model: 'Some untruth anyone can give the lie to,/A nothing no-one need believe is there'. The claim is as contradictory as it is pertinent, and is once again an insight into the constructed nature of history and sense that results from Auden's engagement with history. Yet by unveiling history as construction its power is by no means diminished; and it only gradually becomes evident that its power is not 'natural', substantial, and given, but entangled in ideological discourses, in acts of interpretation, legislation, and so on.[26] The 'nothing' that a concept such as history is, is none the less 'there', since it interferes actively with human existstence.

In terms of poetry, however, behind a manufactured history such as Virgil's narrative of Rome's past, present and future, 'Behind your verse so masterfully made/We hear the weeping of a Muse betrayed'. The betrayed Muse of this kind of historicism is Clio, the Muse of history, and she owes her betrayal to one of her sisters, Calliope, the Muse of epic poetry. In his poem 'Homage to Clio' of 1960 Auden eventually sums up the relation of poetry to history in a poetic form. What does the Muse of History have to say to the poets? According to Auden's poem, nothing. The Muse is silent in 'Homage to Clio'. The poets may 'dream as we wish/Of phallic pillar or navel-stone/With twelve nymphs twirling about it, but pictures/Are no help' (*CP* 463–5). They are no help, because what history really presents is a silence that is always already there 'Between us and any magical centre/Where things are taken in hand'. The Muse of History is a source of inspiration because she is an absence which invites completion. She is not so much an explanation, an ontology explaining origins or a teleology providing a perspective for the future or justification for prescribed actions, as she is the desire for such explanations. The silence of the Muse is the desire for sense. And in their sense-making activities, poet and historian are intimately related.

By creating a representation of history, however, the historian as well as the artist deadens it, reifying and stabilising it unduly. The eyes of Clio, the poet claims, provoke description: 'How shall I describe you? They/Can be represented in granite'. It is clear that granite as the epitome of solidity is an inadequate material for the depiction of history. But would any other material be better suited? Would poetry offer the necessary form as well as flexibility? The poem seems to deny this, instead claiming to have seen history in the shape of a photograph: 'I have seen/Your photo, I think, in the papers, nursing/A baby or mourning a corpse'. This should not be read as a symbolic retreat of poetry in favour of journalism. Even in the apparent depiction in the newspaper, history 'had nothing to say'. The silence of history can neither be represented nor filled with even the most outrageous act or artifice. This silence 'No explosion can conquer but a lover's Yes/Has been known to fill'.

If the Muse represents the desire for sense, self and continuity, then, Auden's poems suggest, it is the task of both poetry and historical writings to fulfil this desire. However, both are obliged to keep an eye on their premises; they must refrain from a mythmaking that obscures the fact that their products are artefacts, that they write histories as stories, stories that are neither anchored in an autonomous self nor in mythical inevitability. Even the apparent lapse into a Romantic 'lover's Yes' in Auden's poem still acknowledges the fact that it is not an autonomous 'I' that creates poems and histories. It reiterates that the connection between 'I' and 'You' throughout history is one of tension, potential betrayal and struggle, but also one of possible fulfilment. This fulfilment need not be a merely personal one, but it can – via the acknowledgement of history as tensional – encompass both a politics of sceptical humanism and a faith that is not so much doctrinaire as understanding.

6

Displaced Voices:
Post-War Auden

IDENTITY AND SUBVERSION

The quest forms one of the dominant structures in Auden's poems. But, as we have seen above, it is never exclusively a personal one, nor is it merely one for political change, a search for spiritual fulfilment or the right ordering of culture, as in the modernist poems of Eliot and Pound.[1] In Auden, as the previous chapters have demonstrated, we find a complex entanglement of all these yearnings. More than merely being intertwined, they actually clash in the search for individual identity as part of a just society. To combine this search for personal fulfilment and a social role with sexual fulfilment is certainly a common topic with poets. In Auden's case it also represents a continual attempt to come to terms with homosexuality. Though frequently treated in a humorous vein, as in his often obscene short poems, homosexuality has serious implications for the formation of identity in his poems. It is one of the reasons for the blurred distinctions between 'us' and 'them'. The enemy is always also the potential lover and vice versa. The Other only exists in a close resemblance to the self, and seriously disturbs its conceptualisation. Homosexuality is also a decisive influence behind the images of the secret agent, the traitor, and the spy, all of whom live adapted lives in enemy territory. It is most important for the use of codes, a secret language only accessible to the initiated, a description that could easily be applied to the whole of Auden's early poems.[2]

The secret codes are not so much subversive as protective. Some of the most obscure poems in Auden's early *oeuvre* deal with homosexuality in terms of delineations and their transgression and their – usually painful – consequences. 'Suppose they met, the inevitable procedure', one of the most unintelligible of his early poems, discusses the topic in relation to the Christian concept of guilt, when it

115

invokes a 'doddering Jehovah' who manages to 'show them to their rooms' and to make them sleep apart 'though doors were never locked' (*EA* 22–3).

Transgression of the norm leads to punishment. 'To have found a place for nowhere', for instance, illustrates, though in deliberately exaggerated form, the restrictive mechanisms of society in lines such as 'But now they come/With girls and guns/And letter home' (*EA* 43–4). It couples the female with the lethal and both with the schoolboy nightmare of the letter to the parents. The suppression of homosexuality, on the other hand, leads to neurotic symptoms as described in 'Sir, no man's enemy', and is therefore equally undesirable. Most of Auden's love poems illustrate the tragic lack of identity in love – which eventually leads to a questioning of its very existence. 'This lunar history', for example, begins in the manner of a seventeenth-century Metaphysical poem praising the beauty of the loved one, only to dissolve in its very first stanza:

> This lunar beauty
> Has no history
> Is complete and early;
> If beauty later
> Bear any feature,
> It had a lover
> And is another. (*CP* 57)

'Love by ambition' goes even further by adding to the already enormous dilemma the question of the desirability of successful love. Its result is envisaged as 'Views from the rail/Of land and happiness,/Assured of all/The sofas creak' (*CP* 45). It describes the relapse into a certainty that is otherwise so vehemently rejected in the poems. Already the form of the quest with the triumphant return as its successful conclusion is a contradiction of what the poems so eagerly strive for: the achievement of something new and detachment from the past. Auden's poem 'This loved one', written to commemorate one of Christopher Isherwood's affairs, is at first glance a congratulation, but becomes highly ambiguous when read under these assumptions. Its first half describes almost prototypically the successful quest with the eventual discovery of the desired object. It talks about the abandoning of family as well as history, the crossing of frontiers, and gradual impoverishment as prerequisites to finding 'this last one', 'this loved one' (*CP* 44).

The second stanza of the poem then takes back all promise of a real change. On the contrary, it regards the achieved as a mere return to the old standards in a vaguely disguised but in fact even worse form. It culminates in an ingenious pun on the problematic feature of homosexuality, when it calls the newly found love 'no real meeting/But instinctive look/A backward love'.

Identity, as should have become obvious, does not have an easy stand in Auden's early poems. It is the continual victim of contradictory structures, denied existence by the farewell to the Romantic idea of wholeness, desired by the urge to attain a stable centre on which to base the vague notion of a new reality, and discarded by the justified suspicion that this reality as well as the desired identity can only be achieved by succumbing to the old values, by an orientation towards tradition, a giving-in to the discourse of the Other. When identity is present in speakers and others, loved ones or enemies, it is undermined by a setting that is constantly on the verge of collapse into surrealism.[3] When it is absent, the ordered and realistic imagery not only demands it, but virtually creates it in implicit representations In both cases, the poems suffer from their contradictions: either their logic and coherence is distorted or their intelligibility threatened. The real absence of identity would indeed be the collapse of poetic discourse, its sliding into a discourse of madness. It would bring about the end of the poems' message and thus the end of the poems themselves.

This, however, is exactly what the poems must achieve if they really want to escape the discourse of the Other, comment on it without being subverted by it, and create something new without being a mere extension of tradition, a tradition that is also the modernist one with its continual internalisation of reality. Identity must be abandoned in order to express the new reality that resembles that of a neurotic, an unceasing flux which finds its equivalent in many features of life in the twentieth century. As Jacques Lacan puts it, 'In effect, it is in the disintegration of the imaginary unity constituted by the ego that the subject finds the signifying material of his symptoms.'[4]

Auden's poems find their own expression of the dilemma in 'Consider', which ends with the unpleasant alternatives for identity: 'To disintegrate on an instant in the explosion of mania/Or lapse for ever into a classic fatigue' (*CP* 61–2). One could be malicious and apply these lines to Auden himself. There we would find the 'classic fatigue' of some of his later works with their own reworkings of the classics in the shape of Horace, Propertius, Byron, and Goethe. We have also already encountered one very radical attempt to go the other, explosive way in the shape of *The Orators*.

ENGLISH WANDERERS

One of the attempts to deal with an impossible positioning of subject in Auden's poetry is the symbolic escape into fantasies of migration. In his very liberal version of the Old English poem 'The Wanderer' he not only uses the subject-matter of his beloved Anglo-Saxon verse, but also manages to infuse the traditional theme of human suffering with a very contemporary edge.[5] In fact, he turns the message of the original upside down: rather than wondering about the paradoxical optimism generated by being cast out from the company of friends and protectors and subjected to unpredictable nature, Auden's poem starts off by declaring exile a necessary condition. 'That he should leave his house,/No cloud-soft hand can hold him, restraint by women' (*CP* 62). Exile appears to be a specifically masculine condition, while women stand for home, but also for restraint.

The male exile is caught up in a contradictory attitude: he yearns for the stability of the domestic and 'dreams of home,/Waving from window, spread of welcome, Kissing of wife under single sheet'. At the same time in his exiled wanderings he hears 'through doorways voices/Of new men making another love'. The poem eventually shifts into prayer form (a minimal reference to the wholly religious tone of the Old English original) and asks for the protection of man as well as his house, concluding in a vision of joy linked with the 'day of his returning'. The contradictions could not be greater. Edward Mendelson uses the poem's confusion to establish another sly link with the Old English model when he claims that 'while the archaic words of "The Wanderer" give Auden a living poetic language, they offer him no further comfort. He knows that what makes them contemporary is the persistence of the sorrow they proclaim, a sorrow that will never pass away.'[6] But what is this sorrow exactly?

Monroe K. Spears rightly claims that 'the wanderer is in one aspect the middle-class intellectual, doomed by his political awareness to leave his intellectual and spiritual home and endure hardship and isolation'.[7] But the contradictions of the text reach much further:

they deny a viable speaking position to its protagonist, and, indeed, speak about him rather than granting him a voice. While the Old English model is a personal narration, Auden's poem is an impersonal verdict. It is not the doomed individual who utters his predicament in the poem, but the rupture, the borderline that makes itself heard in it, describing the quest as a basic condition as well as outlining the fact that it derives essentially from a contradictory impulse: the desire for stability, and the inability to accept it.

Apart from uniting personal and political goals in a problematic way, the quest motif also reflects back on the genealogy of Auden's poems as texts. After all, 'The Wanderer' is as much an attempt to anchor a new poetics in established forms (here Old and Middle English models) as it is a decisive break away from these forms and an assertion of something contemporary and new. This is clearly recognised by Mendelson when he compares Auden's technique with those of another 'translator' of Old English poems, Ezra Pound: 'The Seafarer's world, for Pound, may be gone for ever, but its powers are recoverable in the poet's heroic transforming imagination, and only there. For Auden, in contrast, "The Wanderer" is thoroughly available to the present.'[8] The reason why it is 'thoroughly available', however, is the fact that there is a tragic analogy between some existential conditions in the Old English text and the twentieth-century poem. The parallels lie in the fact that individuality as well as textuality can only be envisaged in terms of exile. In contrast to Pound's synthetic yet assertive modernist speaker, the displaced voice becomes a dominant feature in Auden's poetry.

In 'The Exiles' (*CP* 64–6) Auden develops a detailed contemporary analogy of this condition. Its images of frozen fjords and labelled luggage eerily prefigure his personal displacements in the later 1930s and after the Second World War, as well as predicting the fate of so many women and men in the upheavals of the twentieth century. Yet more than that, they elevate the marginal position of displacement to the status of a life-source and thus also to an origin of poetry: 'The marginal grief/Is source of life.' 'The Witnesses' (*EA* 126–30; *CP* 71–2) is another example of a poetry that turns the quest from personal initiation ritual into a political and, eventually, cultural pattern in the broadest sense. Earlier and later versions of this poem differ significantly, and yet are concerned with similar issues. In the early version the scenery is a strange fairy-tale England of 'banks of roses', 'Lords who sit at committee tables', 'grooms in riding stables', solicitors, doctors, reporters, bishops (the complete entourage of Auden's early plays, in fact), as well as steeplejacks, shepherds, and tramps.

Into this idyll Prince Alpha is born in the early version (the shorter later one only has nameless 'Young men'). His name marks him immediately as a hybrid: he is both part of an outdated tradition, a prince, and stands for a new type of man. Socially privileged, intelligent, and good-looking, he none the less abandons his luxurious surroundings and embarks on a quest into a hostile exterior of ice, gravel, and jungle. He performs the usual feats of rescuing maidens and defeating giants, but his achievements fail to make him happy: 'He came to a desert and down he sat and cried.' He complains that his actions give him no satisfaction and eventually declares, 'No, I am not the truly strong man' (EA 128), before he dies. But why is he not the truly strong man, and why does he have to die? To this the two rocks between which he has positioned himself pretend to provide an answer. They declare that they have been watching him and are in fact watching everyone. They know personal weaknesses as well as the futility of human actions. In the end they threaten both with traditional images of natural disasters and supernatural events (the woods approaching and surrounding people, as in Macbeth), but also with contemporary images such as the removal van, 'women in dark glasses, the hump-backed surgeons/and the scissor-man', the latter probably Freudian castration anxiety (EA 129; CP 73 – where the women become mere 'hooded women', but the Scissor Man is capitalised).

Despite the fairy-tale connotations, one must take seriously those stones, who also call themselves 'guardians' and 'the Two'. Their pronouncement as well as the entire parable of Prince Alpha are prophecies concerning the problems of developing a new voice and of embarking on new political and aesthetic endeavours. If these attempts are meant to be successful, they must remain aware of their weaknesses and limitations. Yet this creates a paradox that mirrors one encountered earlier in connection with authority and tradition. If one aims to distance oneself from one's background and environment, one must have an awareness of this environment in the first place. This, however, demands immersion in it, and this in turn compromises the attempt. Applied to the concept of the truly strong man, it creates the paradox that only an awareness of weaknesses makes a man truly strong.

An escape from the dilemma is not very seriously sought in Romantic death, since at least the voices of the guardians survive and apparently warn new generations of Prince Alphas. It will take Auden a few decades before his poetry manages to turn the limit into a productive force. Here, already, it is the generator of movement, a movement of protagonists as a quest, but also a movement of texts (or rather, voices) between dialectical positions. All of these positions are displaced ones. None is authentic, but their interaction forces the reader (who is directly addressed and thus brought into play by 'The Witnesses') to position him- or herself – and consequently register the threat that his point of view might also be one of exile.

In the poem that bears the title 'The Witnesses' in Auden's later *Collected Poems*, 'the Two' also tell of the necessity of this paradoxical quest of displacement: 'For walk he must the empty/Selfish journey/Between the needless risk/And the empty safety.' It, too, culminates in a dubious piece of advice: 'Be clean, be tidy, oil the lock,/ Weed the garden, wind the clock; Remember the Two.' If this advice sounds like the eventual victory of domestic security, there still remains an element of tension. Why oil the lock? In order to lock or to unlock it, to lock oneself in or to escape? Halfway through the poem, when 'the Two' introduce themselves, they make it clear that they do not address an individual, but many: 'You are the town and We are the clock.' The clock regulates lives with mechanic rigidity. But it also has to be wound. The advice of the guardians therefore contains an acknowledgement that their power derives from the cooperation of the individuals they control. They describe hegemony. Once again, Auden's poem is undecided whether to believe in an external fate (that can include mythical determination as well as class background) or in individual responsibility. Displacement and quest are the means of negotiating this dilemma textually.

In the long poem of 1936, *Letter to Lord Byron*, Auden eventually takes the theme of wandering, exile, and Englishness to a logical conclusion when he addresses the embodiment of the English wanderer and does so from a position of self-imposed exile. *Letter to Lord Byron* originally formed part of *Letters from Iceland*, a travel book (in the loosest sense of the term) that Auden produced together with Louis MacNeice. In the project of *Letters from Iceland*, a number of related but superficially contradictory aims collude. On the one hand, the journey to Iceland is the fulfilment of one of Auden's fascinations with Old Norse sagas. More than that, since the Auden family (quite certainly falsely) believed that the name Auden had

Icelandic roots, the trip is a personal pilgrimage to his imaginary origins. It is also the attempt to escape, at least temporarily, from the tensions of Europe in 1936 to a region seemingly untroubled by the conflicts.

However, the very composition of the travelling group of Auden, MacNeice and their favourite pupils turns the adventure into a very English school trip, and the style of several parts of the eventual book bears testimony to its obsession with Englishness. Furthermore, as in *Letter to Lord Byron*, the trip becomes an opportunity for poetic self-assessment and self-positioning inside the canon of English literature for Auden. Geographic displacement is used for asserting rather than unsettling cultural and personal identity.[9]

Letter to Lord Byron begins like a rather disrespectful fan letter to the Romantic poet. But it soon becomes clear that its author considers himself on equal terms with Byron, when he complains about having to read his readers' unsolicited confessions over his breakfast toast. Eventually, he declares his intention 'To chat about your poetry or mine' (*CP* 77). That the writer of the letter should find *Don Juan* 'fine' is as derogatory as may be expected, since Byron's hero – in unison with the earlier Childe Harold – provides a model for the exiled Englishman whose effortless superiority is merely highlighted by foreign locations and characters, and whose exile makes him all the more attractive to an English audience. There is certainly an element of biographical experiment at work here that sees Auden toying with his role as an established author.

The trip to Iceland is completely relegated to the background, when apart from the concerns about poetry the state of England in the 1930s shifts into the focus of the text in its second part. Under the pretence of keeping Byron informed about the developments since his death, *Letter to Lord Byron* undertakes an assessment of British culture and civilization – from technological advances via class structures to lifestyles and literary fashions. The section gives the overall impression of an uneasy celebration of the democratisation of culture; 'The porter at the Carlton' (*CP* 84) may be the writer's brother, but he will only wish him a good evening if he pays. One of the problematic consequences of this democratisation is that everyone now considers themselves little: John Bull has made way for Mickey Mouse, Englishness is in danger of being Americanised. But more importantly, instead of heroism there is now only an anti-hero who only dares to kick the tyrant in his dreams. As a consequence the poem laments susceptibility to totalitarianism, and even imagines the possibility of seeing 'Lord Byron at the head of his storm-troopers' (*CP* 86).

The poem shifts from a social mode into an artistic one in its third part, and reflects in great detail on the role of the poet in a democratised environment, in which even 'The humblest is acquiring with facility/A Universal-Complex sensibility' (*CP* 90). Auden's poem argues for a dual perception of art that has its origin not in some totalising history of mankind, 'the scratches in the ancient caves', but in the English eighteenth century. There it sees art developing as a dialogic force between the 'quick and graceful, and by no means holy', reliant on patronage and destined for the upper classes, and the 'pious, sober, moving slowly,/Appealing mainly to the poor and lowly' (*CP* 91). Yet by doing so it implicitly situates itself on the side of privilege. It also upholds the class structures that caused so much havoc in the Britain of the twentieth century, and eventually it asserts once again an essentially English model of culture.

Letter to Lord Byron is at the same time disrespectfully analytic and utterly conservative. It has to bestride these contradictory positions if it wants to resist the hegemony of what it sees as the overpowering force of the present age. 'Goddess of bossy underlings, Normality!/What murders are committed in thy name!/Totalitarian is thy state Reality' (*CP* 97). The historic context of the poem indeed proved that the attempt to overcome social distinctions did not lead to increased freedom for the forcibly homogenised populations of Stalin's Russia and Hitler's Germany, but to oppression.

Returning to England and to art, the neat dialectic of a witty upper-class art and serious lower-class one was threatened, the poem continues, by commercialisation, which severed artists from patrons and subjected them to market forces. But not for long. The result of this pressure, the poem claims, was a split into those artists who settled for established positions as critics, and those that formed 'the Poet's Party' of élitist snobbery and self-declared intellectual superiority. Of course, the writer of Auden's poem would want to claim both positions for himself. He starts this section by declaring 'I'm setting up my brass plate as a critic' (*CP* 88), only to denounce his own criticism as whimsical and irreverential. Trying to encompass both sides of the postulated dialogue leads to a sitting on the fence of art and society.

The fourth section of *Letter to Lord Byron* is unashamedly personal again, but personal in a very English sense. Without having engaged seriously with Iceland, the destination of the excursion, it declares

'I've done with the Icelandic scene', only to conclude two stanzas later with the most condescendingly English of qualifications: 'All things considered, I consider Iceland,/Apart from Reykjavik, a very nice land' (CP 94). By escaping temporarily from England, the text manages to reassert an essential Englishness as well as the privileged position of its speaking voice. 'The line I travel has the English gauge' (CP 100), it concludes by returning to its starting position. As an attempt at cultural relativisation it is a complete failure. Yet it provides a rich tapestry of self-aware analyses of the formative cultural and personal forces behind Auden's writing. The dislocated voice becomes an analytical one.

'Dover' is another poem that uses geography for an assessment of Englishness under threat (CP 124–5). 'Aeroplanes drone through the new European air/On the edge of a sky that makes England of minor importance'. Dover, itself on the margin of Britain and the closest port to the now dangerously unstable Europe, acts as a lens that helps focus on what 'England' means.[10] Earlier versions added the date '1937' to the poem's title to emphasise historical specificity (the Spanish Civil War was raging in the background). The border produces nothing material ('Nothing is made in this town'), but it specialises in travellers and their martial equivalents in displacement, soldiers. Its border position sharpens the view of both normality and its margins. The poem was actually written while Auden and Isherwood were co-writing *On the Frontier*.[11] Dover is simultaneouly the epitome of Englishness ('Like twin stone dogs opposed on a gentleman's gate') and 'breakwaters', yet one where still 'English is properly spoken'. Dover thus becomes an emblem of the marginal position that Auden's poetry manoeuvres itself into, a displacement that actually enforces the link with what it distances itself from.

The outside might be exciting, like the full moon over France in the poem, but it is also cold, and only achieves importance when the 'homecomers' (a concept already encountered in 'The Wanderer') bring it back to the England of yew trees, children's parties, and Georgian houses. Yet this England is also the England of the normality that appeared in such a sinister shape in *Letter to Lord Byron*, a normality in which 'Everything must be explained'. Its normality also normalises violence and war, when it enables the soldiers to kill time in pubs rather than killing enemies or being killed themselves. The poem's last three stanzas culminate in sinister pronouncements that England in the late 1930s must not forget that it is of 'minor

importance' with 'half its history done'. The poem's surprising final
line 'Not all of us are unhappy' encompasses once more the ambivalence of the margin and the perils of displacement: it may lead to
increased analytic insight, but the achieved insight (into the displaced self or the normality it distances itself from) might only be
one into helplessness and unhappiness.

'Journey to Iceland' (*CP* 126–7), the poem that succeeds the first
part of *Letter to Lord Byron* in *Letters from Iceland*, sums up this ambivalence. One of its first claims is that 'North means to all *Reject*' . It
clearly sets up the position of exclusion and displacement. Yet after
this declaration of rejection, the poem quickly arrives at the confession that this exclusion was consciously sought. In fact it is escapist
in tendency, and what is meant to be left behind is the current political situation. 'Europe is absent: this is an island and should be/a
refuge', the poem continues, only to contradict itself soon afterward:
'But is it'? Displacement does not answer the pressing questions,
'*Where is the homage? When/shall justice be done? Who is against me?/
Why am I always alone?*' In a typically Audenesque vein, these mix
personal and public concerns. When at the end of the poem 'some
driver/pulls on his gloves and in a blinding snowstorm starts/upon a
fatal journey', he is compared cynically to 'some writer' who 'runs
howling to his art'. Displacement that is fatal for some might, after
all, be a mere textual manoeuvre for a poet like Auden. Rather than
separating him from the stifling discourses of the time it might drive
him back to them in the shape of 'his art'.

The poems reprinted under the heading *A Voyage* in Auden's *Collected Poems* derive from another exercise in displacement. In 1938
Auden and Christopher Isherwood set out to produce another travel
book, *Journey to a War*. This time the journey did not take them to a
corner of Europe seemingly removed from contemporary politics,
but to a remote corner of the world (at least for European eyes), yet
one that was fully implicated in the political turmoil of the decade.
They travelled to a China that was suffering under partial Japanese
occupation. Consequently, the initial question of the poem 'Whither?'
(*CP* 143) or 'The Voyage' in the original edition (*Pr* 496), 'Where does
this journey look', has a more worrying tone than the lighthearted
reflection about Iceland as a nice land. None the less, even this voyage to what must have appeared as the actuality of history is quickly
transformed both into a general and again a personal quest: 'Does it
promise a juster life?' (the original version was even more insistent
with 'Does it still promise the Juster Life?'; *Pr* 496).

What the quest is about is Auden's fetish of 'the Good Place', yet what the traveller discovers is 'nothing'. The poem unravels the problem behind the quester itself: 'he does not want to arrive./His journey is false.' The poem depicts the imagined, just existence as a feverish dream, and the illness behind this fever as the only reality. Solace is found not in actual places, but in remembered ones. Yet the poem does not simply drift into regression, into images of a happy, sheltered childhood, for example. On the contrary, it forces these memories of fulfilment into interaction with the present. In this present 'maybe, his fever shall find a cure', but the cure would also be the end of the true journey – which is not so much the actuality of displacement, but the yearning for it. Displacement as an actual experience is not productive, but must be understood as desire. Like desire, its aim is not fulfilment, but deferral, a deferral that is the condition of all identities, personal, political, and cultural.

As a consequence of the discovery that the journey is not so much an actual geographic one as an internal one, the remaining poems that form *A Voyage* in Auden's *Collected Poems* and the section 'London to Hongkong' in *Journey to a War* are capable of using actual places, such as Macao and Hong Kong, as points of meditative reference, and mixing them with symbolic forces of orientation, such as the Sphinx, who stands for the Oedipal riddle of self-knowledge. The Sphinx neither accuses nor pardons. As the embodied reminder of desire and lack, it merely confirms that isolation and suffering are the inevitable conditions of the individual. Still, outside these personal insights into lack and desire, history continues and has to be dealt with. In the poem 'Hong Kong' neither the Westernised businessmen nor their and the poem's attempt to anchor themselves in a 'Late Victorian hill' manage to obscure the fact that 'off-stage, a war/ Thuds like the slamming of a distant door' (*CP* 144).

In 'Macao', too, the personal weaknesses, the 'mortal sins by which the strong are killed' ('major sins by which the heart is killed' in the early version; *Pr* 498) are placed side by side with men and governments that are 'torn to pieces'. Internal and external violence and suffering must be seen in unison. Even when the poem ends ironically with 'nothing serious can happen here', it can say this because it presents the perspective of Macao, 'the weed from Catholic Europe', an exotic 'fruit', as that of a child. The voice of the poem is unashamedly patronising and colonial. But the perspective also reflects back on a poetry that is forever caught in a struggle against its own ogres and dragons, whose function *Letter to Lord*

Byron describes as 'scaring him [the speaker and wanderer of the texts] back to childhood if he can' (*CP* 87). In 'A Major Port' (a poem which originally formed poem XXV in the sonnet sequence *In Time of War*; *Pr* 679) a scenery is eventually developed very unlike the marginal yet reassuring one of 'Dover'. It is a scenario of absence and loss: 'No guidance can be found in ancient lore' ('Nothing is given: we must find our law' in the early version; *Pr* 679), 'We have no destiny assigned to us,/No data but our bodies' (*CP* 145). Once again, the really loved, that is, whole ones are children. But even for them the poem predicts a future in which 'We' (the voice of the poem shifts subtly to include its speaker and readers) 'learn to pity and rebel'.

The twenty-one poems in the sequence *Sonnets from China* (originally twenty-seven plus a Commentary entitled *In Time of War*) are further evidence that displacement need not lead to insights into problems outside the personal sphere, but might simply produce a narcissistic refocusing on the old issues with the help of exotic props. The sonnets are deliberately abstract and therefore unmimic Chinese verse. But they are not concerned with Chinese culture. Neither are they interested in the plight of contemporary war-torn China. Instead they are once again psychological assessments of personal development, from childhood via adolescence, to first attempts at writing – 'He, though, by naming thought to make connection' (*CP* 150 – 'that was his projection' in the early version; *Pr* 668) – to marriage and material security (contrasted with images of oppression). The sequence is in many ways a relapse into Auden's narcissistic self-analysis that is only thinly disguised as an impersonal inquiry into the patterns of cultural and personal development. One encounters once more the fairy-tale images of king, shepherd, giant, dragon, kobold and magician.

Only in the twelfth sonnet (number XVI in the original) does the sequence manage to return to contemporary reality, when it suddenly declares 'Here war is harmless like a monument' (*CP* 153; the early version has 'simple'; *Pr* 674). But it soon abandons any interest in actual politics when it jumps back into generalisations in claims such as 'Yet ideas can be true, although men die' and 'maps can really point to places/Where life is evil now./Nanking. Dachau' (*CP* 154). This is a very problematic coupling of Auden's fetish, the map that is capable of outlining and defining everything, with the metaphysical concept of evil and its actual manifestation in massacres and concentration camps. The equation is too simple.

It is so simple that it instantly permits global generalisations. From Nanking and Dachau the journey goes to places 'Far from a cultural centre', to different epochs and eventually reality and 'Our global story' itself (in sonnet XIII in *Collected Poems* and sonnet XVIII in *Journey to a War*). This line is a much worse act of colonisation than the characterisations of Macao, for it implies that personal history, here a privileged middle-class English perspective, is the same as that of the invaded China. As a prophecy, this might have some bearing – Austria, China, Spain, and soon France would indeed be linked – but, again, it is an English prophecy. The perspective is parochial rather than global, as the final sonnet makes abundantly clear. It originally formed the preamble to *Journey to a War*. Not only is it addressed to E. M. Forster, the embodiment of Edwardian England, but it culminates in the revealing statement: 'Yes, we are Lucy, Turton, Philip: we/Wish international evil, are delighted/To join the jolly ranks of the benighted' (*CP* 157). Even when *Sonnets fom China/ In Time of War* wish to use Chinese reality to shake England out of its paralysis or accuse it of silent complicity, they are still firmly engaged with England – and not with the suffering in Nanking (or Dachau). Moreover, the England they are engaged with is that of Edwardian garden parties and petty intrigues, in which the most drastic embodiment of evil is Miss Avery who 'Comes out into the garden with a sword' (*CP* 157).[12]

PLURAL PERSPECTIVES

Even before Auden emigrated to the United States in 1939, there is an interesting shift in the perspective of his poetry which paves the way for an escape from the Oedipal trap of Englishness. Poems such as 'Brussels in Winter', 'Musée des Beaux Arts', and 'Gare du Midi' provide first glimpses of what – via an American exile – would develop into a new European perspective in Auden's writing. The speaker of 'Brussels in Winter' (*CP* 146) has lost the prerequisite that even the most endangered borderline dwellers of Auden's early works possess. He has lost his imaginary map: 'Wandering through cold streets tangled like old string,/Coming on fountains rigid in the frost,/Its formula escapes you.' The scenery does not embrace him, and neither can he project it onto childhood memories or compare it to images of Englishness: 'it has lost/The certainty that constitutes a thing'. It is simply alien, and the only way it can be embraced by a stranger is by paying. This apparently cruel materialist reduction of exile, however, goes hand in hand with a new perspective. In it 'A look contains the history of man'. It is not ancestry, biology, or personal and cultural history that are decisive, but observation and realisation of the present.

This observation is not itself cold and disinterested. It sees 'the old, the hungry and the humbled' and almost envies them their sense of place and belonging. But it also observes the glow from the windows of rich apartments. The interested glance does not abstract completely from the personal position, yet it avoids a narcissistic, all-embracing regression. Instead it tries to unite itself and its surroundings in an objective relationship, a view that is capable of producing 'A phrase [that] goes packed with meaning like a van'. The emerging perspective is that of a meaningful materialism, or, as will be shown in the next chapter, a sceptical humanism that does not rely on metaphysical foundations.

'Musée des Beaux Arts' (*CP* 146–7) is another example of this shift in perspective. It displaces the view several times: from a museum in Brussels to the most general feeling of suffering, via the specifically European 'Old Masters' to images of normality and even banality, and eventually to a specific painting, *Icarus* by Breughel. The poem discusses the relation between individual tragedy and suffering in the context of both art and normality. Only this time, there is no bogey man; neither is there a privileged position for any of these points of reference. There is nothing specifically Audenesque or English about the points of reference either. In the same way that a museum frames art, the beautiful arts normalise suffering. Yet none of them performs an act of deception, since existence itself is constituted of 'dreadful martyrdom' as well as of people going about their business.

The poem is irritating in its argument, until one realises that its postulation of the 'human position' of suffering about which the Old Masters apparently knew everything places this suffering simultaneously in two exclusive positions: it is both daily event and exceptional tragedy. The poem also refrains from integrating suffering into a larger explanatory, indeed mythical narrative, along the lines of Yeats's historical gyres or Eliot's layers in *Four Quartets*. Its message is: normality and suffering coexist and may indeed be inseparable. Yet neither of the two justifies the other. Art must not try to achieve a reconciliation with suffering: on the contrary, it must expose the contradictory coupling and leave judgements to its percipients.

'The Novelist' projects this new perspective back on writing, making the prose writer rather than the poet the protagonist of the struggle for this involved and interested perspective on the vagaries of existence. While the poet is 'Encased in talent like a uniform' and becomes a victim of his own myth, the novelist must be 'plain and awkward', because his duty is to remain as close as possible to the boredom, vulgarity, filth, but also love that characterises human existence (CP 147). This condition is neither God-given nor in other ways essential, but depends on the historic, social, and political forces that create its material as well as spiritual environment.

Of course the poem works in two ways. It implicitly conveys an accusation of dullness against such 'realist' novelists, but it also contains a challenge to poetry to break out of its narcissistic shell. This is a challenge that Auden's writings address to themselves. His writings would soon turn to other forms, such as the long verse play, the 'Baroque Eclogue' of The Age of Anxiety. They would also look in the direction of music and subordinate themselves (at least seemingly) to the demands of another art form. All these structural experiments must be understood as part of a self-relativising endeavour that at the same time aims at a broader, but not totalising and totalitarian perspective.

In 'The Composer' (CP 148) Auden sketches this emerging distrust for poetry, while at the same time slyly preserving a province for it. 'All others translate' is the first assertion of the poem, and with this claim it insists on the entanglement of painting and poetry in the perils of existence that provide material, but also shackle artists to those things 'that hurt and connect'. Music, on the other hand, is regarded by the poem as 'pure contraption', 'the ultimate gift'. Its 'presence' and 'delight', however, not only clash with the silence and the doubt that characterise the working environment of painter and poet; music's miraculous presence is also mute and ineffectual when it comes to coping with existence. Without words 'You alone, alone, imaginary song,/Are unable to say an existence is wrong'. When 'The Composer' therefore closes by granting music the power to 'pour out your forgiveness like wine', it ends on an ambiguous note. Wine has a redemptive ritual character (see its function in the Eucharist), but it is also a drug that makes one forget injustice and error rather than encouraging one to rectify them.

The 1940s not only marked the end of the 'low dishonest decade' that had culminated in the start of the Second World War, but also stood for a further displacement. The 1940s saw Auden in New

York, looking back at Europe from outside its immediate concerns. This geographic displacement was coupled with a personal and artistic one. Auden's self-imposed exile had created hostile responses in Britain. He was accused of leaving 'the sinking ship of European democracy' as well as abandoning his position as an influential poetic force.[13]

In the sonnet sequence entitled 'The Quest' Auden reflects on the position that places him together with all intellectuals of the time at a crossroads: 'who can tell/These places of decision and farewell/To what dishonour all adventure leads' (*CP* 224). The most fascinating aspect of this long poem is that the object of its quest remains completely abstract. In its very first stanza it talks about a vague 'future' as well as 'Enigmas', that it then couples threateningly with 'executioners and rules'. Two stanzas further on we are in the fictional world of *Alice in Wonderland*, where we encounter Alice crying over her minute size compared with the vast expanse of the Wonderland she has just encountered. The poem is again concerned with the effect of displacement on the individual. It describes the loss of orientation and points of reference as well as the actions that are meant to remedy the situation, for which the term 'quest' acts as a shorthand. Any preparation for this disorientation is ridiculed in the second part of the poem, because the confusion is not simply external but internal: 'In theory they were sound on Expectation,/Had there been situations to be in;/Unluckily they were their situation' (*CP* 224).

Since the problematic 'situation' is identical with the displaced identities subjected to it, what is really sought in this poem is determination, self-determination as well as guidelines. The term that summarises these desiderata is 'Necessity'. Yet far from declaring the lacking orientation to be an externally imposed condition or predestination (in the sense of some Protestant teachings), the poem again shifts necessity to a dialectical position between individual and exterior. The belief that 'Necessity by nature is the same/No matter how or by whom it be sought' (*CP* 225) is exposed as wrong. This concept of a universal necessity that fits every individual is challenged in the poem by the city – whose plurality shows that necessity corresponds to individual shortcomings, for which 'grief' is the umbrella term. Consequently, mastery of existence is individual, too, and it consists paradoxically not in overcoming individuality but in giving in to the suitable temptation.

In the final section of the present chapter and in the following one I will use this insight to challenge the notion of Auden as a Christian poet. At this point it is important to see that the farewell to overall concepts of determination and sense goes hand in hand once more with an evaluation of his own artistic position. In Section 6 of 'The Quest' there are thinly disguised references to a 'He' who ends up being ashamed at succumbing narcissistically to his grief, and attempting to overcome this unhealthy attachment by joining 'a gang of rowdy stories where/His gift for magic quickly made him chief'. Auden, who used to be called 'Uncle Wiz' by his friends, uses these lines to characterise his own biography and its personal and political excesses as necessary escapades. Yet he also criticises the position they helped him to achieve as the perceived leader of a new poetry, the 'Auden Group'.

In a manner that prefigures the discussion of alternative lives in the later poem 'In Praise of Limestone', 'The Quest' goes on to expose various responses to lack. The intellectual, the power broker, and the sensual person are shown as equally incapable of turning their desire into necessity. Heroism in any form is criticised as shallow when it is compared in Sonnet 11 to 'an Average Man/Attempting the exceptional'. In the exceptionality of the average, Auden's later poems find a different form of elevation, one that manages to step out of the straitjacket of the concept of the 'truly strong man'. Truth that merely derives from focusing on the individual and then subtracting its deficiencies, i.e. the Nietzschean concept of the superman, so seductive to the classical modernists, is clearly rejected by 'The Quest'. 'And how reliable can any truth be that is got/By observing oneself and then just inserting a Not?', Sonnet 14 correctly asks. The quest must be transformed from a negative one that merely leads away from something, to a positive one that embraces positions.

Stability must not lead to a giving-in to one's surroundings, as it did in the trap of tradition in the earlier poems; instead, it has to be employed for a simultaneous appreciation and critique of existence. Displacement must not become a mere escapist withdrawal, but has to lead to a voicing of difference inside a plurality of situations. Existence must bear this displacement and make it fertile for its surroundings – rather than merely projecting it backwards on what has been left behind. Whether this acceptance of necessity leads into the arms of established religious frameworks will be questioned in the next chapter. The American title of the collection in which 'The Quest' first appeared, The Double Man, should caution against such an appropriation.

In terms of Auden's displaced voices, the final sonnet of 'The Quest' reiterates the necessity of engagement when it declares the journey to be over: 'All journeys die here: wish and weight are lifted' (*CP* 231). Yet this end of the journey does not lead to a renunciation that merely disguises a nostalgia for an unlived past, as in Eliot's *Four Quartets* (the 'old maid's desolation' and the roses that 'have flung their glory like a cloak' in Auden's poem could be read as ridiculing Eliot's rose-garden visions). When in the final line of 'The Quest' the 'centre of volition' of the questers shifts, the poem indicates that the new quest will be about self and others in the here and now – rather than the then and there of some political utopia or metaphysical never-never land.

DIASPORA AND DIALOGUE

The rarely discussed poem 'Diaspora' (*CP* 234) uses a poignant equation to develop further the concept of displacement. In the poem displacement leads via suffering to an implicit call to attempt forms of true identity and existence without the crutches of easy delineations. Originally applied to the scattering of the Jewish tribes, 'diaspora' has a particular pertinence in the 1940s when it describes the Jews who are lucky enough to escape the atrocities of the Germans and their allies, and whose presence was particularly felt in the United States. The poem uses the persecution of the Jews as its allegory for the violent creation of identities through exclusion and delineation. It also shows that the scapegoat never attains sufficient stability, because the concept rests on a basic lack and anxiety in the persecutors: 'he drew their terrors to him'. Spatial exclusion ultimately proves as futile as the projection of presumed difference onto the body via the concept of race. In the same way that the exile in the earlier poems merely led to a refocusing of the problems (and at best to their critique), here the ultimate stab at the necessary Other turns out to be a stab at the self: 'they plunged right through him/Into a land of mirrors without time or space'. The Freudian unconscious comes to mind, or Lacan and Julia Kristeva's imaginary.[14] As long as the attempt at finding certainties and identities fails to take into account that it is generated by, as well as designed to fight, an inherent lack, it is not only doomed to fail; it also violates the principles of what it means to be human, and becomes terroristic: 'And all they had to strike now was the human face.'

It is not coincidental that the two poems that follow 'Diaspora' in Auden's *Collected Poems* are 'Luther' and 'Montaigne'. 'Luther' introduces the great Reformer as a paranoiac: 'With conscience cocked to listen for the thunder,/He saw the Devil busy in the wind' (*CP* 235). Judgement to him is like a bomb whose fuse is already lit, but against it he also only has an 'apparatus' at his disposal. This machinery of salvation consists of mere phrases 'All works, Great Men, Societies are bad./The Just shall live by Faith'. And while Luther cries out these pronouncements 'in dread', 'men and women of the world were glad,/Who'd never cared or trembled in their lives' . The outcome of Luther's efforts is ridiculed. He cannot effect a change in human existence because he has never been in communication with others; his struggle is with himself. Without dialogue there is no change, only theatrics.

A similar verdict is directed against Montaigne. He is shown as terrorising the 'gentle landscape' outside his library window with grammar (*CP* 235). Once again, exile (here intellectual detachment) that does not lead to dialogue is shown as unproductive. However, it spawns something in Montaigne's case, and that is the French Revolution. Yet the effect of the Revolution is precisely to support that for which Montaigne does not stand: he gives 'The Flesh its weapons to defeat the Book'. Both intellect and religion fall victim to excess of isolation, when this exile leads to a failure to communicate with one's environment. What the poem recommends as a remedy is the re-establishment of love 'from the sensual child', doubt, *belles-lettres*, and laziness, indeed everything that Montaigne is not. Only in the dialogue of extremes lies a possibility for an existence that is liveable, not in the totalisation of a single conviction.

'Atlantis' is another poem advocating dialogue and/in displacement, yet refraining from asking for convictions, solutions, or salvation. What is recommended is first and foremost an acceptance that the very desire to reach the promised land leads onto a Ship of Fools. Its journey may take one to places of wisdom or sensual enjoyment. None the less the teachings of the wise that may be encountered must be taken with care: 'Thus they shall teach you the ways/To doubt that you may believe' (*CP* 245). The distractions of pleasure must not distract from the search for Atlantis. At the same time, and this is the crux of the poem, this search should be accompanied by the awareness that it will never reach its goal: 'honour the fate you are,/Travelling and tormented,/Dialectic and bizarre'. Displacement is once again the fate of the individual, only now it is fully evident that the dislocation is not imposed from the outside, by a resistance to the Oedipal forces of ancestry or by political necessity, but is a condition of the self.

The journey itself brings its own salvation, yet only in the shape of 'a poetic vision'. The poetry of failure is its own reward. This is very unlike the apparently similar rejoicing in failure in Eliot's *Ash-Wednesday*, for example. While Eliot's poem claims that it rejoices because it must construct something upon which to rejoice, Auden's refrains from offering a construction that transcends the text. In fact, it docs not even offer a positive poetic vision, only one of failure. While classical modernism tries to create a renewed mythical integrity out of its failure, Auden's postmodern poetics creates nothing but poetry. Even when it invokes God as the 'Ancient of Days' and asks him to bless the doomed traveller in its last stanza, it sets Him side by side with 'Hermes, master of the roads' (but also god of merchants and thieves) and 'the four dwarf Kabiri'. Even religion is a place of dialogue in Auden's poetry, where Christianity and paganism enter an untroubled alliance, yet one that by no means guarantees individual happiness and fulfilment.

One form of describing the dialogue inside which Auden's further poetic development can be viewed was used by Auden himself in 'Under Which Lyre', a poem written for Harvard University in 1946. It celebrates the end of the Second World War only to announce that, at least on university campuses, another war has instantly been declared. This is the one 'Twixt those who follow/Precocious Hermes all the way/And those who without qualms obey/Pompous Apollo' (*CP* 260). It is not difficult to guess that Auden's own poetics sees its allegiance to lie with the unreliable, mercenary, but also open and playful Hermes. The purity, self-importance and closure of an aesthetics as embodied by Apollo is alien to Auden: the importance of Hermes lies mainly in his in-between status. As the messenger of the gods, he negotiates between and connects not only the gods themselves, but also gods and mortals.

None the less Auden's poem does not totally elevate Hermes above Apollo. This would in fact contradict Hermes' nature as relative and dialogic: 'If he would leave the self alone,/Apollo's welcome to the throne', the poem exclaims, only to continue darkly with the reminder that Apollo loves to rule 'Fasces and falcons'. The Second World War had hardly ended when another, the Cold War, started, in which 'falcons' stood for aggressive politicians. Yet the poem also acknowledges that 'The earth would soon, did Hermes run it,/Be like the Balkans'. On the other hand, the idealistic Apollo is also a great leveller who favours the banal and the common. Existentialism is the intellectual movement that puts into practice Apollonian asceticism and its totalitarian aesthetics. Auden's poem is convinced that the monolithic nature of Apollonian thinking can be its downfall. The playful irreverence of the 'Hermetic Decalogue' is introduced as a humorous antidote to aesthetic absolutism. Auden's favouring of light verse (of which 'Under Which Lyre' is itself an example), culminating in his editorship of The Oxford Book of Light Verse in 1938, is the most obvious artistic consequence of the convictions elaborated in this poem. What is rejected is a poetry of and about absolutes; what is recommended instead is a poetics of tolerance and chance, one that is flexible and humorous and, most importantly, open to dialogue and capable of accepting dissent.

DISPUTES OF WILL AND LOVE

That the dialogic principle becomes dominant in Auden's poetry, a principle that develops interacting voices out of the dissenting and conflicting ones of his earlier poetry, is even demonstrated in projects that should, at least in theory, embody the monolithic voice of tradition. In For the Time Being: A Christmas Oratorio, written between 1941 and 1942 and dedicated to Auden's recently deceased mother, a very unusual version of the nativity is presented (CP 269–308). The text not only transports the beginning of Christianity into the present age of darkness, the ongoing Second World War; it also suspends Christ's birth poetically between opposing voices that negotiate its importance. A chorus and a semi-chorus compete with a narrator in the invocation of inertia and despondency, while a recitative counters their position with a paradoxical notion of hope – one of the traditional Christian tenets of faith, the credo quia absurdum, the belief in spite of its absurdity. Yet the hope that emerges is by no means a clear-cut Christian one: it is composed of muscle and mind, of a self that – in order to become one – must rebel against circumstances. In the end its rebellion encompasses its own convictions, and thus arrives at the acceptance of hope in a hopeless situation. The path is paved for a very unusual annunciation, one in which the miraculous is replaced by the psychological; but even the psychological fails to rule supreme – and instead enters a relativising dialogue.

The annunciation proper is consequently undertaken by the four faculties, of intuition, feeling, sensation, and thought, both in unison and individually, in order to highlight once more the struggle between, and also the interconnectedness of, positions. When the traditional protagonists of the annunciation, the Archangel Gabriel and the Virgin Mary, enter the scene, they, too, perform rather unusual roles. Rather than meekly receiving the miraculous news of being chosen, Mary enters into a theological dialogue with Gabriel about the problem of free will in relation to universal love, culminating in Gabriel's message that it is up to her to choose to be chosen.[15]

In a similar vein the subsequent 'Temptation of St. Joseph' removes the biblical story onto a mundane contemporary plane by making Joseph tell his side of the story as one of an interrupted courtship in which polished shoes and pressed trousers, a grey crowd, and the police feature side by side with a fallen star. Joseph even ends up waiting for Mary in a bar, Auden's favourite setting for displaced individuals since 'September 1, 1939', while the chorus tries to instil doubts into him. What clashes in his mind is his individual love for Mary, whom he continually refers to as 'My own true love', with a Divine love that he finds hard to envisage and trust. But it is this Divine love that exceeds the personal sphere of the will, that Gabriel eventually asks him to accept without a single 'Important and elegant proof' (*CP* 281). Yet just as the dialogue between Gabriel and Mary lacks a definite outcome, so here Gabriel's blunt command 'Be silent and sit still' (*CP* 282) remains unanswered. It is the narrator and several choruses that provide an uneasy finale to the section, one that is far from a conclusion, but rather a prayer for one. While the dialogue escapes the totalitarianism of mere order, it is also potentially open-ended and devoid of firm solutions.

The star of the Nativity, which opens the subsequent section entitled 'The Summons', consequently calls itself 'that star most dreaded by the wise', because its function is to end dialogue and to deprive men of choice. Its message is a gloomy one: rather than announcing great joy, as one would expect, it talks about allegorical dangers it has in store: glassy mountains with no footholds for logic, a 'Bridge of dread/Where knowledge but increases vertigo' (*CP* 285), loneliness, and exposure to confusion and pain. In short, it highlights the negative aspects of faith. The Three Wise Men are none the less eager to follow the star, because it enables them to abandon their own limited certainties for an unlimited faith that is also boundless uncertainty. The first of the Wise Men is an empirical student of

Nature, who none the less discovers in Nature merely disjointed answers and no solution to the question how to be truthful. The second one is a historian who had thought real assurances were to be found in the trust in 'Time's constant/Flow' (CP 285), but discovered that facts do not endure, nor does the study of history provide a teleology, answers to the question of how to live in the here and now. The third Wise Man is a student of the body and its senses. He follows the star because his inquiries have failed to provide any insight into love.

The Three Wise Men eventually sum up their position in a very down-to-earth way. They are 'three old sinners' (CP 286) who find the journey too long and troublesome, who miss their wives, books, and dogs and only have 'the vaguest idea why we are what we are'. What unites them is the attempt to 'discover how to be human now' (CP 286). This double insistence on 'human' and 'now' is important for distinguishing the message of Auden's wise men from a mere orthodox repetition of Christian dogma. What Auden's 'Christmas Oratorio' is concerned with are questions of an ultimately humanitarian nature, not the miracles of faith. Rather than eternal truth, it discusses actual necessities, even though the point of orientation in a love that transcends the individual will might be similar. *For the Time Being* must be taken seriously as the title of the piece – and not be reversed into the existentialism of Heidegger's *Being and Time*, or a search for a being that transcends time.[16]

That the text is concerned with actual needs and necessities is further demonstrated by its immediate return to the pressures of the time, here embodied in the demands of authority ('the voice of Caesar', CP 287). This earthly authority, the one that ordered the biblical census, has overcome necessity and fortune by endurance and skill, the benchmarks of power. The order he establishes extends from Seven Kingdoms via Tom, Dick, and Harry right up to the linguistic rules of inflections, accents, prepositions, and word-order. Once again Auden's text insists on the location of power in signification rather than essences. Yet this ordering power only provides answers inside its discourses, as the example of the exact but none the less purely symbolic solution of mathematical equations demonstrates. In the final consequence, power and its 'answers' combine in a tautology in which being great and being right depend on the acceptance that Caesar (or any form of power) is great and right.

The repeated concluding claim, 'God must be with Him', is therefore hardly convincing. The narrator and the final chorus of the section demonstrate that the search for truth and certainties through power merely leads to the wish to silence doubt through violence. Brutal fact is eventually invoked paradoxically to persuade the chorus to pursue 'Adventure, Art, and Peace' (*CP* 289). The displaced, faceless voices of *For the Time Being* yearn for authority and orientation in facts. Yet this would entail the end of the dialogue that is a necessary aspect of their freedom, the will that makes their request as well as their yearning possible in the first place.

The shepherds, whose vision the subsequent section of *For the Time Being* represents, are the masses whose acquiescence to authority is shown as motivated solely by their conviction that its days are numbered. Their voices are a return of the working-class opinions of Auden's earlier works, and at times it is difficult to decide whether they are awaiting the birth of Christ as the redeemer, or a proletarian revolution. Their main function is to remind the reader that the search for salvation and redemption must never lose sight of the mundane issues of daily practice. Once more, if there is a Christian message in this text, it is by no means an orthodox one. Its vision of salvation encompasses physical needs, such as 'Light, water, and air', as well as the end of established 'Authoritarian/Constraint' (*CP* 292), rather than projecting the fulfilment of those demands into a metaphysical elsewhere.

'At the manger' is the sequence of *For the Time Being* that depicts the adoration of the Magi and the shepherds. It is also the hitherto most orthodox section of the poem, in that it starts off with Mary's already sombre meditation on Christ's sacrifice which is inherent in the very human form that she has given him. The Wise Men and the shepherds then go on to reflect on the existential changes that the birth of Christ means for them. None the less, even this section of the poem is not without its ambiguities and challenging openness. Mary's meditation eventually focuses on the dream as the human form of wish-fulfilment, where 'earth ascends to Heaven/Where no one need pray nor ever feel alone' (*CP* 293). Her speech implies that the Divine dream of salvation is Heaven descending to earth in the shape of Christ. None the less, this neat reversal grants a rather dubious status to the Divine plan. Is it perhaps as undirected as a dream – or as transient? If Heaven is a place where communication through prayer is no longer necessary because of the achieved proximity of souls and Creator, then what does Christ's presence on earth mean in terms of communication? Is not every word spoken about the Divine presence then superfluous? Does it not, indeed, show a misrecognition of the event? And where does that leave a 'Christmas Oratorio'? Even in its seemingly orthodox sections, Auden's text manages to undermine its very right to exist and argue its point.

A similar problem emerges from the speeches of the Wise Men and shepherds. Their common theme is the release from an unsatisfactory existence through Divine love. Yet when it comes to describing this love, contradictions soon emerge. For a start, this love, despite its enormity, does not 'will enraptured apathy'. Contrary to fate, it 'Can doubt, affirm, deny' (CP 296). Once again, the emphasis is on negotiation and dialogue rather than monological and monolithic certainty. This is further emphasised when the poem goes on to describe love as not afraid of anarchy, but expressing obligation 'With movement and in spontaneity', all of which are features of dialogue rather than certainty. None the less, if this Divine love shifts into a close proximity with free will, as the above quotation signals, then it is in danger of losing its universality and of becoming reduced to an individual emotion again.

In the speeches of the shepherd the problem achieves a very drastic political edge. The first shepherd, after talking about 'the great boots of the rich on our faces' (CP 296), then advocates a truth of their abuse in their own abuse. What is going on? A little later the shepherds demand a replacement of hate by 'the poetry of hate'. How does this fit a 'Christmas Oratorio'? And how does a pronouncement of Divine Love look when it is described in an obvious proto-Lacanian formula: 'Love's possibilities of realization/Require an Otherness that can say I'? For the Time Being seems a far cry from a 'distinction Auden makes in his criticism between the pre-Christian and the Christian world', as George Bahlke suggests with reference to Auden's foreword to The Portable Greek Reader of 1952.[17] Rather than shifting his thought clearly into the realm of orthodox Christianity, Auden pushes it over the top and into his familar territory of psychoanalysis and sociology. Yet rather than suffering from this intellectual betrayal, Auden's poems gain from it: they achieve a level of significance through their openness that makes them palatable and, indeed, provocative for Christians and non-Christians alike.

'The Meditation of Simeon', a section that echoes Eliot's 'A Song for Simeon', once more takes up the biblical model (Luke 2: 25–35) in order to infuse it with contradiction and dialogue. In Luke the Holy Ghost reveals to Simeon that he will not die before he has seen

Christ. He encounters Jesus in the temple and identifies him as the Saviour in front of Jesus's astonished parents. Auden's Simeon, on the other hand, is first and foremost a sceptic. First, he doubts the factuality of the biblical Fall from a historical perspective; then he questions its necessity from a psychological point of view and a political one, in order to manoeuvre the argument into the direction of self and soul. Yet in the narcissistic enclosure in which the self mirrors itself and believes to be perceiving its perfect soul, there is no consolation either. This consolation lies, interestingly enough, in vagueness.

For this meditation Auden uses images quite similar to those of the poetic philosophy of space and time developed in Eliot's *Four Quartets*, especially 'Burnt Norton'. Yet rather than following Eliot in leading the manifold to a synthesising oneness – in which past, present, and future merge – Auden insists on the dialogue of one and many. This excludes simple determinism. It abstains from certainty, too, and these two rejections have direct consequences for language and poetry. In connnection with the word of God and its reception by the prophets, the meditation continues, 'their witness could only be received as long as it was vaguely misunderstood, as long as it seemed either to be neither impossible nor necessary, or necessary but not impossible, or impossible but not necessary' (*CP* 299). The complex formula reiterates the crucial belief of Auden's early poetry that signification reigns supreme, yet that it reigns only through excess, deferral, and thus ultimately through failure: failure to set up natural correspondences, for example. The misunderstanding that is the essence of prophecy reflects back both on a poetry that must be self-contradictory and ambiguous, and on its voices, that must remain dejected and dislocated even when they are in a truth that they can never hope to express.

Rather than merely developing a coherent Christian belief that leads out of the impasses of Auden's earlier poetry, 'The Meditation of Simeon' becomes itself a dialogic text under whose surface-orthodoxy runs a suspicion that it is nothing more than what it is, a meditation and therefore not the truth, but a questioning of the truth; in short, a quest once more. Even though the meditation seems to end in an acknowledgement of God's presence and an advocating of surrender rather than pursuit, it adds that it is still following Him, and admits to anxiety rather than peace. The section is also not the conclusion of *For the Time Being*, but its deferral, and it is itself followed by the very opposite of peace and resolution. It is succeeded by 'The

Massacre of the Innocents' and 'The Flight into Egypt', by violence and further displacement.

Eliot is once again not far away when 'The Massacre of the Innocents' opens with a soliloquy by Herod that echoes the beginning of Eliot's conversion poem, *Ash-Wednesday*. Where Eliot's speaker moves from an acceptance of the impossibility of change to a paradoxical hope generated artificially out of this impotence, Auden's Herod accepts only his bewilderment at the fact that things are what they are. Indeed, he is most worried by the absence of visible disorder. Existence is orderly. Normality is firmly in place. And still he is troubled by the suspicion that the population will demand more, that security and normality will breed restlessness and upheaval. Out of the desire for the 'more' that transcends routine, he fears, irrational wishes and desires will be born, and he sees the belief in the birth of the Messiah as a first sign of this epidemic of irrationality. 'Reason will be replaced by Revelation.' 'Idealism will be replaced by Materialism.' 'Justice will be replaced by Pity' (*CP* 303). The consequence will be the collapse of civilization. This leaves Herod in an impossible position. As a self-declared liberal he should, in principle, be permissive towards people's desires and even accept the follies of their wills. But as a liberal he also cannot accept the emergence of a system of belief like Christianity – which would indeed spell the end of liberalism and introduce strict rules of behaviour and norms of right and wrong. The conflict is similar to the one between Apollo and Hermes in 'Under Which Lyre'.

Herod's conflict is pinpointed by his actual position of power, which puts him in a Catch-22 situation: even if he rejects the Christian God, either by having the innocent children of the Jews slaughtered or by brushing off the news of Christ's birth as a rumour, he is still following this God's teaching of free will. Pagan belief would simply rely on predestined fate. Yet a decision has to be made, and this puts him in the impossible position of being given the power to kill God. 'And for me personally at that moment it would mean that God had given me the power to destroy himself. I refuse to be taken in. He could not play such a horrible practical joke' (*CP* 304). Herod becomes a precursor of Nietzsche, a Nietzsche that spelled out the possibilities of a modernity that both gives itself its own rules and unconvers them as fictional: a Nietzsche, also, who went mad. Herod's credo is that of the modern liberal, and it echoes the death-throes of the middle class in Auden's earlier works. It also sums up the self-destructive dialectic that characterises the modern, or perhaps the modernist, self, a self that is caught in its own binary oppositions and uses a monologic and monolithic self to govern others rather than to enter a dialogue with them: 'I'm a liberal. I want everyone to be happy. I wish I had never been born' (*CP* 304).

In 'The Flight to Egypt' it is this flight from the self-enclosure of a modernist, self-destructive self that Mary and Joseph exercise. The means of their escape, which is once again a form of exile, are the overcoming of mirror and echo, devices of self-knowledge, which none the less permit only a narcissistic regard of self for self. Anonymity and loss (the 'Kingdom of the Robbers' and the 'waste of the Anonymous', *CP* 305–6) are preferable to the monadic state of monologic existence. In a sequence in which Mary and Joseph speak in often funny rhyming couplets, and unidentified 'Voices of the Desert' develop surreal scenarios that mock images from Eliot's poetry (a well-run desert, canals, cigarette ends, times of the night), a farewell is sketched to the problematic attachment to the past that threatened every concept of future in Auden's poems. A new life that is no longer merely the antithesis of the old one is to be developed, but it will entail losses as well, the loss of the old insecurity, for example, the paradoxical feeling of belonging that relied on the presence of threat.

The finale of *For the Time Being* sketches this new life as one devoid of vacuous idealisms. In a pragmatic move, the clearing up after Christmas is used as a foil on which the hopes generated by Christ's birth are symbolically relativised. In the same way as the narrator reports the failure 'To love all our relatives' as an indication that we have 'Grossly overestimated our powers' (*CP* 307), Christ's sacrifice is devalued by the weakness of those who receive it as a gift. As a consequence, the 'unpleasant whiff of apprehension at the thought/Of Lent and Good Friday' is already in the air. Yet again the 'time being' that is now made an issue is not a metaphysical one or one of eternal failure and damnation – in the same way that it was not the promise of eternal salvation in the earlier sections of the poem either. The time being is a time when will, decision, and love have to manifest themselves in the everyday world of paying bills and learning irregular verbs. These mundane activities, rather than idealistic gestures, are what redeem the time being from insignificance. Even in terms of faith, it is neither its loss nor its victory that is to be expected, but 'A silence that is neither for nor against her [the soul's] faith' (*CP* 308). In this silence of absolutes, however, the dialogic and contradictory voices of self, will, and love make themselves heard – not as certainties, but as negotiations.

This they do also in the concluding chorus of *For the Time Being*, in which orthodox Christian doctrine (that calls God the Way, the Truth, and the Life) blends with typical Audenesque fairy tale images of allegorical lands and kingdoms, rare beasts, adventures, and even the successful quest – whose conclusion is the return to a great city in which a marriage feast awaits the quester. The mixture is deliberately relativising, yet it does not become self-destructive as in many of Auden's earlier poems ('The Wanderer', for example). What the choral finale suggests is that faith and allegory work together. One is the expression of the other. At the same time certainty and poetry insist on their difference – which actually enables them to enter a dialogue which leaves room for interpretation, decision, and freedom – rather than blending into the totality of certainty.

7

From Eros to Agape: The Philosophy of Auden's Later Works

PREMATURE EXTRAPOLATIONS

The previous chapter began to challenge the notion entertained by some critics that there is a proper conversion to Christianity in Auden's biography that finds unequivocal expression in his writings. Auden himself mentions the incisive event of a sudden feeling of agape he experienced as early as 1933. Agape means 'brotherly love' without any sexual elements, and refers to the early Christian practice of a love-feast commemorating the Last Supper. The experience is described in the poem 'A Summer Night'.

Yet far from giving the impression of an overtly religious text, 'A Summer Night' in fact blends in remarkably well with the rest of Auden's poetry of the 1930s, in that it is an assessment of the status of the self in relation to others.[1] It moves from 'I' to 'we', and in the process from the viewpoint of an individual position to that of a privileged group that is exempt from the threats that the European situation has in store. The poem also contains a further shift, that from the 'tyrannies of love' (*CP* 103), which creates a hierarchy of desire and power, to a feeling of equality in the company of colleagues.

The poem, indeed, employs some vaguely religious terms, such as 'congregated' (which is applied to leaves, however), 'chosen' (a reference to the workplace of the speaker), and 'dove-like' (describing the light), an arrangement that culminates in the rather hyperbolic 'And Death put down his book'. Yet from Stanza 5 onwards, we are firmly in the familiar terrain of Auden's early poetry, when the text mentions 'healers', 'brilliant talkers', 'eccentrics' and 'silent walkers', in order to move on towards England's position in the alarming political uncertainty of the time, and then once again towards fairy-tale monsters and issues of parental authority.

145

If there are first glimpses of religious motives here, then they are those that are already evident in Auden's earliest writings. They are ambiguous and only ever appear in deflated form, reduced to materialistic insights or obvious hyperbole. Not even the shift that Auden himself saw in the poem, that from erotic love with its inevitable undertones of egotism and potential failure to a brotherly love embodied in agape, is completely evident. The 'good atmosphere' of the text (in itself a rather transient form of the good place that Auden's poetry constantly yearns for) is indeed described as composed of 'the sexy airs of summer and the bare arms'. Rather than saying farewell to eros and embracing caritas, the text shows the two as intermingled. Critics who follow Auden's own wilful appropriation of this poem as the starting-point of a personal 'conversion' are, indeed, required not to read the text, and must merely take its author's biased reading for granted.

Yet despite the continual deflation of positions, there is an ongoing debate about the status of love and sexuality versus society in Auden's writings. There is also a clear interest in questions of religion – an interest surfaces not only in Auden's biography, but also in his admission of uneasy feelings when he noticed the closed churches in Spain during the Civil War or the fact that he started going to church again, on an experimental basis, as he claimed, usually leaving before the sermon.[2] What is easily mistaken as a conversion narrative in his writings, however, is more likely a reworking of personal and existential concerns into a new framework, one that no longer aspires to universal significance or complete fulfilment. It is more likely a pragmatic reduction of the anxieties of his early phase into a form that proved personally manageable – and therefore artistically honest. This chapter will try to outline the development of this framework in Auden's writings. It will also show that, far from integrating his thought into established religious patterns, be they Protestant or otherwise, Auden retains an openness and polyvalence that has more in common with postmodern thinking than established religiosity.

The conflict of eros and caritas, or sexuality and a love that is more than idealistic, egotistic (and perhaps even narcissistic) is, as I have claimed above, present from Auden's earliest writings. Yet the solution of the problem must not be sought in a rejection of one for the other. This would merely support a binarism of right and wrong, good and evil, that creates the tensions between the two concepts in the first place. Auden himself wrote that 'Agape is the fulfilment and correction of eros, not its contradiction'.[3] His much anthologised love poem 'Lullaby' should consequently be read as a reconciliation of eros and caritas – or at least as an acknowledgement of the force of interested, sexual desire together with its relativising and integration into a more mundane daily practice that actually accepts the desire of the Other in more than narcissistic, ego-supporting ways. What starts out like a traditional, perhaps even Metaphysical love poem is already undermined by its second line. It adds two great levelling terms to the love it describes, 'human' and 'faithless' (*CP* 131–2). The two seem to be intimately related.

The poem continues by undermining another staple of love poetry, beauty. It sets individual beauty – which is reified and objectified, and therefore temporal – against the beauty that lies, traditionally, in the eye of the beholder. Here, however, the text goes beyond another cliché by amalgamating the beauty that the loved one embodies for the speaker with mortality and guilt. Together they add up to 'the living creature' that is the love object in this poem, a love object very different from idealistic metaphysical elevations. The notion of boundless body and soul is then satirised as part of the 'ordinary swoon' that love produces. It is as much a delusion as 'supernatural sympathy' and 'universal love and hope', but is also 'abstract insight'. Once again, there is no simple construction of hierachies and binaries in which one element is elevated over another. There is, on the contrary, a continual undermining of these metaphysical concepts, concepts that are outside the realm of daily practice, beyond 'the living creature', and therefore either useless or even potentially harmful for it.

The poem's third stanza then evokes classical modernist images, the stroke of midnight from Yeats's 'Byzantium', the madman from Eliot's 'Rhapsody on a Windy Night' and the 'dreaded cards' from *The Waste Land*'s 'Burial of the Dead' as examples of attempts at transcending daily life and practice. It sets them against its own universe, which is a much reduced one that knows only 'this night' and its whispers, thoughts, and kisses. Rather than transcending these mundane elements in the direction of a 'truth' about love, the poem merely wants to cherish them for themselves.[4] It distrusts metaphysics and is happy with existence. This is corroborated in its fourth and final stanza, which prays for the possibility of finding 'our mortal world enough' and emphatically places its love not with a universal one, but simply with 'human love'. And it goes even further by adding to the inconspicuous and yet so challenging term the adjective 'every'. This human love is not merely available to the isolated individual alone, which would simply make it the equal of egotistical passion, but is accessible to every one. In this anti-metaphysical love that is none the less far from anti-erotic and asexual lies a key towards the bridging of the abyss between individuals. Here self and society can join forces, but only when eros and caritas merge rather than cancel each other out.

The German theologian Martin Buber calls this attitude 'the hallowing of the everyday'. Edward Callan's perceptive study *Auden: A Carnival of Intellect* adds two more modern thinkers to those who provided the concepts for Auden's new perspective: Dag Hammarskjöld and Karl Jaspers. Jaspers, Callan summarises, defines an authentic response to life 'as the determination to affirm life again and again; the willingness to persist in creative activity in spite of seeming futility'.[5] Hammarskjöld put this philosophy into practice as Secretary General of the United Nations during the difficult years of the Cold War, until his death in a plane crash in 1961.

MULTIPLE CODES

In *New Year Letter*, dated 1 January 1940, Auden not only says farewell to the 'low dishonest decade' which 'September 1, 1939' had labelled the 1930s, but also attempts a first full-scale assessment of what the beginning of the long poem calls 'A common meditative norm' (*CP* 161). This places its point of departure between the three options of 'Retrenchment, Sacrifice, Reform'. Although undoubtedly echoing wartime rhetoric (Roosevelt's, for example), retrenchment also reiterates the narcissistic regression into the Oedipal triangle of father, mother, and child which characterised so many of Auden's early poems. The term 'retrenchment' encompasses the dilemma produced by this attitude, for it leads both to aggression and to paralysis, since there is no escape from the entanglement with one's personal as well as social, cultural, and political past other than its rejection (and thereby its implicit acknowledgement) or its wholesale adoption. In the same way, sacrifice is no option either. As self-sacrifice it would be the denial of personal fulfilment, be it sexual, materialist, even spiritual. It can also function on a social scale, where it produces heroic, but deeply problematic leader figures, whose detachment from the masses and failure to become 'truly strong men' was discussed in detail in Chapter 3.

Reform stands for a more productive attitude, since it involves compromise and negotiation. None the less, its practicality and viability must have seemed doubtful at a time when the Second World War had just started to be a real war rather than a phoney one. *New Year Letter* is aware of the precariousness of its speculation, since it posits itself in the rift between the pre-war era ('Twelve months ago in Brussels', *CP* 161) and the martial reality of its present. None the less, it manages to use its anchoring in a problematic 'now', the existence so cherished in 'Lullaby', for a productive assessment that is neither reduced to immediate responses nor escapist in its attempt to remove itself from the immediacy of the threats it describes. It places a variety of limited positions next to one another, the position of 'a man alone', the seemingly unmotivated and uncontrollable events of a ship changing its course and a train making an unwonted stop, the not-so-unmotivated crowd that smashes up a shop, and eventually the totally planned patterns of generals (*CP* 161). Coincidence, subtle manipulation, and obvious strategy are shown as linked in the complexity that is daily practice. And even though time might moderate its tone and seemingly have different messages in store for the singular individual, perhaps a thinker trying to make sense of historic events, the poem still insists that all are part of the same messy reality that finds its most drastic expression in the generals' 'sharp crude patterns'.

Linked, too, are those that reside in an apparently cosy exile, in America or, more specifically, a cottage in Long Island, where culture is so safe that listening to Buxtehude can affirm the belief in a *civitas* composed of assent (an anticipation of Habermas's concept of the communicative action).[6] The third stanza of *New Year Letter* presents the Enlightenment credo of the true, the beautiful, and the good: 'For art had set in order sense/And feeling and intelligence,/ And from its ideal order grew/Our local understanding too' (*CP* 162). Yet the shift from an ideal order to a local understanding is far from convincing in a text that has just exposed its own setting as a privileged and, in many ways, an escapist one. That the poem does not trust those idealist formulas becomes clear when it takes up the problem of order immediately in its subsequent stanza. There it shows order as equally desired by Eros and Apollo, by life and art, even though their concepts of order are vastly different.

The poem itself runs into trouble when it then tries to define order both as synthesis and process, or even struggle, only ever leading to partial fulfilment – and simultaneously as an end in itself. This is where Auden's poetics of openness, dialogue, and development clash with the Enlightenment and modernism's yearning for absolutes. *New Year Letter* tries, in a typically dialogic, Audenesque way, to reconcile the irreconcilable, to merge life with order. But synthesis itself can turn into closure, thus undermining the very openness and dialogue from which it emerges. That the poem realises this danger is evident when – after having gone through a rather fruitless discussion of the conflict of will and fulfilment – it finds itself forced to sever art from society: 'Art is not life and cannot be/A midwife to society,/For art is a *fait accompli*' (*CP* 162). This is a premature move that denies any social influence to art and also leaves very little space for new artistic production after the pronouncement of art's finite status. The poem makes this more than evident when its discussion continues – which would make no sense if the claim was to be taken seriously. Only a few lines later the text indeed speculates about 'Great masters who have shown mankind/An order it has yet to find' (*CP* 163). This is very much in line with the complicated message of 'Musée des Beaux Arts', where it was also an old master, Breughel, who depicted an order, yet an order only to be found in actual existence, not in metaphysical or theological premises or the promise of an ordered existence yet to come.

This is the crux of *New Year Letter*, a crux that is slyly realised in its very title. It announces something new through the very medium of the letter, but this news is always also an already-realised one, in the same way that a New Year requires the year as an established category in order to be one. It can therefore only ever be partially new, and must carry with it the incompleteness and possible mess of the old. The problem that Auden's early writings debate under the label of tradition resurfaces in his middle phase in the search for a balance of will and order, or singular artistic statement and the society of which it unwillingly forms part. The message that art therefore has in store for the mankind addressed earlier is consoling and unsettling at the same time. After rousing the dreamer by presenting itself as deed, enouraging the striving through the success of its very existence and comforting the mourner by displaying its lasting value, its message culminates in the combined statement and order 'I am. Live.' (*CP* 163).

This doubling of art and existence is also implied in the American title of *New Year Letter*, *The Double Man*, a reference to Montaigne.[7] It contains in its own shape another doubling, that into text and notes. Some of these notes, partly written in prose, partly poetry themselves, ended up as individual poems in Auden's *Collected Poems* ('Diaspora' is one example). They have a very different status from the notes to Eliot's *The Waste Land*, for example, which are afterthoughts and addenda rather than intrinsic parts of the text. Auden's *New Year Letter* uses its original notes to set up another internal doubling, another dialogue of distinct voices and positions. This is the reason why some of the notes are themselves poems. Out of the existence of art as dialogue, at least a minimal dialogue between artefact and existence involves the obligation of the individual to take this existence seriously, similar to the way 'Lullaby' argues in connection with love.

Yet a causal relationship between art's factual existence and the individual's responsibility for his or her own can hardly be found in this statement. Indeed, it must not be found, for otherwise the perfect inescapable order would already have materialised. Its establishment would leave no room for individual existence and, indeed, would take the responsibility for it out of the hands of the individual. *New Year Letter* must remain flawed as an argument in order to make its point a point that also insists that art can have an impact on society, but not in the form of teaching its truths in a straightforward way. One of the reasons why art cannot speak with one voice is indeed that it is made up of a multitude of voices, as the self-reflexive section towards the end of the first part of *New Year Letter* demonstrates. In it Auden goes through a list of capitalised authors ranging from Catullus via Voltaire and Blake to Tennyson, Hardy, Baudelaire, Kipling and Rilke – only to conclude that he himself has adopted what he would disown, other inauthentic voices. But rather than branding this his own particular fault, he goes on to call it 'the sin/Particular to his discipline' (*CP* 165).

The polyphony and intertextuality that produces inauthenticity in poetic and all literary language is, however, also the one that connects it with history and society and, indeed, prevents it from ever becoming a *fait accompli*. With this in mind, it becomes clear that it is not only too restrictive but indeed counterproductive to squeeze *New Year Letter* into a closed philosophical model, as Edward Callan attempts when he simply equates the three sections of Auden's poem with Kierkegaard's triad of the aesthetic, the ethical, and the religious sphere.[8] Although Callan also recognises that *New Year Letter* is a discussion of order, he sacrifices Auden's poetic insights into the problematic of this order by subjecting them to a philosophical model that he tellingly characterises as 'an all-embracing, notional scheme'.[9] Moreover, his interpretation misses the important insistence of Auden's poem on the 'now', an emphasis repeated at the start of each of its sections.

Rather than modelling his poem on an established philosophy, Auden in *New Year Letter* assumes a position that resembles Adorno's views on art. Adorno, too, sees the relationship between art and society in a complex light and refuses to accept it as a simple one. He rejects both the mimetic premise according to which art mirrors society and the simplistic didactic one according to which art holds some straightforward lessons for society in store. Instead he argues concerning the relation of art and its context:

> Context, viewed as the life that inheres in works of art, is an after-image of empirical life. Meaningfulness emanates from the former and illuminates the empirical world. The concept of a context of meaning is dialectical, for the art work is not oriented to a fixed concept but instead unfolds its concept internally, on its inside. What is more, this process does not lend itself to theoretical understanding until after the context of meaning itself, along with its traditional conceptualization, begins to lose its footing.[10]

This also becomes evident in the second and third part of *New Year Letter*. Part Two of the poem stresses the mismatch of human intellect and imagination – which are capable of and eager to show unlimited possibilities and potentials to the human self – and the human situation as an infinitely small and insignificant element inside the universe and even inside human concepts, such as world history. Nietzsche's parable of humankind as intelligent animals who take themselves very seriously until their planet freezes and they are completely forgotten comes to mind, when the poem reminds its reader of the status of humans as 'children of a modest star' (*CP* 167).[11] The problem is not the unlimited potential of imagination, but the adapting of this imagination to the requirements of existence and daily practice. Once again Auden's poem declares its anti-idealism, and once again it couples it with an insistence on change and plurality: 'each great I/Is but a process in a process/ Within a field that never closes' (*CP* 167).

The poem moves on by depicting side by side extreme acts of imagination and egomania. The Dutch astronomer Sitter (1872–1934) who claimed that the universe is expanding, and calculated its size and contents, is placed side by side with eccentrics such as Labellière (who insisted on being buried upside down) and Sarah Whitehead, the infamous 'Bank Nun', all of whom are immortalised in Edith Sitwell's *English Eccentrics*.[12] The power to differentiate between imagination and delusion is then strikingly enough linked with the devil, the 'Prince of Lies' (*CP* 168). Yet, once again, rather than simply adopting an established religious stance, Auden's text contructs its own notion of the devil, a devil that comes extremely close to the very premises that spawn human freedom, will, and imagination in the first place. In fact, if the devil in the second part of *New Year Letter* has an ancestry, it is not so much a religious as a literary one. While common critical agreement locates Auden's attitude towards the problem of free will in his readings of the theological works of Charles Williams and Reinhold Niebuhr,[13] his devil is amazingly similar to a literary rather than a theological one. His model is Mephistopheles in Goethe's *Faust* (with whom he also shares his name). Like Goethe's devil, he is more of an insistent sceptic and experimenter than the traditional embodiment of evil.

Rather than merely representing the stable opposite of God and salvation, in Auden's processual universe this devil is actually necessary to push along human will on its search for salvation. He is part of the inquiry that characterises human existence – even though his presence is also experienced as 'paralysing' (*CP* 169), because it is a constant one and one that steers human inquiry towards mere binary oppositions.[14] None the less, the poem refuses a simple victory of mechanistic thinking – embodied in 'The formal logic of the clock' (*CP* 169) – and reminds its reader that in the same way that concepts are continually shifting, so perception itself 'has shifting contours like a dream' (*CP* 169). The bottom line of the argument is therefore that both a monistic idealism and a simplistic dualism are unproductive – as illustrated in the examples of Descartes and Berkeley, who are both accused of having been unable to practise what they preached. The great point of orientation that the poem sets up against monism and dualism is once again 'Experience', or human practice. Thinking in binary oppositions 'must falsify experience' (*CP* 170). It is eventually held responsible for separating the individual from the community and thereby engendering human isolation and alienation ('O cruel intellect that chills/His natural warmth until it kills/The roots of all togetherness' (*CP* 170).

Yet the poem is on far less stable ground when it tries to come up with an alternative to intellect and its reliance on binary hierarchies and oppositions. Its advocation of 'instinct' and '*Beischlaf*' of the blood' (*CP* 171) smacks of D. H. Lawrence, if not of the blood-based ideology of fascism. It hardly goes together with an equally clichéd '*ordre du cœur*' either – whose link with *mœurs* (morals) is also a mere desideratum. In many ways, though, the text must once again miss its ideal to uphold its overall argument about order as process rather than certainty. In fact, it wraps its ideal formula into a question – and reduces its authenticity by clothing it in foreign languages and thereby turning certainty into quotation. The voice of truth is replaced by the multiple voices of biased positions. Flaubert, Baudelaire, Aristotle, and Rilke form an uneasy debating team, one that does not come up with conclusive statements but decides to turn on the radio instead, not in order to listen to the news, but rather to Wagner's Isolde and her desire. The emphasis is again on deferral and absence of fulfilment rather than the establishment of securities and truths. Once again, Auden's poetics proves to be a poetics of desire and dialogue rather than of monological truth.

In a characteristically devious move, the poem then scrutinises its own logical set-up in order to expose it as similar to that of the dialectic devil. In structural terms, the text performs the modernist act of self-reflection, but not in order to ascertain its closure and simultaneous universalism or to assert its 'intolerance of all externality'.[15] Rather, it performs what it advocates by becoming a process itself. It also spots the devil of dialectic in historical processes: Washington crossing the Delaware or Wordsworth mistaking the fall of the Bastille for the Second Coming (albeit of liberty instead of Christ) are placed in an analogous position to visionaries and eccentrics. They, too, are taken in by their own imagination, and in the case of Wordsworth this delusion actually leads to a politics that is in obvious contradiction to the original ideal. Another worldly advent listed in the second part of the poem is the Russian Revolution. It is seen to prefigure 'the potential Man' (*CP* 173), an ideal of Auden's middle phase that is very different from the 'truly strong man' of the early poetry, and has less in common with Nietzsche's detached superman than with the self-relativising and sceptical practitioner first encountered in poems such as 'Brussels in Winter' and 'Musée des Beaux Arts'.

This potential man is seen through a Marxian lens, yet it is also made clear that while Marx's writings produce mere complacent intellectual response, the Russian Revolution set into motion something very different: less thought than action. Its underlying Marxist ideas are questioned in a manner that would resurface after the collapse of the Soviet Union in the 1980s: 'What if his hate distorted?'

and 'What if he erred?' (*CP* 174). At the same time Marx is partly excused, since he is still portrayed as entangled in his own Oedipal struggle against a 'father-shadow' and the victim of psychosomatic effects of suppressed love. In short, Marx is turned into an Auden-esque hero – or rather, into the now-obsolete 'strong man' of his earlier writings. He is both treated with sympathy and eventually discarded: and his mistake is his attachment to pure ideas. Theory, the poem makes clear, is detached from action and reality: 'Expect-ing the Millenium/That theory promised us would come: It didn't' (*CP* 175). But pure thought is difficult to leave behind. Consequently it is now specialists who 'must try/To detail all the reasons why'. Once again, not a monolithic reason determines events, but its dialo-gic and messy entanglement with another force, that of Eros. The poem uses a genetic paradigm to make its point:

> The rays of Logos take effect,
> But not as theory would expect,
> For, sterile and diseased by doubt,
> The dwarf mutations are thrown out
> From Eros' weaving centrosome. (*CP* 176)

The products of the dialogue are dubious. It is not clear whether they, the dwarf mutations, are the sterile and diseased ones, or if theory is so afflicted. The end of the second part of *New Year Letter* continues to elaborate this insecurity. It denounces those entangled in a narcissistic enjoyment of their own dialectic split as 'moral asymmetric souls', 'either-ors' and 'mongrel halves', implicitly hold-ing them responsible for the state of affairs and the far-from-realised freedom. At the same time it points out that 'half-truths' also contain the gift of a 'double focus'. Incompleteness, bias, and the need to complement oneself and one's position can lead to a different kind of enlightenment. The explanation that the poem offers for this hid-den potential, however, is 'hocus-pocus'. By having recourse to images of Aladdin's magic lamp that must only be used correctly, the logic of the poem is not much more convincing than the fairytale solution of a poem as early as '1929'. The focus is now obviously broader, but the means of achieving and securing a stable philo-sophical perspective on the interaction of reason and libido – or truth and love – are not yet in sight.

Not surprisingly, then, the final, third part of *New Year Letter* shifts music back into the focus of the poem. In the same way as in 'The

Composer', music is seen as miraculously detached from the conflicts outlined in the poem's earlier sections. Music is in fact in the
same privileged position as the speaker and his community in the
poem. It is of course this very detachment that would have provoked a severe criticism from Adorno, had he engaged with Auden.
Adorno's simple claim is: 'While art opposes society, it is incapable
of taking up a vantage point beyond it. Art's opposition is thus in
part identification with what it opposes.'[16] This claim has much
more in common with the dialectic entanglement of art and society
in Auden's poems that the idealistic attempt to find a loophole in the
medium of music.

The memories of a wedding that took place in the same location as
the music, Elizabeth Mayer's house (to whom New Year Letter is dedicated), are used to develop a utopian image of the perfect harmonious
linking of 'the erotic and the logical'. In a move that reintroduces a
Renaissance ideal easily visible in the happy marriages that serve as
conclusions to Shakespeare's comedies, 'food and friendship', a
'privileged community', and 'that real republic' are merged. Not
content with its own fiction of miraculous harmony, the poem then
goes on to find it everywhere and at all times: 'O but it happens
everyday/To someone' (CP 177). That may be the case, but equally
certainly injustice, brutality, and suffering happen to someone every
day. New Year Letter becomes infatuated with its own imagination, in
a manner eerily prefigured by the eccentrics of its second part. Interestingly enough, it is exactly this infatuation that eventually leads to
the critical blindness of the text towards itself that has enchanted
many of its critics, because it seemingly supports the establishment
of belief in Auden that they are so eagerly looking for.

The poem unsurprisingly employs traditional allegories to celebrate the discovery of its ideal. A 'well of life' appears, as does the tree
of knowledge, in thinly disguised form as 'the tree/And fruit of
human destiny' (CP 178), after God has made a guest appearance as
'perfect Being'. The third part of this third and last part is as bland as
can be imagined, and one is almost relieved when the poem returns
to its speculations of will, truth, and lie in Stanzas 4 and 5, even if
one feels that the discussion is not a new one. The rest of this long
third part of New Year Letter now engages in a number of attempts to
condense faith out of the conflicts of freedom of will, doubt, and
desire. But one cannot help but feel that the section is at its best
when it actually takes recourse to the mundane position of the fictional writer of the section rather than to the illustrious assembly of

European philosophers that it recruits as witnesses of its philosophical miracle. This miracle turns out to be nothing but poetry, when the text rather uneasily but very revealingly holds its newly achieved ideal against the well-known concerns and images of Auden's poetry. Limestone and Roman walls, mines and tramways meet the mythical Über-Mother, and all is well because all is Auden and not a second-hand philosophy or a proper religious conversion.

The argument of the poem's finale is a mess, but it is a productive one, productive in a poetic sense rather than a logical one, as the text itself readily admits: 'Our road/Gets worse and we seem altogether/ Lost as our theories, like the weather/Veer round completely every day.' *New Year Letter* veers around fairytale images like the unicorn, doves that represent science as well as faith, the fish as the symbol of Christ, but playfully hidden rather than revealed, Audenesque allegories like the clock and the keeper of the years, hell, the hill of Venus, and the stairs of the will. If it presents an image of faith, it is a faith in assemblages. What goes on in the conclusion of *New Year Letter* is not a succumbing to established faith, but a *bricolage* of images, out of which emerges a *jouissance* that may be divine, but not an orthodox belief.[17] If its penultimate stanza concludes by addressing God with 'O da quod jubes, Domine' (*CP* 193), its final one closes inconclusively with 'The world's great rage, the travel of young men'. It focuses not on reconciliation, but once again on conflict and process, on the particular and personal rather than the universal and impersonal.

DIALOGUE AND ITS DISSIDENTS

The Sea and the Mirror, written between 1942 and 1944, takes the theme of dialogue and polyphony even further. It is subtitled 'A Commentary on Shakespeare's *The Tempest*', and thus assumes a similar position to the classical play as the notes in Auden's *New Year Letter*. It further frames itself by starting off with an address by the stage manager to the critics, another form of dialogue. Moreover, by not only commenting on the play but having the protagonists of Shakespeare's play comment on it and on their own positions in it, *The Sea and the Mirror* achieves a careful exposition of philosophical positions as well as a multifaceted debate on the relation of art to existence. *The Tempest*, as John Fuller points out, used to be regarded as a dramatic treatise on art, philosophy, sensuality, and religion in the nineteenth century.[18] Even if this allegorical reading has become unfashionable, it is none the less clear that the play uses its plot and island setting to explore some consequences of the emerging rational philosophies in connection with issues of magic, as well as learning and power.

The main protagonists of its implicit debate are Prospero, the puller of strings, whose island kingdom merges knowledge, magic, and power; Ariel, his servant spirit; Antonio, Prospero's brother, who has usurped Prospero's Dukedom in his absence; Ferdinand, son of Alonso, King of Naples, with whom Prospero's daughter Miranda falls in love, securing the harmonious ending of the play; Sebastian, the king's brother; plus an assortment of sailors, a cook, and so on. But there is also a character in the play who does not fit in: Caliban, a native of the island, the son of a witch whom Prospero overcame when he took possession of the island. That the dissident voice of Caliban takes up the largest part of *The Sea and the Mirror* will be of importance below.

The Preface that starts off Auden's poem is already much more than an appeal for a sympathetic review that traditional epilogues tend to be. Here, the stage manager addresses the critics not so much in a mercenary vein as in an existentialist one: he talks about terror and lack, and concludes with a metaphor of the relation of art to existence that shows that art can only comment (as does Auden's poem on Shakespeare). Its commentary must be concerned with its own insubstantiality, but not in order to set against it the fullness of life: rather, that which art sets itself up against is the silence of existence. It has no obvious and tangible substance (this is Auden's rejection of empiricism and actionism), but is rather like the other side of a wall that one cannot see and from which no sound reaches the desperate ear. Yet this silence of existence, independent of what it represents (if it stands for anything), still ripens in the poem, until this ripeness becomes all.

The poem cleverly avoids a clear position on existence. It neither assumes a nihilistic stance (there is nothing to be found in it) nor a mystical or theological one (the silence clearly stands for something). Instead it points out that the effect of the absence of certainties shapes human existence, and it can do so in very productive ways, even though its effect may be ambivalent, as the poem continues to demonstrate. Auden's existentialism is once again not one of certainties, not even of the nihilistic certainty of absence and nothingness *à la* Sartre. It is, instead, an existentialism of productive questioning and of listening: in short, once again one of openness and dialogue, even if it cannot be certain of the Other in the equation.

Prospero supplies the first voice in the text's chorus. He is about to abandon his island as well as his power, and that includes the knowledge and learning contained in his books. He wishes to get rid of them by throwing them into the sea 'which misuses nothing because it values nothing' (*CP* 312). Value and related sense-making operations characterise human existence, as he continues to elaborate when he describes his own intellectual growth from dependent child to tormenting despot. He yearns to be free from these traps of the intellect – which in their final analysis helped him to erect a kingdom in which he was all-powerful, but at the price of not being able to escape from it. Prospero becomes an allegory of rationality which, in tandem with imagination, is capable of building complete realities of its own in which it reigns supreme. Yet these embodiments of uncontrolled and uncontrollable logocentrism are also monadic and closed to any external reality. What Prospero also yearns for, strikingly enough, is death, something that an all-powerful intellect can never imagine for itself. He labels Ariel, the spirit, his tool in these operations of logocentric power, and tells this agent of his own rationality how difficult it is to part with it.

After this second philosophical introduction, the second part of the poem then sees the rest of the cast add their particular perspectives to the debate. Antonio is shown to be another outsider in the seemingly harmonious finale. He sees through the conventions, as he points out when alluding to the traditional literary examples of setting things right, the tranformation of pigs back into men from the *Odyssey*, and the happy union of the loving couple that restores harmony on earth and in the universe. Antonio is convinced that these emblems of harmony only disguise the fact that a stable harmony can never be achieved. Human will, he is convinced, must soon raise its ugly head again and restore Prospero's broken wand. The books of knowledge that he wants to cast into the sea will reappear undamaged, because human agency by its very nature stands outside – and thereby creates the inside–outside dichotomy underlying binary oppositions and hierarchies. What the doubting and denying devil stood for in *New Year Letter* Antonio represents in *The Sea and the Mirror*. He is a constant reminder that the mirror wins, because it can even turn the sea into one. That the chthonian chaos of the sea is itself merely an escapist fiction of rationality will later become evident in Caliban's long speech.

Ferdinand, the sailors, Alonso, Sebastian, and Miranda then discuss their individual motivations and beliefs. In the case of Ferdinand, it is his romantically naive conception of love that he both experiences as sensual (and therefore transient) and wishes to elevate into metaphysical dimensions. He represents a traditional concept of love which is quite opposed to Auden's non-metaphysical one, as expressed in 'Lullaby'. Stephano is enclosed in another form of sensuality that threatens to become universalist: he is a worshipper of his stomach, but wonders whether he is the master of his desires or mastered by them. Alonso, the pessimistic doubter with a strong dislike of the supernatural, also has to acquiesce in the seemingly restored harmony, even though he does so without rejoicing. Alonso worries about his son who will rule after their return to Milan. He fears that the trappings of power will distort his view on the realities of power, which is forever threatened by resistance and betrayal, but also by its own blindness, an echo of Prospero's absolute and exclusive rule. Sebastian, the usurper, then discusses the thirst for power as the natural consequence of the trust in will and imagination: 'What sadness signalled to our children's day/ Where each believed all wished wear a crown' (*CP* 323).

Trinculo, the clown, is the one who recognises most clearly that the various complications of will, existence, and power are inextricably linked with language as the means of expressing imagination and desire: 'My history, my love,/Is but a choice of speech' (*CP* 324). He is closest to the traditional image of the poet who recognises the potential terror and danger in his capacity to manipulate language and therefore the imagination, the mundane equivalent of Prospero, the magician: 'A terror shakes my tree,/A flock of words fly out' (*CP* 324).

Miranda eventually complements the chorus of voices with her song. Rejoicing in her newly found love, she uses its positive images to dispell a number of childhood fears, such as the Black Man and the Witch. However, the refrains of her little ditty are themselves ambiguous: 'And the high green hill sits always by the sea' and 'My Dear One is mine as mirrors are lonely'. While the first refrain might simply contain an emblem of eternity and therefore a sign of her trust in her love, the second one brings in the mirror of the poem's title as well as the idea of loneliness – which is obviously antagonistic to the ideal of a happy union. It is also seemingly nonsensical, since mirrors double. It makes sense, however, if one sees it as a further echo of Antonio's insistence that there is no way of overcoming binary oppositions. Harmony and union are only possible as concepts that are set against their opposite, disharmony and loneliness. Even inside happiness lurks the awareness that it is only conceivable in connection with unhappiness and suffering. As Antonio's ominous claims hover over the section, so his words intersperse it. After each statement of individual will there follows his ghostly refrain, which relativises what has just been said by its insistence on his dissident position.

> *Your all is partial, Prospero;*
> *My will is all my own:*
> *Your need to love shall never know*
> *Me: I am I, Antonio,*
> *By choice myself alone.* (CP 318)

This is his first assertion of the egotistical separation of his voice as well as his indomitable will. Still, this separation and dissidence do not spoil the argument of *The Sea and the Mirror*, even though they undercut its pretended harmony. They are necessary to affirm the very insistence of Auden's text on plurality. This plurality must not find its embodiment in the harmonised voices of a group in which the individual positions fade into a unified whole, something which would merely reproduce mythical forms of unity and deny the very separateness of the individual and its will that is the prerequisite of its painful freedom. Dissidence goes hand in hand with harmony in the same way that resistance is inseparable from power. Its denial would undercut the argument by setting up holistic utopian solutions. The presence of dissidence is a positive reminder of the implications of dialogue and plurality as much as a negative reminder of the continuation of hierarchies, injustice, and oppression.[19]

Caliban, of course, is the most poignant reminder that there is something left over and, indeed, left behind in all the ostensibly achieved harmony of *The Tempest*'s finale. He lived on the island long before the arrival of Prospero and Miranda and the establishment of their logocentric realm, and, indeed, is both the anagrammatised canibal and Caribbean of the emerging rational project of Imperialism of which Shakespeare's play is an early indication. At the same time he is not essential either: he is neither nature, body, desire, nor sexuality. He is himself already separated from an earlier wholeness. While Caliban has to be taught language by Prospero in Shakespeare's play and thanks his teacher by cursing him, Auden's

Caliban speaks in the elaborate style of Henry James, the author who takes rationality to its logical extreme in his style and thereby paves the way for the tumbling of this rationality into the abyss of modernism, modernity turning in on, or indeed against, itself. Caliban has a lot to say. His speech, the only prose section of the text, takes up at least as much space as all other sections taken together. The dissident voice is shown to be not marginal but central, central to the establishment of a real dialogue, but also as incapable of really becoming independent from what it stands against.

Surprisingly enough, rather than singling out his voice as the deviant and unrepresentative, Caliban assumes the position of authority in his very first statements. This authority goes beyond that of a mere individual voice, but claims to represent, if not the author of *The Tempest*, Shakespeare himself ('our so good, so great, so dead author', *CP* 325), then at least the 'very echo' of the audience's demand to be made privy to the author's intentions. Once again, the text argues in favour of seeing existence as the desire and yearning for answers, and of regarding these answers as nothing but the echoes of insistent questions. The answer Caliban gives to the questions once again emphasises plurality. His defence of the theatrical muse as at least apparently non-exclusive culminates in the image of the 'mixed perfect brew' (*CP* 326). Yet if the Muse of theatre is the perfect symbiosis of existence and art, if she is capable of suspending the limitations of history, geography, and sense through her charm, as Caliban argues, she must still exclude and oppose one thing. (And which of the three theatrical muses does he have in mind anyway? Melpomene, the muse of tragedy, Thalia, the muse of comedy, or Terpsichore, the muse of choral poetry?) The harmony of art must remain the enemy of 'unrectored chaos'.

> Just because of all she is and all she means to be she cannot conceivably tolerate in her presence the represented principle of *not* sympathising, *not* associating, *not* amusing, the only child of her Awful Enemy, the rival whose real name she will never sully her lips with – 'that envious witch' is sign sufficient. (*CP* 327)

It is of course Caliban himself who is the only child of the witch Setebos, who has been deprived of her rule over the island by Prospero. But he is not chaos himself – which would turn him into an essence or nature. Rather, he is a 'represented principle' and thus already partly entangled in the logocentric systems that he opposes. His aim is therefore suspiciously close to that of reason. He does not wish to be in direct contact with chaos ('We most emphatically do not ask that she should speak to us, or try to understand us; on the contrary, our one desire has always been that she should preserve forever her old high strangeness'; *CP* 327–8). Reason requires chaos as its Other – and the strangeness is needed as a label to differentiate it from the familiar. All the same, the reasonable dissident against reason, Caliban, speaks with reason's voice when he requests 'that for a few hours the curtain should be left undrawn, so as to allow our humble ragged selves the privilege of craning and gaping at the splendid goings-on inside'. Reason is infatuated with its Other, but this Other is already a construction. Behind the curtain, the beginning of *The Sea and the Mirror* has informed us, is silence. Yet even the marginalised, constructed Other of reason cannot help but think in logocentric terms and speak in a logocentric voice.[20]

Art and chaos are not mere opposites; they are indeed linked. Yet while the principle of reason prefers to remain without obvious representation, it represents itself negatively by giving a discrete outline and limiting shape to its opposite. Ariel is a spirit, but Caliban is a brute animal. None the less, they are entangled in their mutual constitution, as becomes evident when Caliban worries about the permeation of their two realms: 'For if the intrusion of the real has disconcerted and incommoded the poetic, that is a mere bagatelle compared to the damage which the poetic would inflict if it ever succeeded in intruding upon the real' (*CP* 331). But this is, of course, what has happened from the very start, when the imaginary (and therefore poetic) distinction divided chaos and art, instinct and reason, existence and will. The effect of the damage is the continual desire of reason for the opposite it has created but can now no longer reach, because its very existence depends on the separation of the two.

This becomes evident in Ariel's love song to Caliban, which forms the surprising conclusion of *The Sea and the Mirror*. There Ariel, the spirit of logocentrism, calls itself a mere shadow of the mortality embodied by Caliban. The refrain of his love song mirrors Caliban's self-characterisation as the echo of the desire of the questioning audience. The 'I' that ends each stanza of Ariel's song is the echo of its penultimate lines. It is at the same time the fragmented echo of three forms of utterance, the reply (the effect of dialogue), the cry (the reduced monologue), and the sigh (the sad remainder and reminder of lacking communication as well as self-confidence). In language, the Siamese opponents, art and existence, meet, yet their encounter is as unsatisfactory as that between Narcissus and the nymph Echo.

ALLEGORIES OF ANXIETY

In the title of his Christmas oratorio, *For the Time Being*, Auden had already expressed man's anxieties in time. His next major work, another long poem which used verse forms going back to the beginnings of English verse, to *Beowulf*, *Deor* and *Piers Ploughman*, displays its concerns in its very title, *The Age of Anxiety*. It describes the meeting of four strangers in a bar on 3rd Avenue in New York during the Second World War, and indicates that Auden had transformed the approach of his works rather than changed its orientation in that these strangers are symbolic representations of the four psychic faculties according to the psychoanalytic theories of Freud's rival, Carl Gustav Jung. They stand for thought, feeling, intuition, and sensation. *The Age of Anxiety* exercises the very opposite of the explosive dissolution of identity in *The Orators* or the unresolved entangling of voice and dissident echo as exemplified in the finale of *The Sea and the Mirror*.

The 'Baroque Eclogue' describes the attempted 'integration' of a group of strangers to something resembling the agape of Auden's experience of 1933. The text, indeed, takes up the theme of agape explicitly when it describes the gathering and *rapprochement* of its characters in the following terms: 'For it can happen, if circumstances are otherwise propitious, that members of a group in this condition can establish a rapport in which communication of thoughts and feelings is so accurate and instantaneous, that they appear to function as a single organism' (*CP* 371). The prerequisite of this miraculous merger is described by the text as 'semi-intoxication', drunkenness, which can enhance 'our faith in the existence of other selves'. Once again, the text is concerned with the awareness of others, with the link between self and community. However, its attempt is rather different from the earlier ones encountered above. What *The Age of Anxiety* attempts is not a display of polyphony but a miraculous merger. The text is set on All Souls' Night, and thus signals both a spiritual universalism and a Christian approach.

But does the text deliver what it promises? Some early reviewers of *The Age of Anxiety* seemed to think so, like M. L. Rosenthal, who discussed the poem in the *New York Herald Tribune* in 1947. He claimed that the reader's 'attention will be absorbed by the various centers of concentration along which the "plot" is strung, each of them one aspect of a continuous, straining effort to get at the heart of the human condition and trace the lines of possible (or impossible) salvation'.[21] Yet if it attempts to represent the anxiety of an age, or, vice versa, a special period of anxiety in human history, it chooses for it a framework and protagonists that counteract a possible universalism from the very start. The text is framed in multiple ironies. Its subtitle, 'A Baroque Eclogue', is the first indication that its message must be taken with a pinch of salt. 'Baroque', as Rosenthal grudgingly acknowledges, might indeed be a rather cheap pun on the poem's setting. The bar that made a first, important appearance in 'September 1, 1939' is a particularly dubious setting for an experience of agape, since it commonly stands for alienation, anonymity, and commerce. The 'Baroque' of the poem's subtitle further hints at the length of *The Age of Anxiety*, which rather contradicts the conventional meaning of an eclogue – a usually short, often dialogic poem, which employs a pastoral setting. Dialogic the poem certainly is, even polylogic, yet it is neither pastoral nor short – and it also has little in common with the idylls of Virgil, the poetic prototypes of eclogues.

Rather than an eclogue, *The Age of Anxiety* is an allegory. It tries to mirror its message in its shape and represent an abstract idea, the anxiety of its title, in its structure. It corresponds to an earlier technique of Auden's *oeuvre*, the parable, used, for example in '1929'. Yet while the didacticism of the parable is clothed in an underlying narrative – and therefore functions through metonymic fragmentation and recurrence – the allegory attempts a metaphorical fusion, which in *The Age of Anxiety* merges place (the New York bar), time (All Souls' Night), and its protagonists. Since its aim is holistic rather than procedural, it is also more manipulative, as Rosenthal's uncritical projection of 'the heart of the human condition' into the text aptly demonstrates.

The protagonists of the poem are themselves allegorical representatives of particular types: Quant, Malin, Rosetta, and Emble. Critics have rarely overlooked the obvious symbolism of their names and tend to associate Quant with quantum physics, Malin with the French word for ill will, Rosetta with the undecipherable Rosetta Stone, and Emble with the concept of the emblem itself. Yet a closer look at their monologues (for even after they start talking to one other in the poem, they rarely respond to one another) reveals that their characterisation – as the arbiter of rationality who seeks the explanations science cannot provide in mythology; the (self-)destructive cynic; the embodiment of sensuality and the need to please and be loved; and the naive young man whose only thirst is for a life he hardly understands – is neither thorough nor entirely convincing. Indeed, what the characters have to say and how they say it seems very similar. Their cases differ, but their anxieties are the same.

One could take this to signal that the poem is indeed on the right track, that the age it depicts shares common problems and the feeling of crisis. However, the fact that the characters are mere facets of a common problem rather undermines the need for a merger that the text pretends to achieve and illustrate. Another indication of a short circuit that prevents the rather grandiose project of a poem for the age from succeeding is therefore the absence of real dialogue – something that *The Sea and the Mirror* and even *For the Time Being* achieved. Another case is point is the clumsy framing of the monologues in explanatory prose. When Caliban speaks in the style of Henry James in *The Sea and the Mirror* there is a structural reason for his stylistic dissidence. In *The Age of Anxiety*, the prose explains that which the poetry is meant to deliver. The very first section, indeed, outlines what the whole text is meant to stand for. The framing is not dialogic, as in *The Sea and the Mirror*, but reinforces the attempted didactic monologue of the text. Needless to say, the poem does not live up to the generalisations outlined in its prose prologue. It is still too poetic, too open, and full of contradictions for this. It is also too playful, and never manages to maintain its earnest proselytising tone for very long before it lapses into favourite Audenesque images, such as the illicit glance through keyholes or the unmotivated introduction of 'limestone heights' (*CP* 347).

A further structural feature that is designed to homogenise positions and integrate them into a larger pattern (rather than accepting difference and separateness) is the reference to the Renaissance concept of the seven ages of man, from infancy via adolescence, maturity, to old age, in Part 2 of the poem. It is then echoed in 'The Seven Stages' of the poem's third part. These stages stand for an allegorical journey that the protagonists undertake, through a mountainous region via a valley and a pass to a tavern, from the tavern to two ports, over the sea, inland again by air and rail to a city and eventually a big country house, to a graveyard, to hermetic gardens, and eventually into a mysterious forest. Their paths separate and unite

several times during this journey, and eventually, when they expect
to be completely lost in the forest, they are again reunited. But their
quest is not over yet. Wondering whether they can ever succeed in
finding what they cannot know, because they are carrying it inside
themselves, they are eventually reunited with the world. From this
world their quest has led them away on an escapist journey.
Facing the world is their ultimate challenge, and it is quite clear that
being reunited with it is far from pleasant.

Eventually the quest is unveiled as a vision when the four characters find themselves in the same bar in which the story began. Yet
again the mirroring of the issues of restlessness, lack of orientation,
and simultaneous yearning for directions and certainties in the various parables of *The Age of Anxiety* does not add nuances and facets to
the story. It merely repeats a monolithic message, even if this message speaks of fragmentation and absence of meaning. The poetic
equivalent of this quest that leads nowhere because it is never seriously undertaken would not be *The Waste Land* so much as Eliot's
seemingly most desperate poem, 'The Hollow Men'. It, too, manages
to achieve a remarkable stability in its absences, and also does this
mainly through repetition.

The next steps in *The Age of Anxiety* use rituals as their foil. Part 4
employs the religious ritual of the dirge; Part 5 the secular one of the
masque. Part 4 sees the voices united in a chorus of bleakest pessimism and denial. It is the closest Auden's poetry comes to nihilism,
and it is a nihilism based on the Nietzschean postulate of the death
of God. In 'Dirge', the protagonists mourn 'Our lost dad,/Our colossal father' (*CP* 394), even though there is still a trace of irony in the
familiar term. Without Him truth is no longer linked with time, the
'world-engine' that is 'creaking and cracking' in a metaphysical
metamorphosis of the engines of Auden's early poems, because it no
longer has an appropriate engineer. Yet as was already implied in
the term 'colossal father', here the reference to the absent force as
'watchman' makes it abundantly clear that the presence of a metaphysical ordering principle introduces not only security, but also the
other aspect of authority, domination, and potentially terror. Even
in its most metaphysical sections, *The Age of Anxiety* retains an element of ambivalence concerning its losses and desires.

'The Masque' contrasts the nihilistic existentialism of 'The Dirge'
with an emphasis on appearance and its elevation over essences.
Sincerity, the section claims, is the preserve of animals and angels,
but not available to human beings. Being human means being an

actor. Consequently the characters enact little rituals, all of which are connected to their individual desires. Rosetta and Emble express their mutual physical attraction by dancing. Malin builds an altar out of sandwiches! Yet rather than pure blasphemy, this altar is once again an allegory of Auden's aim to reconcile the mundane and the metaphysical. Its sacrifice is an olive, and the god that it means to invoke is Venus. Venus is indeed conjured up, both in the sense of eros and agape. Emble and Rosetta break into a surreal duet of love vows, first to allegorical structures ranging from the 'Four Faces Feeling can make' via the three 'Grim Spinning Sisters', the fates, the 'Heavenly Twins' (Castor and Pollux, rather misplaced), to 'that Oldest One whom/This world is with'. But instantly the metaphysical is replaced by the mundane again: 'If you blush, I'll build breakwaters./When you're tired, I'll tidy your table' (*CP* 396).

In the same way that the bar proved a rather unsuitable setting for a feeling of agape, now Rosetta's flat becomes the scene of the mutual feeling of communion. And since agape was traditionally a love meal, their sharing of loves of various kind and quickly prepared sandwiches and drinks is indeed its contemporary equivalent. Quant, the empiricist, consequently directs his prayers for the couple not towards God or mythical figures, but towards the bugs and viruses of the household. Malin, the cynic, invokes the restrictions of love when he reminds Rosetta of the child that shapes the man (an echo of the old Oedipal entanglement in Auden's verse). Eventually they all become overwhelmed by their feeling of communion and their hope that it could be projected onto the entire world. When they declare in turn their faith, their declaration is not a re-enactment of the liturgic ritual, and the list of their beliefs and hopes remains a solidly mundane one that is even childish in places. Emble, for example, declares, 'Nor money, magic, nor martial law,/ Hardness of heart nor hocus-pocus/Are needed now on the novel earth' (*CP* 400), at the same time as asking for 'Barns and shrubberies for game-playing gangs' (*CP* 401).

When Malin and Quant eventually leave the happy couple, the idea of communion is further challenged. After exchanging addresses in the Epilogue of the poem and immediately forgetting each other's existence, they head home to their own places. Allegorical again, the poem asserts that communion is transient, a feeling rather than reality. Living one's life is a task left to the individual alone. None the less, both Malin and Quant have gained something from the experience. Malin finds that, contrary to what the managers of the mirror

claim, we don't learn from the past, there is something worth learning, and that is that one must not 'refuse the tasks of our time' (*CP*
407). Depite the pressures of arbitrary authority and the terror of
contingency, it is action rather than narcissistic despair that is called
for. Quant, too, learns to balance scientific knowledge and unscien-
tific yearnings, such as that for security, and interpret them as related
ways of dealing with existence.

Even Rosetta, whose sexual union with Emble is prevented when
Emble passes out drunkenly on her bed, is not betrayed and
deprived of fulfilment, but sees the event in a positive light. Sexuality would have been merely another mask that the following morning would have destroyed. As Auden claimed in an early journal
entry, it would merely stand for something else: intimacy.[22] This
intimacy was already achieved in *The Age of Anxiety* when Rosetta
gained an insight into Emble's existence and into her own, even
when this moment of communion convinces her of their separateness. The strangers of the poem have undergone a psychic journey
together which brings them insights into their respective personalities as well as their common anxieties, but afterwards they go their
separate ways. The world has not been changed – as it certainly
would have been had one of the modernists, Eliot, for instance,
worked the same plot into a poem. (The cosmic overtones of *Four
Quartets* once more come to mind in this respect.) Despite the multiple allegories, beginning with the title, integration is only ap-
proached, and it remains temporary. *The Age of Anxiety* earned Auden
a Pulitzer Prize in 1948. Leonard Bernstein used it as the basis of one
of his symphonies. The poem attests that Auden did not give up the
great themes, neither did he say farewell to his analytic and even scientific approach. But he worked themes and approach into relative
frameworks that he linked with the actuality of existence, with
everyday practice.

IN PRAISE OF THE LIMIT

One of the most striking changes during the shift from idealistic
concepts to practice in Auden's writing is the changing role of the
limit. In the early quest poems, the limit (often allegorised, as in 'The
Quest') stood for restrictions that were beyond the control of
the individual. Together with the Oedipal attachments to the past, limits
of various kinds were the reason for the failure of the 'truly strong

man'. Yet even in Auden's early writings there is an element of ambivalence in the limit. In the shape of the frontier, for example, the limit also generates adventure and excitement. It enables those who risk an encounter with the limit to be on two sides simultaneously, to gain insights into self and Other, even if this knowledge proves costly.

In the poem 'In Transit' of 1950, there is already evidence that the frontier will become a positive force in Auden's later works. Rather than seeing the transit across cultural and political barriers as a displacement that leads to loss – and must therefore be countered with an emphasis on identity, Englishness, the past – the poem discovers in the no-man's-land that is the transitional abode of its speaker a place for reflection. 'Somewhere there are places where we have been' (*CP* 413), he remarks, signalling that the transit, the crossing of borders, does not lead to a simple abandoning of the past. At the same time it refrains from seeing the new as an area of unlimited opportunity, even though it invests it with typical Audenesque imagery: 'I admire a limestone hill I have no permission to climb.' What is even more important than this balanced view is that the speaker of 'In Transit' realises that his condition is not particular to him. He manages to envisage another person on the other side in exactly the same state of reflection: 'maybe an ambitious lad stares back,/Dreaming of elsewhere and our godlike freedom'. The godlike freedom is also that of Auden, the American citizen, in a postwar Europe.[23] Yet the term 'godlike' is clearly over-determined; the speaker is sceptical towards his position, while he simultaneously enjoys the encounter with his cultural Other, the lad, and with 'Italian sunshine, Italian flesh'.

The poem is set in an explicit 'nowhere', but it is not the nowhere of pessimistic absences, as in *The Age of Anxiety*. Even though the speaker abstains from considering the effects of his visit on this nowhere and does not even attempt to connect with it ('unrelated to day or to Mother/Earth in love or in hate; our occupation/Leaves no trace on this place') and in fact sees his presence as potential aggression, there is still a possible consequence of the encounter. It affects both speaker and environment: when he is taking off by plane, the nowhere is transformed from a 'congested surface' into a 'world'. Only from the outsider perspective can reality achieve its full significance. At the same time, the surface that the speaker leaves behind, a reality in which 'wrongs and graves grow greenly', the slaves of this reality feel the urge to live, even against their will. Existence is stronger than will, and this existence is affirmed by 'a loose bird', the plane of the speaker as well as his song, the poem itself. In the disconnected and possibly unconcerned or even hostile experience of otherness, existence affirms itself, even though this affirmation does not automatically lead to happiness. There is no promise inherent in the contingencies of existence. It can spare cities through prayer – or it may open old feuds again.

'In Praise of Limestone' is in many respects the happier version of 'In Transit'. It is a poem of multiple dialectics, yet eventually manages to break free from these dialectic oppositions into an area of affirmation that is neither reducible to logic nor miraculously elevated into metaphysics. The poem is also an assessment of Auden's own poetry and its past obsessions. Yet rather than once again setting up (or setting itself up against) an Oedipal trap, it treats the addictions that shape it in a loving and humorous vein. The first stanza of the poem is concerned with the paradoxical constancy of inconstancy. It starts from a position that Auden's early poems strive to achieve or signal demonstratively without much conviction: it talks about a 'we' that is characterised by a common homesickness. This homesickness is the equivalent of the striving encountered in poems such as *For the Time Being*, *New Year Letter*, *The Sea and the Mirror* and *The Age of Anxiety*. It is Auden's reduced version of certainties, their eventual shift from metaphysical promise to existential presence, even though this presence is one of absence and yearning. In the desire for that which is simultaneously in the past and in the future, homesickness manages to reconcile tradition, parents, and child with utopian hopes. It also achieves a loving rather than a critical, detached, or dismissive stance.

Consequently, in the metaphor of the limestone landscape, childhood memories, the allegorical mother figure, the young man who yearns simultaneously for Oedipal attachment and for an existence of his own, and language as the forever shifting basis of poetry meet. And this meeting does not exclude external reality either – which is represented in surface fragrances and images of butterfly and lizard, evasive and transient objects that are beyond the control of the individual will. Culture and wilderness, too, meet in the shape of 'hilltop temple', 'appearing waters' and 'Conspicuous fountains' (*CP* 414) in a poem which moves 'from a wild to a formal vineyard' without setting up hierarchies and proper oppositions. The tableau of its first stanza indeed ends in the image of a child pleasing and teasing alternately in order to receive attention. From its very start the poem relativises its own exercise and presents itself as dependent on its reader(s) and not as a detached statement, personal or metaphysical.

Its reconciliation, of contradictions continues in its second stanza. There, a 'band of rivals' is seen climbing up and down the allegorical landscape 'at times/Arm in arm, but never, thank God, in step'. This is the ultimate expression of Auden's agape. It unites the libidinously charged images of his early poetry, the homosocial and often homo-erotic bonding of males. Only now they are neither clearly male nor are they united by their adoration of a leader figure. They are indi-viduals who overcome their rivalry, their individual wills, only tem-porarily, but do this because they have things in common, anxieties at least, and are therefore a band too. They are the products of the interaction with the sheltering yet flexible limestone landscape. Their belief is not in an overarching god, but in one 'whose temper-tantrums are moral', a god who is neither the Old Testament nor the New Testament one, while uniting both. He can be 'pacified by a clever line/Or a good lay' and is therefore also a Classical one, similar to Greek and Roman deities. All of this turns him into a postmodern concept, one that functions as a quotation from the Bible and the classics and a simultanous reference to the cleverness and occasional smuttiness of Auden's own poetry. It remains local ('Adjusted to the local needs of valleys') and forgiving, because it is relative in the sense of remaining in tune with existence rather than standing above it.

Alternative allegories are used to describe negatively this differ-ent, because relational rather than absolute, belief. The believers in 'In Praise of Limestone' do not live in awe of a volcano 'whose blaz-ing fury could not be fixed', nor of a jungle of 'monstrous forms and lives'. Their existence is that of valley dwellers, civilized and circum-scribed, but also connected to their lives and environment 'where everything can be touched or reached by walking'. The poem yet again rejects metaphysical detachment in favour of localised exist-ence ('Their eyes have never looked into infinite spaces'). The price that the inhabitants of this happy middle ground have to pay is that their moderate soil does not attract 'the best and worst'. Yet the poem is not convinced that these extreme Romantic positions are desirable. For those who uphold their search for essence and mean-ings, other soils are available: the hard granite wastes for the 'Saints-to-be'; the clay and gravel plains for 'Intendant Caesars'; and the ultimately ungiving sea for 'the really reckless'. The sea's message is for the existentialist nihilists à la Sartre. It asks and promises nothing,

nothing but setting the individual free through nothingness. Buddhism's rejection of desire comes to mind. Yet even Auden's nihilistic sea cannot quite free itself from a sly look toward love, even though it ends up rejecting it: 'There is no love; There are only the various envies, all of them sad.'

Rather than rejecting these positions, 'In Praise of Limestone' achieves its aim by actually embracing them all: 'They were right, my dear, all of these voices were right.' It accepts plurality and different positions, but of course it also questions the validity of their exclusive stances by the very fact of its being pluralistic. Furthermore, it achieves its own act of dissidence against totalising perspectives by accepting the non-existence of love, while addressing its acceptance to 'my dear'. This 'my dear' is not the Romantic fairytale prince; it is not 'my love'. It is, rather, its conventionalised and reduced version, yet one that is attainable without sadness and envy. It is undramatic and homely. It is also backward, and perhaps even suffers from tunnel vision, but fulfils its 'worldly duty'. Its very existence, though, 'calls into question/All the Great Powers assume; it disturbs out rights', not the rights of individual, mind, but the binary concepts of right and wrong. It even challenges the poet, who – at least in his Romantic and classical modernist guise – displays a tendency to fall victim to his own puzzles, to elevate his constructions to truths and universes. The poem calls these synthetic worlds 'antimythological myth'.

'In Praise of Limestone' does not completely refrain from offering its own 'anti-mythological myth', though, even though it slyly claims to know nothing of the forgiving of sins and the rising from the dead. Yet its myth is merely an allegory, and a personal and contradictory one at that. Its limestone landscape is its vision of 'faultless love/Or the life to come'. Yet, as the poem has declared earlier, the limestone landscape is not without its tensions, nor is it concerned with a life to come – rather, its concern is with the one that is already there. Yet through its multiple contradictions 'In Praise of Limestone' has already achieved its own utopia: the poem is its own poetic paradise, and one that need not fear a Fall, because it thrives on falls.

Other, later poems take up this theme of achieved paradise within actual existence, a paradise based on contradictions and tension. 'Ode to Gaea' is such an ode to a reality, consisting of *'partibus infidelibus'* rather than certainties or idealist goals (*CP* 424). Humorous texts, such as 'The Love Feast', with its conclusion 'Make me chaste,

Lord, but not yet' (*CP* 466) that echoes St Augustine, even show that, in order to be convincing, this vision of an existential paradise in the here and now must be able to step back and ridicule itself.[24] Auden's continual exercises in writing short and irreverent poems is a further indication of this happy and relaxed relativising of established certainties, including that of the status of his own poetry. 'Ode to Terminus', a poem written as late as 1968, summarises his relative and pragmatic existentialism in an address to the 'God of walls, doors and reticence' (*CP* 609).

Terminus is not a major god in the Roman pantheon. He is rather a household item, a god with a use-value rather than the indomitable forces of Venus and Mars. It is therefore telling that he should be invoked to assist 'gardeners or house-wives' against the threat of a new breed of high priests, those armed with 'telescopes and cyclotrons'. In the postwar world, it is the scientists who are the spokesmen of a new faith, yet one that is just as hostile towards existence as the old extremist religions. Scientists as the believers in the unlimited power of human intellect and reason 'keep making pronouncements about happenings/on scales too gigantic or dwarfish/to be noticed by our native senses'. In short, their teachings and interests are directed away from existence and are not in touch with it. The poem holds against these concerns of extreme rationality 'the world we/really live in', and it is a world that is irrational and non-scientific, where surfaces count and limited beliefs may be ridiculous, but provide spiritual as well as physical sustenance.

'Ode to Terminus' argues in favour of accepting limits and using them to learn to cope with existence. It does not promise answers, but through the acceptance of locality, particularity, and limitation it sees the possibility of community, at least on a small scale, and of an understanding that is a translation and a relationship. The praise of the limit is also seen as a counterbalance to the exploitation of the planet, a plundering and poisoning that results from a belief in unlimited progress. What the limit has to offer may be a translation; it may even be a lie. Yet its relativising power helps to see that the rational explanations of scientists are on a plane equal with the 'tall story' of 'self-proclaimed poets'. Its limiting influence, in which rationality and poetry come together, can make existence livable, rather than continually promising a better existence elsewhere or in the future, while destroying existence physically and spiritually in the here and now.

8

Last Things

A TRUCE BETWEEN SUBJECT AND OBJECTS

An acceptance and appreciation of the here and now, as described in the development of Auden's thinking in the two previous chapters, goes hand in hand with an interest in objective reality – and the very things which make it objective. Very much in the manner of Baudrillard's prediction of the end of metaphysics through the 'revenge of the objects', Auden's poetry executes its poetic *coup de grâce* towards idealist metaphysics by concerning itself with the things that make up existence.[1] Yet the result is not a rampant rejection of human subjectivity and the concerns of the subject; it is rather a relaxed, but also challenging truce between object world and self. It leads to the relativising of human concerns, in particular the concerns of the will, or rationality, and libido, or love and sexuality. On the side of the object world, what happens is described by the German theologian Martin Buber as 'the hallowing of the everyday',[2] except that in Auden's late work this hallowing takes place without a necessary reference to definite religious beliefs.

If one compares poems such as 'Ischia' with earlier depictions of places, such as 'Dover' or the poems from Iceland, it becomes evident that a symbolic use of settings is no longer the aim of Auden's writings. Now the writing shifts towards attempts to do justice to phenomena. While 'Ischia', the poem describing Auden's summer abode since 1948,[3] begins in a still symbolic vein by mentioning a time in which 'then sword decides', that is, with symbolic references to the recently finished war, it quickly moves on 'to praise the shining earth' (*CP* 416). The speaker of the poem in fact explicitly refrains from generalising and advocates the appreciation of the specific:

> Dearest to each his birthplace; but to recall a green
> valley where mushrooms fatten in the summer nights
>   and silvered willow copy
> the circumflexions of the stream

is not my gladness today: I am presently moved
by sun-drenched Parthenopea, my thanks are for you,
Ischia, to whom a fair wind has
brought me rejoicing with dear friends

The poem continues its specific appreciation by evoking the island's 'twisting paths' and vistas. Even Vesuvius, a tempting opportunity for an allegorical or symbolic excursion, remains resolutely part of the object world; in fact, it is domesticated rather than elevated in its description as 'like a massive family pudding'. The perspective is firmly on the present, and this present is the immediate environment – without any pretension towards allegorical generalisations. The only god of the poem is the pleasure that reigns in neighbouring Capri, and as a deity it is a rather tame and commercial one. The pleasures of Ischia are the simple ones of resting in shadows, tasting honey and wine.[4] Yet this is not an island Arcadia, an earthly paradise. The small pleasures never make the visitor forget that he remains a stranger and that 'all is never well' (*CP* 417). The good life of the poem is framed by the awareness that there is no perfection in life, yet imperfection can be appreciated too.

'Cattivo Tempo' and 'An Island Cemetery' are further explorations of the potentials of the mundane. 'Cattivo Tempo' merges an Italian setting with a reflection on the perils of being a writer. 'Sirocco brings the minor devils' (*CP* 419) into this existence, but it is not so much migraine and depression as 'Nibbar, demon/Of ga-ga and bêtise,/Tubervillus, demon/Of gossip and spite'. Their effects are not merely transient, a bad poem or a hurtful joke. Part of their evil influence is to banish the poet into his isolated bedroom, 'Manufacturing there/From lewdness or self-care/Some whining unmanaged/Imp of your own.' The demons of poetry are seclusion and narcissism. By inflating the concerns of the self for itself they eventually create concepts that become unmanageable, obliterate their individual origin, and present themselves as universally valid and relevant.

The antidote that the poem recommends is surprising, yet completely adequate. Rather than beating poetic imagination with its own traditional means, conquering one imaginative concept with an even more successful one, 'Cattivo Tempo' advocates the use of the banal and obvious: 'The proper riposte is to bore them.' Yet what it calls banal is also that which breaks through the isolation of the poetic imagination. It is communication, correspondence, and chat, and the obviousness of its concern for the mundane is that which both outwits hell and makes the results of this new reduced poetics 'human'.

'An Island Cemetery' (*CP* 421–2) uses its observation of Italian burial customs for a reflection on the ultimate touchstone of human existence, death. The poem rests on an unexpected comparison: the way in which the islanders deal with the restricted space in their cemetery is paralleled to the cultivation of crops. Decomposition is equalled to ripening. Yet the effect and tone of the poem are neither sinister nor grotesque; on the contrary, it appears remarkably balanced and optimistic. In the same way that the restriction of the cemetery offers stability within change (another instance of Auden's poems advocating the limit), the skeletons that humans leave behind 'Are no discredit to our kind'.

While we do not know 'Wherever our personalities go' (the poem refrains from using the term 'soul'), we can at least be sure of what we turn into after our death, 'This underlying thing in us/Which never at any time made a fuss'. The final stanza of 'An Island Cemetery' uses this insight for an elaborate pun that links a capitalised yet nondescript 'Love' with the (sexual) ride it needs to reach its end. Yet this end is the certainty of the burial mount 'which has no need of friends'. In the certainty of death, not as a metaphysical goal, but as a material reality, our striving for self and Other and their reconciliation eventually ceases. The poem finds reassurance rather than despair in death's objective, material certainties.

In the collection *The Shield of Achilles* of 1955, the two great poetic cycles are 'Bucolics', modelled after the classical pastoral poetry bearing the same label, and *Horae Canonicae*, based on the monastic rules for the celebration of the hours of the day. In Auden's version, the nature depicted in 'Bucolics' is connected to the psyche, as it had been in his early poems. In fact each poem is dedicated to a particular person. Yet far from illustrating the particular qualities via reference to nature, 'Bucolics' uses its guiding metaphors, 'Winds', 'Woods', 'Mountains', 'Lakes', 'Islands', 'Plains', and 'Streams' to reflect on the communication between human beings and nature, rather than their symbolic equivalence. Although 'Winds' starts off in a tone that is familiar from Auden's early works, when it proclaims that 'Deep, deep below our violence,/Quite still, lie our first Dad, his watch' (*CP* 426) and seems to turn its images at once into psychological, mythological, or even religious ones, it soon becomes clear that it distances itself from this appropriation of self and nature, and refrains from executing a symbolic merger. In fact, it resorts to a seemingly banal, yet programmatically objective tone: 'Winds make weather; weather/ Is what nasty people are/Nasty about and the nice/Show a common joy in observing.'

Rather than introjecting objective reality into the self and using it as an explanatory matrix for the human psyche – or extracting psychological qualities and thus infusing external nature with a symbolic significance – the poem insists on separateness, yet also on connection through observation and even use. If one compares this attitude to T. S. Eliot's early poetry, for example, one finds that the threatening oscillation between passive objectified subjectivities and dangerously animated and anthropomorphised objects (evident, for example in 'Preludes' and 'The Love Song of J. Alfred Prufrock') is the complete antithesis to Auden's truce between subject and objects. The world depicted in Auden's later poems is not one of existential threat; it is one of daily practice.

Yeats's later poetry, in which objects provide the symbols for dealing with existential anxieties concerning ageing, death, and the value of culture, offers another point of comparison. In poems such as 'The Circus Animals' Desertion', objects are simultaneously derided as the source of convincing symbols; at the same time symbols are shown as the inevitable result of human interaction with the object world. Auden's later poems can afford to be relaxed about the status of objects in rationality's sense-making operations. Objects no longer need be forced into symbols, mainly because the need for metaphysical assurance and finalities has been greatly reduced, if it has not disappeared altogether. As in the skeletons in 'An Island Cemetery', if there are traces of symbols left in Auden's later poetry, they are basic ones and never far from the objective status of the things on which they are based. Reassurance is not sought in that which exceeds human existence and practice, but that which affirms it: human nature (not as an essential entity, but as a mixture of imperfection, lack, and desire), and objective reality, unstable, ever-changing, of spurious value, but none the less there to be perceived and utilised.

When 'Winds' in 'Bucolics' takes up the theme and even the phrasing of the earlier 'In Praise of Limestone' in its lines declaring 'When I seek an image/For our Authentic City', it shows an awareness that the desire it expresses is one for poetic images, not for metaphysical certainties. The 'good place' has metamorphosed into the 'Authentic City'. There are still echoes of symbolism here – and

the intertextual link with St Augustine's City of God. Yet the adjective 'authentic' has a very different quality from ethical concepts,
such as 'good'. 'Authentic' describes a relation of practice – and
nothing beyond existence. It also includes an insight into its make-
up, and therefore remains firmly on the territory of the poetic text.
This is demonstrated when the poem indulges in a pseudo-symbolic
wild goose chase for which 'brigs of dread' and 'gloomy galleries'
and 'old men in hall-ways' (CP 426) provide fitting horror story
ingredients. Yet all this parody of an existential search for the transcendental leads to is merely the inspection of a drain-pipe by a
paterfamilias after breakfast. The signals are clear: the poem advocates
a focusing on the everyday rather than an escapist search for certainties beyond existence. When it presents a father figure in a domestic
setting as a positive image, one should note that in this truce of subject and object world Auden's poetry eventually manages to lay to
rest the ghosts of its own past and its continual struggle against family and tradition.

The poem concludes with a summary of its intentions and concerns. Its third and final stanza addresses a 'Goddess of winds and
wisdom' that Spears links with Robert Graves's White Goddess,
witches, and the unconscious.[5] The spokesman of this badly defined
power, the poet, is flawed, has 'bodily ticks' and only invokes her
unconsciously. What the problematic prayer asks for is therefore not
so much divine inspiration or an existential change brought about
by a supernatural power; rather, it is an address to a natural force,
and the request is for an awareness of nature (internal as well as
external) as 'unable/To name or to structure'.[6] Contrary to a proper
religious force, this simple objective presence does not lead to miraculous transformations, but merely to verbal rites without any outspoken validity beyond themselves. Yet it is important that they are
fittingly done, not because this makes them achieve any magical
power, but because it shows an understanding 'Of what is excellent/
Yet a visible creature'. This awareness of what is excellent in existence – rather than beyond it – is yet another equivalent of Buber's
'hallowing of the every day'.

The poem concludes by listing Earth and Sky as examples of
excellence in existence. They are natural phenomena that are linked
by wind. Yet even when the poem includes them in its argument, it
carefully avoids appropriation. Aware that its own power is only
that of textuality, but that even and especially in textuality an appreciation is possible, it calls them 'a few dear names'.

'Woods' continues the farewell to a symbolic appropriation of external reality combined with an attempt to cherish the world humans inhabit in an appropriate way. This fitting way is always a dialogic one: there is no appreciation without an awareness why things such as woods are cherished. At the same time there is a distinct difference between appreciation and abuse. The poem outlines a history of the appreciation of woods, starting with the etymological idea that woods harbour everything that is savage. Even this early concept, Auden's poem shows, displays an understanding that 'savage' refers both to the creatures supposedly lurking in forests, and also the human drives for which the forest offered shelter and licence: 'Guilty intention still looks for a hotel/That wants no details and surrenders none;/A wood is that' (CP 427).

The poem is drastically optimistic when it counters ideas of Romantic enchantment not only with pragmatic modern images, such as the hotel catering for dirty weekends, but also with the demystifiying idea of snapshots taken during picnics. Yet despite its debunking of symbolism and myth, the poem continues to insist on an intrinsic connection of man and nature, even though it is not the magical one of manipulation and transformation or the related Romantic one of elevation and purification. Auden's Pan talks in morse code; his doves 'rear their modern family of two'. 'Woods' sees the relation of man and nature as one of care. Yet this care does not derive from a human superiority over the object world nor a Heideggerian concept in which care is merely the care for Being in Existence (and thus a completely anthropocentric concept).[7] In Auden's poem 'The trees encountered on a country stroll/Reveal a lot about a country's soul'. This soul is by no means an essential nationalism, but the relation of human beings to one another and to their environment. 'A small grove massacred to the last ash,/An oak with heart-rot, give away the show', claims the poem in images that evoke wars as well as the problems of the self, yet without elevating them to symbols of these conditions. The poem's final claim reasserts the separateness from which comparison and eventually learning can emerge: 'A culture is no better than its woods.'

'Mountains' are a more problematic test of Auden's philosophy. This is not because they represent an antagonistic element, but because, by being perceived and appropriated by human beings, they easily permit identification with views that are opposed to his insistence on openness and productive limits. Mountains invite appreciation by Romantic concepts of absolutes and extremes: they are a wall rather than a border. In Auden's early poetry they provide the vantage-point for doomed, isolated, and potentially dangerous leader figures. Here, too, 'perfect monsters – remember Dracula – / Are bred on crags in castles' (*CP* 429). Mountains can be made to stand for the opposite of civilization, and they achieve this role by their association with extremes of belief. Yet Auden's poem questions the wholesomeness of such service to absolutes, when it describes its followers as 'unsmiling parties' and asks 'but what God/ Does their order serve?' Any conviction that serves extremes, the poem implies, serves abstractions rather than any god that would merit divine status in Auden's universe.

While Auden's speaker advocates possible mundane advantages of mountains, as refuges, for example, Romatic fetishising turns the wall of mountains into a world. But it is a world in which 'any kind of growth' is detested. 'Mountains' continues in what might be a subtle joke at the expense of Yeats's late poem 'Lapis Lazuli'. In Yeats's poem, refuge from the turmoil of history is sought in the contemplation of a sculpture of three Chinamen which are made to represent Nietzschean tragic gaiety, and therefore an elevated superhistorical attitude. In the conclusion of Auden's poem the speaker wonders for how long the presence of a mountain 'Like a Chinese poem' would keep him happy, when nearby 'a real darling/Is cooking a delicious lunch'. Five minutes it grants the mountain, and this irreverence indicates once more that the poem's eyes are firmly set on the here and now and mock any attempt of art to leave the present behind.

'Lakes', too, starts with the image of 'an average father', and the emphasis is once again on circumvention and integration into human patterns of existence. 'Anything bigger than that, like Michigan or Baikal,/Though potable, is an "estranging sea"' (*CP* 430), states the poem, indicating that it is critical of alienation, if it is an alienation from human practice. The reassuring and calming qualities of lakes, the poem continues, are an antidote to Romantic aggression. It also hold lakes responsible for the success of Christianity, when it claims – in terms that are obviously blasphemous for orthodox Christians – 'Christendom did not get really started,/Till [. . .] Her pensive chiefs converged on the Ascanian Lake/And by that stork-infested shore invented/The life of Godhead.' Lakes signal specificity, and that endears them to Auden's late philosophy of particulars. They are also more benign than the formless and impersonal sea. Ultimately, they fulfil the important condition of his thinking: they can be made to relate to the individual, rather than challenging, changing, subduing, or even obliterating it. In poetic terms this means that they are accessible and respond to naming: 'Moraine, pot, oxbow, glint, sink, crater, piedmont, dimple ... ?/Just reeling off their names is ever so comfy.'

'Islands' in many respects counterbalances 'Mountains'. Both cater for isolated egotists, but where mountains confront them with absolutes, islands preserve and accept 'the private code', be it the hermit's or that of prisons. Their separateness is comforting, not frightening; their support of narcissism does not lead to extremism, merely to indulgence. This indulgence can be poetic, as Sappho, Tiberius, and Auden's playful 'I' demonstrate, or merely that of leisure-seeking sunbathers.

'[N]othing is lovely,/Not even in poetry, which is not the case,' concludes 'Plains'. With this Wittgensteinian reminder the penultimate poem of 'Bucolics' summarises the results of its sceptical investigation of the landscape that knows no limits and therefore lacks the necessary dialogic challenge as much as its opposite, the singular mountains, did. Auden's speaker cannot envisage living in these directionless regions, an unsexed space 'where all elsewheres are equal!' By offering equality and therefore sameness, plains inspire neither poetry, nor quest, nor romance. In Auden's landscape, plains are the realms of Caesars and tax-collectors, imposers of abstract order, representatives of the 'They', not the 'I' and 'you'. The self that is never abandoned in Auden's poetry cannot find shelter in plains. Their 'dead centre' defies location and definition and is therefore experienced as antagonistic to poetry as it is hostile to existence in the world, the world that is Wittgenstein's reference point in *Tractatus logico-philosophicus*, from which the conclusion of 'Plains' borrows its final clause.[8] Only from the specificity of facts and their relation to the individual, the poem implicitly suggests, does existence emerge.

'Streams', the concluding poem of 'Bucolics', is also the most positive and harmonious of them all. In streams, Auden's poetics of playfulness, deferral, and also communion and promise find a perfect equivalent. They represent 'pure being', yet one inside existence, not beyond it as in religion or existentialism. If streams are immaculate, as the poem suggests, it is because they are also inconstant. At the same time they display a remarkable constancy, but only towards themselves. When the poem likens the sound of streams to the state of language before the Babylonian confusion, yet also claims that this constancy derives from the fact that streams are only ever talking to themselves, they become the equivalent of poetry: constant in their use of forever the same material, yet forever bending it into new shapes. Poetry as well as streams only submits to domination in an unconcerned way, because it can only ever be temporary – and will eventually be followed by a renewed liberty once the constraints are overcome. As in 'In Praise of Limestone', it is the flowing water, the emblem of constant change, that is responsible for transformation in stability, and in this way makes existence liveable, because it does not respect standstill and certainty.

Unlike Nietzsche, who turns the will as well as the human drive to form metaphors into an all-overpowering force, and the modernists who use a similar mode of thinking, in Vorticism, for example, Auden's streams are not one major force. They are already plural. Their power derives from interaction with their environment, not from the submersion of this environment. If one compares the mythopoeic image of the Mississippi in Eliot's 'The Dry Salvages' to Auden's streams, the difference becomes instantly obvious. (In the occasional poem 'To T. S. Eliot on His Sixtieth Birthday' Auden slyly states that Eliot's poetic strength lay in 'finding the right/language for thirst and fear'; he certainly did not use language, not even images of water, to make existence fertile; *CP* 440). Auden's streams do not take over existence; they accompany it. They give the speaker of the text dreams, but they do not become the dream or the vision of mankind. Auden's 'Bucolics' do not elevate nature to myth. In the traditional manner of bucolics, they employ nature to frame human existence. Its otherness is relative in that there is communication, yet without Romantic communion or merger. Water, the poem concludes, 'run[s] with the human race', and if its effect is a highlighting of the splendour and holiness of 'the least of men', then this emphasis derives not from any magical powers of nature, but from the 'I thought', the perception and imagination of the human subject.

A POETRY COMING TO ITS SENSES

A poetry that declares a truce between subject and objects is also one that comes to terms with the closest union of the two that is at hand in human existence: the body. Auden's early poetry is tellingly unsensual when analysed for its depiction of bodies. Bodies are subordinated to will and desires, and more often than not they frustrate desire rather than condone it. Numb fingers (in 'The Letter', *CP* 39) and tightening jaws (in 'Too Dear, Too Vague', *CP* 45) are the characteristics of a poetry that holds up a notion of the 'Uncertain Flesh' (in 'Easy Knowledge', *CP* 44). Desirable bodies are those of the Other, and an unreachable Other it usually turns out to be, as can be glimpsed from 'the stubborn athletes' in 'The Bonfires' (*CP* 53), 'The smiling boy at the garage [who]/Ran out before he blew his horn' in 'A Misunderstanding' (*CP* 109), and, most crucially, the epitome of the desirable body, the diver in 'No trenchant parting this' (*EA* 21). Although Auden's poetry frequently touches on sexuality as a problematic means of human interaction, it is happy to defer its depiction to materialist reductions, such as creaking sofas (in 'Love by ambition', *EA* 30), or abstractions, such as the even senses in 'For what as easy' (*EA* 113). The body is a potential traitor rather than an ally, and the anti-sensual emphasis in Auden's early poetry is the consequence of its distrust of the senses.

Yet senses are that which link self and world, subject and object. As Auden's later poetry learns to appreciate the particular qualities of things, so, in a similar way, it learns to cherish the faculties that help the self achieve contact with the external world. 'Precious Five' (*CP* 449) is a poem dedicated to the five senses. When the poem labels the nose 'solemn', the reader becomes aware that the appreciation of the object world now includes an appreciation of the most subjective object, the body, too. The nose is praised because it connects the self with the present moment, and is both a point of orientation and a bridge between brow and mouth. For Auden's poem it links time and space as well as memory and hope. This may not be a very convincing way of seeing a nose, yet if one compares Auden's solution for the missing link between memory and hope to Eliot's desperate but eventually futile search for a bridge between memory and desire in *The Waste Land*, one might be tempted to think that the real message of the nose points once again in the direction of the presence and significance of existence. The message would then be: it was right in front of you all the time.

Hearing is singled out in 'Precious Five' for its capacity to be trained. What Auden's text wishes hearing to achieve is such a level of discrimination that eventually all sounds 'Seem natural, not one/ Fantastic and banal'. The effect of the most meticulous discrimination would then be the greatest openness and tolerance. If hearing is granted this crucial potential that is the mundane ideal of Auden's later poetry, this is certainly also because it is the sense that responds both to spoken language and Auden's beloved music.

Hands are the emblems of human activity, and Auden's poem links them with the emergence of culture. It also implicitly connects them with texts, yet not in the straightforward way as the producers of written language that one would expect. Although they cannot read, their deeds are written on them, the poem claims. It distinguishes between action (which is blind to knowledge) and the results of action, which form the basis of knowledge and culture. Because the tactile hands are in a position of ethical blindness combined with responsibility, they share precisely the condition of human beings after the abandoning of explanatory certainties, the grand narratives that justify action. Their responsibility must be towards their actions, and these actions must be creative ones, even though those who will inherit their results, future generations, are not yet to be seen. In this condensed allegory Auden's poem expresses precisely the ethical insight of many twentieth-century theorists of a non-metaphysical ethics of responsibiliy and forward orientation despite one's inevitable blindness towards the future.[9]

The eyes are used in 'Precious Five' for a renewed discussion of the relation of self to Other(s). The section recommends an intense awareness of others – yet without taking them in, without subduing them to the terrorist demands of the self. This self must refrain from a narcissistic communion with itself only, yet without losing sight of the demands of will and libido. It must look 'from inside out'. Furthermore, it must retain a position of difference to others, while remaining aware of their existence and actually admitting to its desire for them: 'Look outward, eyes, and love/Those eyes you cannot be' (*CP* 449). This, in short, is the credo of Auden's later poetry concerning the relation of self to Other.

The tongue comes last in Auden's poem, but by no means least. Its connection with language and communication privileges it among the senses. Its praise is for 'the Earthly Muse', yet the poem also declares that it may use for its appreciation 'by number and by name' (i.e. once again by reference to particulars rather than generalisations) 'any style you choose'. Once again, Auden's poetics insist on tolerance and plurality rather than strict categories. The differences with modernism's exclusive poetics (visible, for example, in Imagism's negative rules) could not be greater. The non-metaphysical earthly muse of Auden's poetry is both fishwife and queen, reason and unreason, and her alternative Wheel of Fortune oscillates between 'appetite and season' rather than fortune and despair. The tongue, as the organ best equipped to relate to this muse, is also both the producer of language and the 'animal of taste', and as such is only interested in 'drink or meal'. After having freed self and objects from their submission to metaphysical concepts, Auden's poetry eventually goes all the way and even rejects the elevation of language and poetry above existence. They, too, are tied to every-day concerns and pleasures, as the further link of the tongue to the penis indicates, its 'twin, your brother,/Unlettered, savage, dumb,/ Down there below the waist' (CP 449). Ariel and Caliban cannot be separated.

Despite the praise of the natural senses that 'Precious Five' under-takes, it refrains from turning its observation into another universal-ist ideal, that of the Natural Law. The poem insists on the local and temporal limitations of its insights: 'Be happy, precious five,/So long as I'm alive.' It does not claim to have explanations for existence that are more than ingenious inventions of the imagination. The sky that it would address with these fictions (note that the text avoids the religiously loaded term 'heaven') would remain unimpressed. If the poem juggles with the traditional link between Divine Law and Nat-ural Law, as its line 'Bless what there is for being' indicates,[10] it settles for neither. The self, it argues, is not made to submit easily to either or both of these universal concepts. Its task, in accordance with Auden's poetics of plurality and debate, is 'Agreeing or disagreeing'.

Two related sonnets, 'Objects' and 'Words', once again take up the relation of object world and the most ingenious way in which the self makes sense of its encounters with it, that of language. 'Objects' defines this life-world very clearly as inaccessible to the limitations of human reason: 'All that which lies outside our sort of why' (CP 473). None the less, this object world poses an existential challenge through its very otherness. It consists of 'wordless crea-tures who are there as well'. Its relation to the self that is endowed with words but also tied to its sense-making operations functions through the senses themselves. This exterior world is 'Remote from mourning yet in sight and cry'. The effect of its challenge of other-ness and alienness is surprisingly positive; it actually exceeds through its very presence even the imaginative powers of the self and, as a result, makes 'time more golden than we meant to tell'.

The power of the object world resides exactly in that which is commonly derided by human reason: it is located in surfaces. This surprising insight contradicts the traditional Platonic distinction of appearance and reality which reappears in traditional hermeneutics as the separation of surface and depth. However, it corresponds exactly to postmodern theories that propose a thinking in surfaces and skins. Baudrillard's insistence that the seeming secrets of the life-world are buried 'deep inside the surface' and Lyotards's attempt to think in surfaces on which exchanges happen that constitute exist-ence and the responses of rationality to it, are illustrations of this move away from depth and essences.[11] The depth of the surface, Auden's poem claims, derives not from any essential quality, but only tom the human longing for it. Even the otherness of the object world is not an essential quality, but a relational and perceptive one. It therefore falls both within the scope of textual and artistic enquiry and remains outside its appropriating desire and potential: 'If shapes can so to their own edges keep,/No separation proves a being bad.'

Once again 'Objects' takes up the theme of care, but again not as a relation to an absolute Being (either subjective or divine). Its care is triggered by the awareness of transience, the temporality which forms the link between object world and self. In mortality, the self ultimately realises its object status. Yet the silence of loss, with which 'Objects' ends its inquiry, is not a metaphysical absence, but a long-ing of the self for 'a soul' which is 'somewhere' and forms the 'Light' in the bestial substance, the animal nature of the human being which is encapsulated in the body. One could read the poem's con-clusion in a religious vein were it not for the preceding discussion of the nature of depth as the result of the longing for it. If Auden's poem stubbornly insists on a soul, it is a soul that is the effect of the desire for one. This desire does not leave the object world behind and degrade it to a secondary phenomenon; on the contrary, it relies on the object world, it depends on the 'bestial substance', and it cherishes this dependence on substantial otherness even inside the self as 'wonder' and not so much as grief. The miracle of exist-ence is again not a metaphysical one for Auden, but emerges from the entanglement in the objectivity of human practice, out of which even the desire for transcending it is generated.

'Words' forms the other side of the debate. If the separateness of object world from the subject triggers the self's rational and libidinal attempts to make sense of existence, then language as the result of these attempts reflects back on the initial split and reponds to it. It can deny the rift by becoming all-inclusive, as in myth-making, be it traditional or modernist: 'A sentence uttered makes a world appear'

(*CP* 473). Inside this fictional world, subject and object are seemingly in harmony, because the control of fiction ameliorates difference. Yet this total control also produces the blindness of fictional systems towards themselves and what Adorno calls their 'intolerance of all externality'.[12] Auden's poem summarises the dilemma in a neat formula: 'Words have no words for words that are not true.'

After having outlined the complete control inside closure, the poem sets out to break up this enclosure, a monadic equation of word and world that is characteristic of modernist master-texts such as *The Cantos* and *Four Quartets*. It insists on the stubborn residual forces that challenge the victory of monadic closure. It introduces first of all in a pun the subject that remains at the heart of these universalist constructions in language: 'One cannot change the subject half-way through.' The subject remains the instigator as well as the miraculous outsider of the nominalist world formulas. Its presence questions the enclosure of the fictional world. At the same time the poem reminds the reader of the inevitable entanglement of fiction in previous fiction as well as in the general conventions of language. Syntax and tenses are its proofs that fictions are internally restricted.

Traditional narrative models are its intertextual evidence of the limitations of fictional myth-making, recalling that fiction is not separate from, but indeed a constitutive part of, the human life-world: 'Arcadian tales are hard-luck stories, too.' As part of everyday life they share the ambivalences and problems of existence. The poem balances fact and fiction, but opts for neither – in a similar way as 'Precious Five' refrained from privileging and indeed accepting a specific order. The poem's critique of monadic myth-making is itself expressed in literary clichés. There is no position outside imagination and simultaneously no viable position outside objective reality either. Once again, negotiation and compromise are the order of the day. When the poem concludes with the established Audenesque image of the quest it not only adds to it a question mark, it also indicates that the quest does not lead out of this existential entanglement, the permanent borderline position of self between objects and imagination, but only ever along this border.

HUMANE ORDER

Horae Canonicae charts the crucifixion, but also the human states of consciousness between waking and going to sleep. Edward Callan claims that Auden echoes the phenomenology of Husserl in this poem, the immediate 'world-about-me' and its interaction with human awareness.[13] Again it is noticeable that the generalised concepts of Auden's earlier poems have become transformed into still-rational observation, but now the observation concerns practice rather than concepts.

'Prime' describes the feelings of a person waking up, the slow acknowledgement of the existence of body and exterior world and their separation from entangled unity into distinct entities – which eventually leads to the establishment of the self. The body is both the medium of self-recognition and the plane on which the meeting of self and object world takes place. The self wakes first 'without a name or history' 'between my body and the day' (*CP* 475). This moment of unity in separation is called 'holy' and 'wholly' by the poem, because it encapsulates the self's awareness of itself at the same time as its reassuring realisation that it is surrounded by 'a world' and therefore 'not alone'.

'Prime' ingeniously fuses this awareness of the self in its relation to the world with Christ's acceptance of his self-sacrifice in the garden of Gethsemane. Subtly, the poem moves towards this double focus when it introduces 'gates' in its first stanza and 'complete obedience' in the second. Yet, despite having been prepared for a religious message through the poem's title, the reader only realises that there is a second entangled plane of reference when the end of 'Prime''s second stanza introduces Adam before the Fall. In the third stanza the doubling becomes even more evident when the seemingly opposed images of Paradise and death are evoked and eventually the accomplice turns into an assassin, a thinly veiled allusion to Judas Iscariot.

Yet despite its clever intermingling of everyday phenomena and the story of Christ's arrest, the poem refrains from becoming a symbolic and religious one. Its counterprojection works both ways. By projecting Christ's sacrifice as a human being onto the self-realisation of the human being every time one awakes, it signals that Christ's sacrifice brings into contact the Divine and the mundane in the same way as human (self-)consciousness contains an acceptance of the self as object together with the realisation of its separateness from the object world. The poem does not lead to an affirmation but to 'our living task, the dying/Which the coming day will ask'. This entails an acceptance of mortality as much as an engagement with life. It permits a religious reading, but it does not enforce it. When the poem summarises its insights in the term 'my historic share of care', it leaves it to the individual to determine their part.

'Terce' contrasts some of these shares, yet rather than shares of care they are shared guilt. Executioner, judge, and poet are shown so entangled in their daily tasks and the mundane desires ruling their existence that they are blind to the significance of their actions. Yet rather than taking a moral high ground, the poem signals sympathy for the concern of all these selves for their immediate reality. It even places the narcissistic gods of its protagonists ('Now each of us/Prays to an image of an image of itself'; *CP* 476) on an equal plane with 'Sprites of the hearth and store-room, godlings/Of professional mysteries, the Big Ones/Who can annihilate a city'. They are equal because they are equally unconcerned, probably because they are equally fictional ('There will be no squabbling on Mount Olympus,/No Chthonian mutters of unrest' states the poem sarcastically). The selves, too, are far from supreme rulers: 'At this hour we all might be anyone.' None the less, they are entangled in a greater scheme of things that will turn this particular day into 'a good Friday'. The irony is basic, since it concerns the projection of the Christian concept of the Divine plan of salvation onto 'the machinery of our world'. Yet the irony also leaves it open as to which interpretation the individual, both as a protagonist of the poem and as its reader, will opt for.

'Sext', too, is ostensibly concerned with the specificity of existence. Its examples are drawn from professions. Entangled in their daily tasks, their practitioners forget themselves in their function. The poem echoes Victor Shklovsky's claims concerning habitualisation of experience:

> Habitualization devours works, clothes, furniture, one's wife, and the fear of war. 'If the whole complex lives of many people go on unconsciously, then such lives are if they had never been.' And art exists that one may recover the sensation of life; it exists to make one feel things, to make the stone *stony*. The purpose of art is to impart the sensation of things as they are perceived and not as they are known.[14]

Yet rather than moralising, the poem once again leaves its argument in suspense. Habitualisation leads to the forgetting of the self, yet it also leads to the introduction of Christian saints in the place of classical deities. The history of civilization itself is thus characterised as an interplay of habit and disruption. The poem claims that 'there should be odes,/to the nameless heroes' who took the first steps in the direction of civilized existence. This civilized existence is characterised by a turning away from the merely mundane. In Bataille's terminology, it rests on excess and activities which have their end in themselves.[15] The 'first flaker of flint/who forgot his dinner,/The first collector of sea-shells/to remain celibate' are the instigators of the poem's history of civilization. Yet this civilization then creates its own norms and habits. Without it there would be no 'basilicas, divas,/dictionaries, pastoral verse' and 'the courtesies of the city'. These habitualised ordering mechanisms that are summarised in the three terms '*Fortitudo, Justicia, Nous*' (strength, justice, intellect and/or common sense) ultimately lead to Christ's sacrifice, too. Suddenly the mundane images drawn from present-day court-rooms achieve once again a religious significance and vice versa. Out of the habits of civilization emerge community, authority, and power, but also the powerlessness of the individual, oppression, and juridical murder.

The third section of '*Sext*' discusses the relation of individual and group. The crowd subsumes the individual as it swallows the individual's view of the particular. What the crowd sees is not the world of things and its causes and effect. Its vision is on something that the crowd itself generates: 'the crowd sees only one thing/(which only the crowd can see),/an epiphany of that/which does whatever is done' (*CP* 479). These cryptic formulas refer to the complex interaction of discourse and power – forces that are connected with and generate each other. What the circular interaction produces is analogous to what Jean Baudrillard calls the 'simulacrum': by no means an imitation or reproduction, but, on the contrary, an effect that has no identifiable cause, marking the end of cause and effect and the abandoning of the Platonic hierarchy of appearance and reality.[16]

In political terms, the implications of the simulacrum generated by the crowd (Auden's thinking is here clearly concerned with mass culture) are double-edged, if not paradoxical, and certainly potentially dangerous. On the one hand it produces the only feeling of belonging that is possible in a secularised society in which even idealistic notions of society have become fragile. What 'Sext' claims in its tautological formula was expressed in an apparent contradiction in 'September 1, 1939': 'There is no such thing as the State/And no one exists alone' (*EA* 246). On the other hand, this simulacrum of belief that the crowd creates is irresponsible, because it does not know individual guilt; in fact, it does not even recognise the value of the individual. Here very different mass ideologies function in a remarkably similar way, be they the openly homogenising ones, such as fascism and Stalinism, or the ones that function through a pretended individualism, but subordinate the individual to the hegemonic demands of a mass market, such as consumer capitalism and its related media empires.

Contemporary human beings must live with the contradictions produced by the life of the crowd, the poem signals when it rejects idealistic alternatives: 'Few people accept each other and most/will never do anything properly.' If the poem still goes on to claim that 'we can say/all men are our brothers', it qualifies this optimism by an admission that this is only possible because 'the crowd rejects no one, joining the crowd/is the only thing all men can do'. Yet despite this seemingly fatalistic embracing of the loss of individuality, the poem upholds its dialogic position by stubbornly concluding with a question and a riddle. Its question splits the unified vision into an 'us' and a 'they'. They are apparently too entangled in their mundane activities to perceive that what is happening is of a possible spiritual significance. Yet the potentially morally superior speakers worship 'The Prince of this world', usually the epithet of the devil in Auden; and in the last two lines of the poem 'at this noon, on this hill', he dies analogous to Christ.

'"It was a monster with one red eye,/A crowd that saw him die, not I"' (*CP* 480), is the reaction of the dehumanised individual to the recognition of guilt and confusion in 'Nones'. Lying, storytelling and mythmaking fall into one, in the way that the German philosopher Odo Marquard describes:

> the mythical technique – the telling of stories – is [...] the art of bringing available truth within the reach of what we are equipped to handle in life. For the truth is, as a rule, not yet there when it is either (like the results of the exact sciences, as, for example, formulas) too abstract to connect with or (for example, the truth about life, which is death) unliveably awful. In such cases, stories – myths – not only can but must come forward in order to tell these truths into our life-world, or to tell them, in our life-world, at the kind of distance at which we can bear them.[17]

But it is the objective reality of 'This mutilated flesh, our victim' that challenges the myth of the guiltless masses, and at this point

Auden's truce of subject and object clearly generates a call for responsibility rather than blissful harmony.

It is again possible to read this section of the poem in religious terms. It would then discuss the problem of sin and redemption. But it can also be read as a debate on historical, social, and political responsibility. The text again insists on a multiple perspective in which individual and collective view relativise each other without cancelling each other out. It merges the appeal to the Madonna with references to 'Pile-driver, concrete mixer,/Crane and pick-axe', and thereby makes it clear that 'our projects under construction' are as much mundane ones as they encompass spiritual dimensions. But so will be 'our completed work': it will include the return of blind daily routine after atrocities as well as the lasting consequences of our deeds. The awareness of this entanglement of life, guilt, and punishment (be it spiritual or physical) accompanies human existence and leads to attempts at imaginary escape. Yet even these attempts of 'our dreaming wills' lead merely to a wandering on 'knife edges', as in Andersen's *Little Mermaid*, one of Auden's favourite fairy tales, but also in his poetry of borders, frontiers, and painful separations.

'Vespers' is an exercise in such a separation, yet is also a dialogue between Auden's anti-idealist conception, that the text calls 'Arcadia' and 'Eden', and the rational modernist one that the poem labels 'Utopia' and 'New Jerusalem'. The conflict is embodied by the speaker of the text, who describes himself as a pot-bellied Aquarian, the flexible water sign, and his counterpart as a narrow-mouthed Scorpio, the (self-)destructive fire sign. If the believer in Arcadia is hooked on an anachronistic and eclectic culture in which Bellini, miners' choirs, and Oxford tow-paths meet, the supporter of the New Jerusalem dreams of a post-revolutionary society of justice and equality. This utopia, however, looks remarkably like the abandoned old order, only that now all the 'right' thinkers are in positions of power. Auden's Edenic vision is unconcerned about power, and therefore certainly naive. Yet in connection with openness, plurality, and an insight into its own restrictions and bias, it is presented as a good deal more humane than the perfect but cold order of the New Jerusalem. In 'Dingley Dell & the Fleet', an essay on mythopoeic imagination, Auden explains the distinction: 'Eden is a past world in which the contradictions of the present world have not yet arisen; New Jerusalem is a future world in which they have at last been resolved' (*DH* 409). Contradictions, however, are what feed the dialogues that keep Auden's worlds liveable. Their resolution produces monologue and death. The essay consequently goes on to state that the motto over the gate of Eden is 'Do what thou wilt is here the Law', whereas New Jerusalem lives according to the guideline 'In His will is our peace'.

'Neither speaks. What experience could we possibly share?' is 'Vespers' description of the non-interaction of the extreme positions. None the less, it is itself an exercise in dialogue, even though a biased one. The experience that the opposites share, as the beginning of 'Vespers' makes evident, is the very fact of being human and citizens. Vespers is, after all, the time of the day devoted to the evening meal, and in connection with Auden's ideas concerning the love-feast of agape, it would be surprising if the text completely upheld its divisions. Indeed, its conclusion asks whether the encounter of the opposites was not that of accomplices. On the conflict of their seemingly irreconcilable views 'our old bag of democracy' is founded. And even though the conflict is bloody and will demand victims '(it must be human, it must be innocent)', it alone guarantees civilization – which is embodied in the image of the productive limit, the 'secular wall'.

'Compline' takes back the poetic cycle almost full circle to its beginning. Where the self gained consciousness at the beginning of *Horae Canonicae*, the body now 'escapes,/Section by section, to join/Plants in their chaster peace' (*CP* 485). Yet the mundane conclusion of the day does not automatically provide a solution to the questions that this day has posed. The poem realises that 'the whole thing' should make sense in an 'instant of recollection' (this is also, in a nutshell, the hope of modernist texts with their insistence on moments, apparitions, and epiphanies). Yet what this moment delivers in Auden's poem is merely the memory of 'doors banging,/Two housewives scolding, an old man gobbling,/A child's wild look of envy' (*CP* 484). Still, even this contingent moment of recollection is far from empty. It once again emphasises plurality, individuality, and the productive effect of limits (the doors), conflict, mundane desires, and even aggression and guilt. Yet the insights that can be gained from this plurality are not easily convertible into 'plot/Or meaning', mainly because they 'could fit any tale'. Their openness to interpretation is their power, but it is a power that is linked with practice rather than dead knowledge. It is also an openness that makes ignorance and forgetting possible. The speaker tellingly claims, 'I cannot remember/A thing between noon and three', the time of the Crucifixion.

Yet despite the absence of monological sense, the self is still neither left to itself nor in isolation. It is still surrounded by 'a sound,/A heart's rhythm, a sense of stars'. The body and the exterior world provide a point of orientation and dialogue: 'I can measure but not read.' Perhaps this dialogue even entails the implicit confession of the individual's part 'In what happened to us from noon till three.' Still the poem refuses to turn even this possible feeling of guilt into knowledge. In the same way as it can imagine that the stars might have a message, all it can do is 'accept our separation'. The only certainty it possesses is that of absence: 'For the end, for me as for cities,/Is total absence', and this is 'Past measure or comprehending'. The poem is not even certain that the storytellers, and that includes those who tell the story of absence and annihilation, can be miraculously exempt from it.

Classical modernist voices who speak their own destruction tend to gain a miraculous longevity from their activities (see the sibyl in Eliot's *Waste Land*, the dead voices of his 'Hollow Men', or 'E. P.' in Ezra Pound's *Hugh Selwyn Mauberley*, happily supervising the erection of his tomb). In Auden's 'Compline', poets as well as 'men in television' (any sense of artistic élitism has vanished) must live with their doubts and uncertainties, even concerning the addressee of their hope. Their prayer is therefore a difficult one, even though Auden turns its difficulties into something approaching humour, when he makes his own prayer both particular by including 'C (dear C)' and contradictory by also asking for liberation of 'all poor s-o-b's who never/Do anything properly'. The hope of Auden's prayer is also, characteristically, not spiritual redemption, but permission to 'come to the picnic/With nothing to hide', even though the dance that is part of the picture is labelled 'perichoresis' and thus refers to the concept of the Trinity.[18]

'Lauds', the final section of *Horae Canonicae*, acts as a lyrical summary of the preceding discussion. In a tightly woven and repetitive form that Spears identifies as a medieval Spanish poetic mode,[19] it renews the insistence on the recognition of the external world (of birds, leaves, the sun, and mortal creatures), one's neighbours, oneself ('The crow of the cock commands awakening', CP 485), civilization, and religion ('Already the mass-bell goes ding-dong'). Yet, again, it does not unite its findings in a clear rule or message, but creates unity in separation. The resulting poetic openness leaves it to the reader to take his or her own pick.

THANKSGIVING

Tied up with practice, Auden's late poems are often in danger of appearing banal – as, for instance, in their insistence on depicting every room and its functions, including the toilet, in his collection *Thanksgiving for a Habitat*, which celebrates his final home in Kirchstetten in Austria. Yet far from being merely playful and irreverent, the poems of *Thanksgiving for a Habitat* combine neatly his ideas concerning the relation of subject and object and the insight into the limited yet humane order that can be derived from a focusing on human practice.

A habitat is indeed a further reduction in size of Auden's good place, its final destination after its metamorphosis into the 'Authentic City' of 'Bucolics'. The community has further shrunk from the citizens of *Horae Canonicae* to the self and its friends and close acquaintances. This could rob *Thanksgiving for a Habitat* of political and social relevance. Yet the poem steers clear of becoming a fully private one. It is prefaced by a line from Psalm 16 that translates as 'The lines are fallen unto me in pleasant places; yea, I have a goodly heritage' in the King James Bible. The psalm deals with heritage and its enjoyment, and acts as a further reflection on the appreciation of existence and the reconciliation of present and past. But Auden, an avid reader of liturgical texts, cannot have overlooked the pun of 'lines' that links inheritance with writing and tradition with literature.

The Prologue of *Thanksgiving for a Habitat* is entitled 'The Birth of Architecture', and it, too, links a discussion of the private sphere with the development of civilization, personal enjoyment or displeasure with impersonal masterplans. The two natures, as the poem calls them, are linked: tomb, temple, shelter, and safes are both the expression of the private need for shelter and serve public functions. They are the limits that make the self possible, but that also determine its interaction with others.

'Thanksgiving for a Habitat', the title poem of the sequence, takes as its starting-point Randolph Hearst's fairytale castle in San Simeon on the Californian coast to formulate its ideas of housing as an expression of individuality and its perils. In the same way as mythological self-creation through storytelling can take over the self in its totalising, artificial environments that are simultanously a world of their own, all-inclusive, and exclusive ('believing footmen don't hear/human speech'; *CP* 519), architecture is regarded critically by the poem. Although fantastic habitats have a similar fascination as ideal bodies, they remain outside the realm of everyday human interaction and practice. 'To be overadmired is not/good enough', claims the text; and the 'enough' is important, since it hints at the lack generated, paradoxically, through excess, a lack of contact and usefulness. The poem goes on to reject the other side of the coin, too, the overtly rational creations of Bauhaus architecture and its many inferior spin-offs. They result in 'a pen/for a rational animal', and this the poem ridicules as 'no fitting habitat for Adam's sovereign clone'. Architecture, too, must enter a dialogue between the human attachment to everyday needs and the equally human aspirations to transcend this groundedness in the mundane. 'Territory, status,/and love' form the challenge, and its ideal is always a compromise, 'not a cradle,/a magic Eden without clocks,/and not a windowless grave, but a place/I may go both in and out of'. The Audenesque good place is again one of interaction and limits. It is not an end in itself, but a place of movement and meeting.

'The Cave of Making' takes this idea further and into unexpected areas, when it applies the relativising notion of the habitat even to the space of artistic and poetic creation. The cave of making merges Plato's cave with a Freudian notion of creativity as uterine regression. Yet even though Auden's study is based on the same archetype as all enclosures (the poem's illustration is Weland's smithy), that is, private and empty, it does not function as the generator of creation in isolation. Even though the text claims, 'Here silence/is turned into objects' (*CP* 521), it invites and, indeed, yearns for company and dialogue. The poem itself is a memorial poem to Louis MacNeice, Auden's friend and collaborator, who had died in 1963, a year before 'The Cave of Making' was written. The poem invites the perspectives of others and, indeed, the echoes of history and literature, into its silence. Despite its initial slogan, it does not subscribe to a mythological or modernist notion of creativity *sui generis*. It is not concerned with 'purifying the dialect of the tribe' (Mallarmé's legacy) or 'making it new' (Pound's pragmatic dream). Or rather, it takes the crucial modernist paradox by the horns and tackles the problem that new creation can only emerge from what is already there, while at the same time it must distance itself from it. The cave, to use the poem's guiding metaphor, has at least one entrance and exit.

The most basic ghost that the poem welcomes is that of the English language itself, and it, too, is neither monolithic nor properly 'basic'. It is 'mongrel barbarian English/which never completely succumbed to the Roman rhetoric'. Because it is a mongrel and not strict and abstract, it can be open and flexible and permit both idiosyncrasy, communication and community, a community that unites the very different perspectives and concerns of authors like Auden and MacNeice. It also tolerates poetry, 'this unpopular art which cannot be turned into/background noise for study/or hung as a status trophy by rising executives' (*CP* 522).

When Auden therefore comes up with a label for himself in this poem that actually stuck, 'a minor atlantic Goethe', he duplicates the mongrel nature of his material in his self-characterisation. He is also not afraid of the playful contradictions of America and Europe, classic and minor. Auden's current status as 'minor classic' is a further reflection of this dialogic balance that is not so much a career accident, but an explicit artistic concern and, indeed, a model of a new poetics, one that one may with hindsight call postmodern. Even the 'egocentric monologue' of poems such as those in *Thanksgiving for a Habitat* are offered as gifts 'for friendship's sake'. They are in themselves a thanksgiving, and combine community with materialism and possible religious overtones with purely individual concerns.

The dialogue becomes implicitly part of *Thanksgiving for a Habitat* when two of its poems are supplied with postscripts, 'The Cave of Making' being one of them. The postscript here is seemingly irreverent, since it defuses the themes into epigraphs of dubious relevance and without obvious links. On closer inspection, however, one realises that they all deal with the status of language, writing, and especially poetry. The very choice of the small form pays respect to the mongrel and the minor and signals a refusal to transform the work into a self-declared classic. None the less, the short poems of 'Postscript' again contain in a nutshell the pluralistic, relativising poetics of Auden's later works.

The first one deals with the 'Timeless fictional worlds/Of self-evident meaning', the myths of tradition as well as the synthetic modernist ones. The poem acknowleges the delight in these fictional worlds, but simultaneously relativises them by contrasting them with, and indeed making them part of, the world of 'our own', which it describes as 'A temporal one where nothing/Is what it seems'. The statement is a simultaneous myth-affirmation and -de(con)struction. The role of poetry is further questioned in the second epigraph where it becomes 'a tall story', yet one that, if it is a good one, 'Makes us want to know'. Once again, no answers or certainties are provided, but a longing for answers is generated.

Thanksgiving for a Habitat continues with its allegorisation of the house by contrasting the Oedipal shelter of the cellar, with its chthonian qualities ('Down There'), with the loftiness of the attic, where established knowledge and our past rests in neatly labelled boxes ('Up There'). Yet both the materiality of the cellar and the abstraction of the attic provide room and shelter for the imagination. 'The Geography of the House' carries an ironic label, because the building in question is the lavatory (its dedication to Christopher Isherwood adds to this irony: Auden used to describe Isherwood as 'a cross between a cavalry major and a rather prim landlady').[20] Digestion and defecation are used in this poem to ground the relation of self and nature in the medium of the body. Auden's poem goes back to Freud's idea of defecation as the first significant act of production for the human being, and uses Luther and the pose of Rodin's 'Thinker' as examples of its predominance in intellect and art.

The main virtue of digestion and its result is that it 'Keep[s] us in our station' (*CP* 527), preventing the excesses of 'Higher Thought'. Yet the poem is by no means an ode to human nature. It concludes by praising modern plumbing, because the stench of excrement easily provokes a rejection of the earthly qualities of human existence. Swift and St Augustine are named as examples of thinkers living in ages where 'a stench of sewage' 'Made a strong debating/Point for Manichees'. Once again, the poem rejects extremes and advocates dialogue and compromise. In digestion, mind and body as well as past and present come together. This is the reason why *Thanksgiving for a Habitat* praises the location of this convergence in 'The Geography of the House'.

The bathroom gets its share of praise in 'Encomium Balnei'. Yet while the toilet is the space where the individual communicates with his or her body and thoughts, the bath is also more pronouncedly a cultural space. Its enclosure would have appeared strange to a classical Roman used to communal bathing. It would have seemed blasphemous to 'St. Anthony and his wild brethren', and perhaps unhealthy to Shakespeare and the monarchs of the Renaissance and Absolutism. In the twentieth century the bath becomes the space where the individual can 'withdraw from the tribe at will', but it remains a civilized space that retains its interaction with the community. One can use it for egotistical pleasure, but this pleasure, too, is part of civilization, in the same way as a hot bath can be the prelude to welcoming friends for dinner. The bathroom, as the space of negotiating public and private, is therefore – with a little hyperbole – linked with 'the Pilgrim's Way', 'the War Path', and 'the Holy City' (*CP* 530).

Kitchen, Guest Room, and Dining Room receive attention in the following three poems of *Thanksgiving for a Habitat*. Brecht's line from the *Threepenny Opera* forms the title of 'Grub First, then Ethics'. But while Brecht uses this claim to uncover the underlying materialist premises of culture in his Marxist analysis of capitalism, Auden's poem is happily celebrating the modern American technology that has found its way into his house in Lower Austria. The poem enjoys showing its fictional guest, Plato, the common state of the art concerning the 'prehistoric hearthstone', and argues, depite the obvious contrast between Plato's idealist shade and its own happy materialism, that cooking and eating possess a civilizing function. They not only bring people together (agape is again not far away), but again link self and world through the body.

The Guest Room in 'For Friends Only' encapsulates the ideal of community in Auden's poem. It is open, yet not undiscriminating, a defined space that none the less remains undemanding, in the same way as friendship is not a tie between people but a negotiation of 'Distance and duties' combined with 're-meeting' as a 'real occasion' (*CP* 532). Its link with language is again crucial here, because it shows how closely poetics and the pragmatic ethics of Auden's later poetry are linked. Both are

> Very difficult to speak well, a tongue
> With no cognates, no resemblance
> To the galimatias of nursery and bedroom,
> Court rhyme or shepherd's prose (*CP* 532)

The language of friendships as well as that of a poetry that negotiates the space between individual and society is neither 'natural', as nursery rhymes and pillow talk, nor can it be purely conventional, as court rhyme and shepherd's prose. It has to carve out a niche for itself without relying on essences or given norms.

The feast that in the shape of agape structures a crucial turn in Auden's thinking attains its habitat in 'Tonight at Seven-Thirty'. Once again the poem insists that at the root of this backbone of civilization lies sheer superfluousness and even madness. Entertaining guests is part of civilization because it is against nature; and yet it negotiates between human egotism and an equally human desire not to be alone. Compromise evolves as the ideal formula from the poem: not a banquet, not even the mythical twelve guests of the Last Supper or Arthur's round table, but six as a 'Perfect/Social Number'. Auden's ideals are again as temporal, local, and pragmatic as they are self-deflating.

The description of the bedroom in 'The Cave of Nakedness' mirrors that of the study not only through the cave of its title, but also in its postscript. If 'The Cave of Making' problematised the mythical notion of artistic creation as a monadic production, so 'The Cave of Nakedness' deflates the myth of the bedroom as the location of erotic encounters. 'Don Juan needs no bed' (*CP* 535). The poem is more concerned with the actual pragmatics of getting sleep in a space that is private: 'Bed-sitting-rooms/soon drive us crazy, a dormitory even sooner'. The bedroom is a refuge both from daily routine and the inflated ideas and ideals that it generates as fictions of escape. 'When they look in their bedroom mirrors', the poem claims,

> Fifty-plus may be bored, but Seventeen is faced by
> a frowning failure, with no money, no mistress,
> no manner of his own, who never got to Italy
> nor met a great one (*CP* 535–6)

The postscript of the section reiterates this pragmatic anti-idealistic attitude. 'Our bodies cannot love:/But without one/What works of Love could we do?' asks the first epigram mischievously. The orientation towards ideals, such as love, can never be abandoned completely, yet the poems insist on their anchoring in everyday reality.

'The Common Life' is the ultimate expression of the pragmatic ideal of Auden's later poetry. This poem to the living room concludes *Thanksgiving for a Habitat*. It is also dedicated to Chester Kallman, Auden's lover and partner. Even there it insists that separation is the necessary prerequisite to relationships and refuses to indulge in visions of a homogenising union. The 'catholic' (i.e. all-embracing) area of the room is also the space where the 'protestant' beings encounter each other in their distinctiveness. The size of the living room makes it a space of interaction, and it makes this interaction civilized ('too big/if it gives them any excuse in a quarrel/for raising their voices', *CP* 537). The biggest miracle, the poem continues, is not that singular lives are drawn together by 'loneliness, lust, ambition', but how they create 'a common world/between them'. The thanksgiving of *Thanksgiving for a Habitat* literally turns into a thanking of the self and the Other. It is also a proper giving, in that it never ceases to pay attention to the mundane, materialist premises on which the community it praises rests. If it is also a religious text, it is this only through its appreciation of existence.

Auden's later works are certainly the products of a successful ageing artist content with life and no longer interested in, and indeed averse to, revolutionary change. But they are never in danger of setting up the universalist concepts familiar from the great modernist writers, and from some of the lifeless excesses of Auden's earlier works. Even his eventual open submission to the Classical models that had shaped much of his earlier poetry must be seen as a relativising of the traditional Romantic idea of poetic creativity. No longer is the act of creation a magical event beyond all daily practice; it is a craft, and one text is only ever the successor of a preceding one in an intertextual chain of translation. In the same way, the text is not justified when relating to abstract ideals and universal norms, but only when it deals with, and indeed participates in, the entanglement of existence in daily practice.

It is easy to dislike much of the conversational poetry of Auden's later phase, the poems that occasionally pose as the detached advice of a mature writer to his readers, the self-satisfied ramblings of an ageing man in perfect stanzas and metres. But Auden's later poetry never forces its ideas on its reader; his poems never present ideas as conclusive and points of view as universally valid. They continue to undermine their own assertions in a subtle, even tender way. The titles of his last and posthumous collections, *Epistle to a Godson* and *Thank You, Fog*, mirror this reduced perspective that still refrains from becoming a purely personal one. He still tackles the great issues in his last poems, the great anxieties of existence, and he still lacks conclusive answers.

But despite all this, he achieves a philosphical and pragmatic perspective. In it, materialism and even religiosity merge, as can be seen in 'Whitsunday in Kirchstetten'. There, the praise to God the creator appears as a quotation, already set at one remove by the German of a hymn. It is instantly linked with the monetary offering accepted by the very real 'Herr Beer' and the funnily named priest 'Pfarrer Lustkandl'. The Anglican speaker of the poem is happy as part of a Roman Catholic mass, in the same way as Western culture has no problems reconciling the Jewish week and the Christian year. Caritas as well as its mundane equivalent, *Gemütlichkeit* (cosiness and homeliness) are based on compromise and chance, as the poem asserts when it explains that the current state of affairs might be very different if Austria had not been conquered by the Allies or if the dollar fell.

The poem declares that its present pluralistic ease is the result of 'Blake's Old Nobodaddy/in his astronomic telescopic heaven,/the Big White Christian upstairs' being dead. This might surprise in a poem set on Whitsunday. But what the poem rejects is all-encompassing belief, be it in divination or one particular form of Christian faith. 'Babel, like Sodom, still/has plenty to offer, though of course it draws/a better sort of crowd', claims the poem jokingly, yet also seriously. Plurality, confusion, and even deviance (the homosexuality traditionally associated with Sodom) conspire to create the complexity of existence. And in this complexity even the Holy Ghost 'does not abhor a golfer's jargon,/a Lower Austrian accent'. Despite the challenges of existence, despite the absence of certainty and fulfilment, in a very un-Romantic and down-to-earth way Auden's poetry continues to be motivated by what is perhaps one of the best motivations of literature: when the final lines of 'Whitsunday in Kirchstetten' admit simultaneous defeat and pleasure in the double statement 'what do I know, except what everybody knows – /if there when Grace dances, I should dance', it states clearly that it continues to be in love with life.

9

Auden's Postmodernism

Rather than subjecting Auden's writings to some fashionable theorems, the analyses of this study have tried to read the texts closely and to use them as their guideline. None the less, it has clearly emerged that the theoretical debates that take place in Auden's writings are analogous to the intellectual discussions that have characterised the last decades of this century. The present study was triggered off by the suspicion that Auden's poetics demonstrate a breaking away from the norms set up by the classical modernism of Yeats, Eliot and Pound. It found evidence for its assumption in Auden's entire poetic career.

The breaking away from a modernist norm could, of course, have led to pre- or even anti-modernist positions. One could have imagined, for example, a poetry that refused to be universalist in a metaphysical or nihilistic sense, and which sided with earlier nineteenth-century empiricism; or a poetry that was disappointed with Marxism which took refuge in established religion. Yet Auden's writings do neither. Rather, they develop some modernist premises, anxieties, and even contradictions further, until they reach a poetic ground that leaves the label 'modernist' behind. His poetry continually pushes itself forward into territory that becomes too unstable for traditional concepts of thought and in which traditional poetic techniques appear lost. None the less, as I hope to have demonstrated, Auden's poetic thought in no way ends up lost and in despair. On the contrary, it arrives at a new relation to existence, in which it is capable of dealing with its old convictions, of overcoming their deadening influence without rejecting them offhand. It is no longer an avant-garde poetry in the sense of a poetry making way for itself, wiping away everything in its path and certainly all that came before.

Auden's poems transform themselves into a writing of negotiation, openness, compromise, and dialogue. Yet in this dialogue of positions they also stubbornly hold on to some positions of their own, though without declaring them to be universally and eternally valid. This final chapter will take up these crucial positions and once again link them with their contemporary theoretical equivalents, the theories that have helped to describe postmodernity.

The introduction of the present study has already mentioned the three starting-points of Auden's writing that he summarised himself under the heading of the 'basic human problem' in a review of a translation of Kierkegaard in 1944. The first aspect of the problem is man's 'present anxiety over himself in relation to his past and his parents'. Auden names Freud as the investigator of this aspect. The second aspect is man's 'present anxiety over himself in relation to his future and his neighbours'. Marx is the spokesman of this challenge. The third one is man's 'present anxiety over himself in relation to eternity and God'. Kierkegaard, the Danish philosopher who combines a religious approach with existential philosophy, is Auden's main reference point for this anxiety.[1] Yet universalising any of these anxieties in isolation only leads to totalitarian concepts. The inflated concern of the self for itself as expressed in the Oedipal struggle with the personal past leads to narcissism and monadic closure. Neither a forward perspective, nor a proper acknowledgement of – much less communication and communion with – others is possible. The endangered self inflates itself until it becomes its own artificial and empty reality.

A related artistic failure can be located in modernist impersonality, the attempt to purge literature from the seemingly crippling attachment to a self. This elimination only leads to the continued ghostly presence of the very authority that undertakes this purge. It also leads to texts that not only foreground the failure of communication but often cease to communicate themselves. Neither the blind acceptance of authority nor the end of communication are ultimately acceptable for Auden's poetics.

The concern of the self for its relations with its neighbours bodes better for a poetics yearning for the good place and an integration of self and society. However, as many of Auden's later poems testify, the total emphasis on social concerns and a rational development of society fails to recognise the continuing demands of the not-always-rational self. These often point in a sensual and selfish direction, and refuse to conform to social interaction and practice. The totalising of this inquiry, for which Marx is one vantage-point and liberal bourgeois concepts of democracy another, leads to the barren utopias of Auden's later writings. Their New Jerusalems are merely the old ones in disguise, except that irrational terror and oppression have become replaced by rational force. An early succumbing to this totalising vision was Auden's line concerning the 'necessary murder' in 'Spain 1937'. In *Horae Canonicae* his poems would have no problems placing 'justified' juridical murder next to irrational slaughter.

The concern for God and eternity is only another vantage-point, rather than offering itself as a culmination of an intellectual development. (This is what many critics would like to see in Auden's works: a development from the infantile narcissist via the juvenile Marxist to the mature Christian.) A monological conception of transcendence also leads to concepts that prove hostile to existence, because they exclude dissent. They violate the important concept of free will that – together with the anarchic libido – never leaves the focus of Auden's attention. Even the desire for absolutes must succumb to plurality in his later works, and it must endure being unveiled as the product of human desire for absolutes rather than the unambiguous creator of this desire. Auden's ontology falls together with teleology, but not in the classical modernist form of the self-enclosed and circular myth that excludes alternative positions. His faith is plural and pluriform, and it does not offer the reassurance of certainty – beyond the certainty of desire.

Rather than privileging any of those three basic concerns over another, Auden's poetics learn to accept their dissonant claims. His writing turns into a chorus of distinct voices and positions, yet without homogenising or forcefully harmonising their concerns. The contradictions that emerge from this pluralistic and dialogic approach must therefore not be read as logical flaws, but as the consequence of a different kind of logic. 'Their Lonely Betters' (*CP* 444) shows this different way of thinking as intimately linked with language. The poem states that vegetables and birds are as incapable of lying as they are unaware of their mortality – or, indeed, in need of this existential knowledge. It is up to 'their lonely betters', human beings, to 'count some days and long for certain letters'. Yet the noises that humans make when they express their existential concerns in laughter and weeping are words, the words that derive from the human need to create order and meaning in existence. The price that has to be paid for this 'conscious' approach to existence is the loneliness that the poem insists on. Language and communication can only ever hope to reach another human being and, by relying on an addressee, remind the addresser of his or her existential isolation.

The creation of order and meaning through language, far from solving issues once and for all, also creates responsibility. Out of concepts emerge action and power, and out of power the need for decisions and bases for decisions, ethics, in short. 'Words are for those with promises to keep', the poem claims. And no matter whether these promises are mundane or metaphysical, the poem asserts that they are firmly anchored in human actions and language. The poem performs the linguistic turn characteristic of modern philosophy since Nietzsche. Yet it does not remain inside a linguistic universe, as both Wittgenstein and Heidegger did in philosophy, the classical modernists in poetry, and Formalism and Structuralism in theory. It insists on the problematic re-attachment of the emerging language to the existence from which it is originally generated.

'First Things First' (*CP* 444) is indicative of this insistence on the primary status of existence. When the self of the poem describes its response to hearing a winter storm while in bed, it is aware that rationality and language combine in their 'work to unscramble that interjectory uproar,/Construing its airy vowels and watery consonants/Into a love-speech indicative of a Proper Noun'. For classical modernism, the achievement of the proper noun would have been an end in itself, as Gertrude Stein demonstrates in one of her lectures:

> Poetry is concerned with using with abusing, with losing with wanting, with denying with avoiding with adoring with replacing the noun. It is doing that always doing that, doing that and doing nothing but that. Poetry is doing nothing but using losing refusing and pleasing and betraying and caressing nouns. That is what poetry does, that is what poetry has to do no matter what kind of poetry it is.[2]

Auden's poem, on the other hand, concludes with the admission that the morning after the storm 'would not say/How much it believed of what I said the storm had said'. It does not care for the sense-making operation of human rationality, but still directs its attention to the cubic metres in the cistern and the insight that 'Thousands have lived without love, not one without water.'

Yet despite this insight, Auden's poetry asserts even in this negative statement that it is still concerned with the self and its need for love and the fate of the masses. It is not an anti-humanist poetry, as for example the poems of Robinson Jeffers, that pretend to care only for a nature devoid of human interference (and create the logical problem that the reason why they care is exactly the continuing presence of the human self). Auden's poetry, rather, upholds a sceptical and self-relativising humanism, inside which human beings are described as imperfect, their rationality is shown as limited and often (self-)destructive, and their eventual destination is uncertain. None the less, his poetics generate not despair or nihilism out of their insight, but playful irony (which derives from ridiculing positions that none the less cannot be abandoned) and even joy.

In 'The Shield of Achilles' (CP 454–5), Auden's poetry eventually returns to one of the modernist stumbling blocks, the work of art. As Adorno shows in his *Aesthetic Theory*, modernism, despite attacking the work and threatening it with fragmentation and dispersal, nevertheless refuses to abandon it – and in fact slyly insists on at least desiring its wholeness.[3] 'The Shield of Achilles' goes in the opposite direction. It starts with the potentially perfect work of art, Hephaestos' creation of a shield for Achilles, the Greek hero. Achilles' mother, the goddess Thetis, asks for the artifact to be produced for her son, whose fate she is fully aware of: he 'would not live long'.

If this shield is the emblem of a poetics that ceases to rely on metaphysical certainties, it is also representative of a poetics that does not put its faith in alternative certainties, that of the creative human subject or the aloof and impersonal work of art. Gathered for battle are an 'unintelligible multitude,/A million eyes, a million boots in line,/ Without expression, waiting for a sign'. The multitude represents the crowd, the negative image of community in Auden's writings. The sign that they are waiting for is also dubious: 'Out of the air a voice without a face/Proved by statistics that some cause was just'. The shield, too, does not conform to the expectations Thetis entertains. She looks to art for images of culture, 'vines and olive trees,/ Marble well-governed cities/And ships upon untamed seas', but what she sees is different. The 'shining metal' of the shield recalls its martial function, and what it depicts are 'An artificial wilderness/ And a sky like lead'. Later she expects images of ritual and piety, but again the shield disappoints her. The poem itself contrasts the expectations traditionally directed towards works of art with contemporary reality in its own form. Thetis's searching glance for the emblems of traditional culture is described in rhymed octets in trimeter. The deflating images of martial reality are contained in septets written in common pentameter.

'Where the altar should have been' is barbed wire. Rather than sacred places, the poem portrays 'an arbitrary spot'. Traditional certainties no longer apply, and art cannot produce sense and coherence where there are crowds and bored officials rather than epic heroes. Yet the poem is not nostalgic for the lost greatness of a classical past. It admits that 'The mass and majesty of this world, all/That carries weight and always weighs the same/Lay in the hands of others'. Mythical stability is now guaranteed by the masses; individual greatness is no longer available when even individual value is under threat and people 'die as men before their bodies died'.

With the disappearance of ritual, notions of community also disappear, and what is left are alienation and anarchy. Athletes and dancers are replaced by a street urchin who inhabits an unkempt, uncivilized world where all available truth is that of brutal experience, the experience 'that girls are raped, that two boys knife a third'. The alternative world 'where promises were kept,/Or one could weep because another wept', a reality of promise, hope, and pity, has become an anachronism. This is the world of the word that 'Their Lonely Betters' depicted as the world of language. It is telling that the work of art that 'The Shield of Achilles' depicts in such a pessimistic way is an example of visual art, and not of poetry. Slyly, inside its hopelessness, the very existence of the poem itself might signal that alternatives are still at least imaginable, that they can at least be yearned for. The closed, complete work of art, however, can only depict the hopelessness resulting from the loss of certainties, not the hopes that might arise out of this loss.

'"The Truest Poetry is the Most Feigning"' tackles the incompatibility of art and existence from the perspective of the shortcomings of art. 'No metaphor, remember, can express/A real historical unhappiness' (*CP* 470) is the poem's central message. Mimesis had already been discarded in 'The Shield of Achilles' as a one-way street; now the contructive aspect of poetry is under attack. What, one is tempted to ask, is left to poetry, if it is not itself a leftover, a useless anachronism in the late twentieth century? The task of the individual, the poem asserts again, is to get on with his or her existence, and here the business is a love affair: 'The living girl's your business'. Yet poetry has the task of enabling the individual to communicate his existence to others in the first place: 'We cannot love your love till she take on,/Through you, the wonders of a paragon'.

The reason why individual existence must be communicated is that this communication, far from merely serving the individual ego, is the basis of community and ultimately culture. Even a seemingly banal issue such as a love affair serves as a counterweight to alienation and its related evil, the dissolution of social responsibility and cohesion. The poem is therefore not entirely hyperbolical when it

envisages as the effect of a conventional and clichéd love poem a
blessing and 'an end to war'. The material that becomes the medium
of this link is language, and by employing its conventions (the paragon, for example), both poet and reader participate in a shared culture.

But again the poetic creation does not turn into a reality *sui generis*.
The goal of the participation in an established tradition is not the
monadic work of art that excludes reality by ignoring it. As the
fourth stanza of the poem clearly indicates, there is a distinct possibility that 'half-way through such praises of your dear,/Riot and
shooting fill the streets with fear'. Poetry is not immune from politics; indeed it might easily become 'suspect with the New Regime'.
The advice that the poem gives in this situation is surprising: it recommends lying as the way in which 'writing may still save your
skin'. This is another explicit farewell of Auden's poetry to the
notion of truths and essences. The plurality, flexibility, and openness of poetry enables it exactly to be inauthentic when it chooses to
be – as a response to the particular pressures surrounding it. Its
ambiguities and obscurities, however, also enable its reader to take
up the position he or she chooses. Like 'honest Iagos', traitors who
succeed by insisting exactly on the truth, they can attempt to uncover
the texts' dishonesty. Alternatively, as deconstructive readers they
can use the contradictions of the texts to point out another layer of
significance.

The inverted commas that accompany the very title of '"The Truest Poetry is the Most Feigning"', a quotation from Shakespeare's *As
You Like It*, would then be put around the poem's ostensible message by
the reader. Even though this would not lead to a definitive alternative
meaning ('*We shall never know/Her name or nature. Well, it's better so*'),
it opens up the poem to resistance within conformity. Projecting its
insights on the entire construction of the 'human condition', the
poem goes on to claim that the human being possesses 'no more
nature in his loving smile/Than in his theories of a natural style'.
Again Auden's poem stabs in the direction of nature and essences
and argues in favour of the inevitable entanglement of human
beings in the constructions and discourses that shape their existence
as well as their understanding of themselves. Auden's shorthand
definition of being human is therefore that of 'The self-made creature who himself unmakes,/The only creature ever made who fakes'.

The circularity of the claim is as evident as its subtle contradiction
between 'self-made' and 'made'. The claim can be read once again in

a religious way or as an analogy of Baudrillard's simulacrum, the copy without original. The difference between this concept and the *sui generis* creations of classical modernism is that Auden's creations really unmake themselves. They even present themselves as fakes, something that the synthetic consciousnesses of classical modernist fiction refuse to do (see, for example, the synthetic figure of Tiresias in *The Waste Land*, who is surrounded by fragmented and unreliable voices, but is himself presented as a miraculously authentic focus of suffering). In Auden's poem there is no disentangling of the contradictions of birth, education, God, self-made man, nature, cultural construction and the tall tales of verbal playing, as in *Thanksgiving for a Habitat*, which characterised poetry, love, truth, and orthodoxy. Itself the least orthodox poem in its message, '"The Truest Poetry is the Most Feigning"' remains none the less a poem. The ultimate twist of its own logic is that it leaves it to its reader to decide whether its message is authentic or to be read 'in inverted commas'.

'A Permanent Way' (*CP* 445) is consequently the least imaginable path for Auden's poetics, and yet it is also the most natural one. While certainty and permanence are destined to remain absences, the longing for them indeed turns existence into a permanent process, into a way. This found its allegorical expression in the quest of Auden's early poems. The problem there was that this quest tended to be circular and therefore regressive and also that it promised a goal and therefore a conclusion. While the limit achieves a very positive role in Auden's later poetics, it still functions as a border along which the search for fulfilment forever continues. When 'A Permanent Way' therefore contrasts the 'new-fangled trails' of 'Self-drivers' with the 'good old train' of dogma, it can afford its ironic detachment, since it is aware that the two are more than related. Being led astray is already implied in way and rail, in the same way as only heresy defines dogma.

The poem can be read as a settling into certainties and norms when it praises the safety and relaxation of established tracks. But it is too full of images of deviation, 'tempting scenes which occur/ Along any permanent way', and sly indications that even established certainty requires force in order to become permanent for the reader not to realise that it is in fact about the dialectic of certainty and chance, norm and eccentricity or even deviance. Even though it projects its detours into a fictional past, it is still aware that there is no greater fun (and 'fun' has clear subversive connotations here) 'Than the inexpensive delight/Of a choice one might have made'.

Even this statement is formulated as a question. Auden's poetics do not lead to affirmations, not even to the affirmation of uncertainty and absence. They ultimately combine questions with appeals to action, and here the action demanded is that of the reader interpreting the contradictory messages of the text.

In this as in many other respects there are no turnings in Auden's poetics. Only the urgent questions 'Why are we here? What are we going to do?' that were asked in *The Orators* (*EA* 61) have now become acknowledgements that we do not know why we are here, and we also have little idea what we are going to do. Yet still we continue to invent ourselves and explanations for existence, as indeed we must, if we want to cope with it. In the same manner, we must act, despite the fact that the justifications available for our activities are more than dubious. Their consequences can hardly be guessed, and yet we are asked to bear these results of our deeds in an ethically responsible way. The postmodernism of Auden's poetics is not the watered-down parody of an 'anything goes' to which traditional and Marxist critics try to reduce postmodernity.[4] The play of signification that his writings engage with has rules, and its outcome matters. Yet by avoiding easy universal answers, the texts open themselves up to history and their readers – and they do this without taking them in and swallowing them in their fictional realities.

The very features that often make Auden's poetry unappealing to readers, its refusal of directness and authenticity, becomes an ethical premise on which a new and responsible form of interaction in interpretation might be based, should the reader decide to accept the challenge of the texts. 'When he looked the cave in the eye', states an epigram in the late sequence of poems entitled 'Symmetries & Asymmetries' (*CP* 549), 'Hercules/Had a moment of doubt.' The reader who engages with the caves of making of Auden's poetry and their often dubious content is also asked to have doubts rather than arrive with a readily available faith, if he really wants to engage with the dialogue that Auden's poetry has to offer.

Notes

1. Taming the Monster

1. Geoffrey Grigson, 'Auden as a Monster', *New Verse*, 26–7 (1937), 13–17 (p. 13).
2. *New Signatures* appeared for the first time in 1932, *New Country* in 1933; *New Verse* was published from January 1933 until January 1939, *New Writing* from Spring 1936 until 1950. See Samuel Hynes, *The Auden Generation: Literature and Politics in England in the 1930s* (London and Boston: Faber & Faber, 1976), pp. 74–5, 102, 114, 198.
3. Richard Hoggart's *Auden: An Introductory Essay* (London: Chatto & Windus, 1951), the first and surprisingly good study of Auden's works, set the tone with the remark 'Auden's poetry is particularly concerned with the pressures of the times', p. 9.
4. François Duchêne, *The Case of the Helmeted Airman: A Study of W. H. Auden's Poetry* (London: Chatto & Windus, 1972) is an unpleasant example of this vivisection attitude that regards the author as a part of the texts and endeavours to supply its reader not only with a textual analysis, but glimpses of the author's psyche. Herbert Greenberg, *Quest for the Necessary: W. H. Auden and the Dilemma of Divided Consciousness* (Cambridge, Mass.: Harvard University Press, 1968) is a more sensitive study.
5. Auden himself proves a perceptive commentator on such attitudes when he writes in the preface to *The Poet's Tongue* of 1935, 'The psychologist maintains that poetry is a neurotic symptom, an attempt to compensate by phantasy for a failure to meet reality. We must tell him that phantasy is only the beginning of writing; that, on the contrary, like psychology, poetry is a struggle to reconcile the unwilling subject and object; in fact, that since psychological truth depends so largely on context, poetry, the parabolic approach, is the only adequate medium for psychology' (*Pr* 108).
6. Grigson, 'Auden as a Monster', pp. 13–14.
7. *New Verse*, 26–7 (1937), p. 25.
8. Rainer Emig, *Modernism in Poetry: Motivations, Structures and Limits*, Studies in Twentieth-Century Literature (London and New York: Longman, 1995).
9. Wolfgang Welsch, *Unsere postmoderne Moderne*, 2nd edn., Acta Humaniora (Weinheim: VCH, 1988).
10. Edward Mendelson, *Early Auden* (London and Boston: Faber & Faber, 1981), although still linking texts and biography, is an important step in the direction of a long-overdue close reading. Stan Smith, *W. H. Auden*, Rereading Literature (Oxford: Blackwell, 1985) manages to place Auden's works in a larger theoretical and political framework. Günther Jarfe, *Der junge Auden: Dichterische Verfahrensweisen und ihre*

Bedeutung in W. H. Audens Frühwerk (Heidelberg: Carl Winter, 1985) is an impressive structural analysis of Auden's early writings, unfortunately not available in translation. The latest additions to this list are John R. Boly, *Reading Auden: The Returns of Caliban* (Ithaca and London: Cornell University Press, 1991) and Anthony Hecht, *The Hidden Law: The Poetry of W. H. Auden* (Cambridge, Mass. and London: Harvard University Press, 1993).

11. I am therefore proposing to take 'poetics' in the double sense of 'underlying structures of poetry as well as the norms created out of them' and 'general structures of transformation and exchange between signifying systems and discourses'. Linda Hutcheon's useful study *A Poetics of Postmodernism: History, Theory, Fiction* (New York and London: Routledge, 1988), while summarising neatly some of the general features of postmodernism, restricts her inquiry almost exclusively to fictional texts, mainly contemporary novels. Her definition of poetics is 'an open, ever-changing theoretical structure by which to order both our cultural knowledge and our critical procedures' (p. 14). While I agree wholeheartedly with this general approach, I would also insist on an inquiry into the area in which openness and change manifest themselves in a self-referential manner, i.e. poetry.

12. Before that, one of Auden's poems had been published in *Public School Verse* (1924), and some others in *Oxford Poetry 1926* and *Oxford Poetry 1927*. John Fuller has traced an even earlier publication in Auden's school magazine, *The Greshams*. See his essay 'W. H. Auden's First Published Poems', *Notes and Queries*, 16 (Spring 1974), 81–6.

13. The relevant section is quoted in Monroe K. Spears' seminal study (written in consultation with Auden), *The Poetry of W. H. Auden: The Disenchanted Island* (New York: Oxford University Press, 1963), p. 178.

2. Early Auden: Farewell to the Signified

1. Justin Replogle, *Auden's Poetry* (London: Methuen, 1969), p. 3.
2. Mendelson, *Early Auden*, p. 33.
3. Ibid.
4. Mendelson suggests that the last three lines describe the funeral, the 'wooden shape' the coffin: Ibid., p. 34.
5. John Fuller, *A Reader's Guide to W. H. Auden* (London: Thames & Hudson, 1970), p. 40. A revised edition is about to appear.
6. William Logan, 'Auden's Images', in *W. H. Auden: The Far Interior*, ed. Alan Bold, Critical Studies (London: Vision Press, 1985), pp. 106–8.
7. For a detailed theoretical discussion of ambiguity and obscurity see Michael Riffaterre, *Text Production*, trans. Terese Lyons (New York: Columbia University Press, 1983), pp. 26 ff.
8. Ferdinand de Saussure, *Course in General Linguistics*, trans. Roy Harris (London: Duckworth, 1983), p. 66.
9. 'The link between signal and signification is arbitrary'; Saussure, *Course*, p. 67; and '[a language as a structured system] exists only by virtue of a kind of contract between the members of a community'; p. 14.

10. Roland Barthes, *Writing Degree Zero*, trans. Annette Lavers and Colin Smith, Cape Editions, 3 (London: Cape, 1967), pp. 48–9.
11. Jean-François Lyotard, 'Answering the Question: What is Postmodernism?', trans. Régis Durand, in *The Postmodern Condition: A Report on Knowledge*, trans. Geoff Bennington and Brian Masumi, Theory and History of Literature, 10 (Manchester: Manchester University Press, 1984), pp. 71–82 (p. 81).
12. Logan, 'Auden's Images', pp. 101–2.
13. Stan Smith also recognises this, yet is overly optimistic when he writes 'But these ghosts can be laid. The way involves memory restoring that which was lost'; *W. H. Auden*, p. 69. Memory, I would argue, is not reconciliatory in Auden's early writings, but more often than not unsettling and threatening.
14. Logan, 'Auden's Images', p. 101.
15. Ibid., p. 107.
16. Jacques Derrida, 'Structure, Sign and Play in the Discourse of the Human Sciences', in *Writing and Difference*, trans. Alan Bass (London and Henley: Routledge & Kegan Paul, 1978), pp. 278–93 (p. 278).
17. Derrida, 'Structure, Sign and Play', p. 280.
18. 'Event' should be understood in the broadest sense, since the concept derives from a general theory of discourse; Paul Ricoeur, *Interpretation Theory: Discourse and the Surplus of Meaning* (Fort Worth: Texas Christian University Press, 1976), pp. 6–12.
19. Hoggart, *Introductory Essay*, p. 14.
20. Mendelson, *Early Auden*, pp. 27–8.
21. Its final line echoes the Anglo-Saxon poem 'Wulf and Eadwacer', and brings in further complication.
22. Mendelson compares the 'deity' of the poem to an electric generator, and adds that the line contains a private pun on Auden's erotic use of the word 'power'; *Early Auden*, p. 87.
23. Spears, *Poetry*, p. 44.
24. Ibid., p. 4.
25. Mendelson, *Early Auden*, p. 87.

3. Libidinous Charades: The Auden-Isherwood Plays

1. Fuller, *Reader's Guide*, p. 13.
2. John Boly rightly points out that the social parity of the families leaves no room for a material explanation of the conflicts; neither do they display ideological differences; *The Returns of Caliban*, p. 65.
3. Jean-François Lyotard describes postmodernity precisely as a farewell to master narratives and an embracing of a plurality of narratives: *Postmodern Condition*, pp. 31–7.
4. This programme note to Auden's *The Dance of Death* of 1933 is reproduced in Fuller's *Reader's Guide*, p. 13.
5. This might be an echo of 'Winter kept us warm' in the 'Burial of the Dead' section of Eliot's *The Waste Land*. Yet what is a personal utterance that symbolises a spiritual state in Eliot's poem becomes a psychological statement that stands for a socio-political argument in Auden.

6. Judith Butler, *Gender Trouble: Feminism and the Subversion of Identity*, Thinking Gender (New York and London: Routledge, 1990).
7. Humphrey Carpenter, *W. H. Auden: A Biography* (London: Allen & Unwin, 1981), p. 172. Yet whether the feet simply represent instinct and reason, as he claims, remains questionable. This view might itself be class-biased.
8. Carpenter draws a detailed picture of the complex writing process behind the plays in *Auden*, pp. 169–73.
9. Carpenter, *Auden*, p. 59.
10. There might be a further implication in this apparent rift between Stagmantle and Britishness. Auden, who repeatedly turns the newspaper barons of the 1930s into figures in his writings, might be alluding to the Canadian background of Baron Beaverbrook and/or the Irish ones of Viscount Rothermere (Harold Sydney Harmsworth) and his brother Lord Northcliffe (Alfred Charles William Harmsworth).
11. Here Ransom echoes some of the sentiments prominent in classical modernist poems of the denunciation of the masses, as in Eliot's *The Waste Land* and its 'hooded hordes swarming', and more explicitly Pound's 'rabble' and 'unkillable infants of the very poor' in 'The Garden' and the frequent outbursts in *The Cantos*. The élitism of the truly strong man is a modernist feature rather than a postmodern one.
12. Sigmund Freud, 'On Narcissism: An Introduction', *On Metapsychology: The Theory of Psychoanalysis*, ed. Angela Richards, The Pelican Freud Library, xi (15 vols.; London: Pelican, 1984), pp. 59–97.
13. I have discussed this problem in the section 'Modernist Poetry as a Universal Compensation Strategy' in *Modernism in Poetry*, pp. 123–32.
14. Hutcheon, *Poetics of Postmodernism*, p. 7.
15. Lyotard, *Postmodern Condition*, p. 10.
16. With reference to another Auden poem, Terry Eagleton writes: 'The plague is all-pervading, but it cannot be seen: it suggests an atmosphere of evil too widespread for analysis, too self-generating for control. As an image of war, the plague relates to the "massive vagueness", at once insistent and elusive, of a "metaphysical" process beyond individual understanding'; 'A Note on Auden', in *Exiles and Émigrés: Studies in Modern Literature* (London: Chatto and Windus, 1970), pp. 179–90 (p. 184).
17. This conflict appears once again in the editorial history of the play: an earlier version of *On the Frontier* apparently ended with the triumph of the workers after the collapse of the two hostile governments (*Pl* xxviii).

4. *The Orators*: A Study of Authority

1. It was reprinted with alterations in 1934. A third edition appeared in 1967.
2. Fuller, *Reader's Guide*, p. 74.
3. Jarfe, *Der junge Auden*, p. 204. The quotation within the quotation is Gottfried Benn, *Probleme der Lyrik* (Wiesbaden, 1966), p. 34 [my translation].
4. Quoted in Smith, *Auden*, p. 55.

5. Ibid., p. 57.
6. Ibid., p. 54.
7. Günther Jarfe, 'W. H. Auden und Sigmund Freud: Ein Versuch über den Einfluß Freuds auf Form, Bildlichkeit und Thematik in Audens früher Dichtung', *Poetica*, 11, no. 1–2 (1979), 176–206 (pp. 191–3).
8. In this connection it remains mysterious why John R. Boly claims that the plot of *The Orators* is easily followed, especially since his study stresses Auden's violations of the reader-controlling aspect of texts; *Reading Auden*, p. 64.
9. On the importance of distinguishing self and other(s) (in the primordial sense of the mother), see the seminal lecture by Jacques Lacan, 'The mirror stage as formative of the function of the I', in *Écrits: A Selection*, trans. Alan Sheridan (London: Tavistock, 1977), pp. 1–7.
10. Lyotard, *Postmodern Condition*, pp. 60–1.
11. Michel Foucault, 'The Order of Discourse', in Robert Young, ed., *Untying the Text: A Post-Structuralist Reader* (London: Routledge & Kegan Paul, 1981), pp. 48–72 (pp. 52–3).
12. Fuller, *Reader's Guide*, p. 56.
13. Fuller's *Reader's Guide*, p. 57, sees a connection with Buchman's Group Movement, a moral rearmament organisation rapidly expanding in the 1930s.
14. Richard Bozorth has elaborated the role of homosexuality in great detail in his essay '"Whatever You Do Don't Go to the Wood": Joking, Rhetoric, and Homosexuality in *The Orators*', in Katherine Bucknell and Nicholas Jenkins, eds., '*The Language of Learning and the Language of Love': Uncollected Writing, New Interpretations*, Auden Studies, 2 (Oxford: Clarendon Press, 1994), pp. 113–36. Yet he overstates (and in fact undermines) his case somewhat by claiming that 'we can understand how and why *The Orators* troubles the standards by which it has been assessed only by exploring its treatment of homosexuality' (p. 114).
15. Spears sees the four parts of 'The Initiates' correspond to 'oration or public speech, statement or scientific exposition, letter or informal style'; Spears, *Poetry*, p. 49.
16. Fuller, *Reader's Guide*, p. 60.
17. Ibid., p. 59.
18. Mendelson, *Early Auden*, pp. 100–1.
19. Ibid., p. 101.
20. Spears, *Poetry*, p. 49.
21. Ibid.
22. The test is actually taken from Wolfgang Köhler, *Gestaltpsychologie* (1930); see Mendelson, *Early Auden*, p. 107.
23. Carpenter, *Auden*, p. 10.
24. The model for the airman could be T. E. Lawrence; Spears, *Poetry*, p. 50.
25. Mendelson, *Early Auden*, pp. 104–5.
26. Ibid., p. 7.
27. Veiled allusions to masturbation and kleptomania are frequent in 'Journal of an Airman' (the themes are obviously taboos), yet often so vague as to fit both transgressions equally well. Examples are 'Yesterday

positively the last time. Hands to remember please, always' (*EA* 84) and 'Whenever temptation is felt go at once to do mechanical drawings'. Others are on pages 91 and 93.

28. Boly also mentions the relation between kleptomania and what he calls 'textual resistance', yet without elaborating the link, in *Reading Auden*, pp. 69–70.

29. W. H. Auden, *Collected Shorter Poems 1927–1957* (London and Boston: Faber & Faber, 1966), p. 59.

30. Mendelson, *Early Auden*, p. 115.

31. Jarfe, *Der junge Auden*, p. 86.

32. The distinction is Roland Barthes'. For him, the readerly work signals an illusory coherence and readability, while the writerly one emphasises the principles of its construction – even at the price of making its reading difficult: *S/Z*, trans. R. Miller (New York: Hill and Wang, 1974), pp. 3–4.

33. Lyotard makes the same point in connection with scientific knowledge in *Postmodern Condition*, p. 8.

34. Jarfe, *Der junge Auden*, p. 87.

5. The Challenge of History

1. Paul de Man 'Literary History and Literary Modernity', in *Blindness and Insight: Essays in the Rhetoric of Contemporary Criticism* (2nd edn., London: Routledge, 1983), pp. 142–65 (p. 161).

2. Günter Jarfe, 'Wandern und Quest als Schlüssel zur Thematik in Auden's Frühwerk', *Anglia*, 97, no. 3–4 (1979), 367–97 (pp. 367–8) [my translation].

3. Michel Foucault, *The Archaeology of Knowledge*, trans. A. M. Sheridan Smith, World of Man (London: Tavistock, 1972), pp. 183–90 (p. 188).

4. They are discussed in *Postmodern Condition*, pp. 27–37. Implicitly, Lyotard also acknowledges that these foundational narratives employ symbolically loaded terms, which he calls 'idealism' (p. 37).

5. Roland Barthes, *Mythologies*, selected and trans. Annette Lavers (London: Paladin, 1973), p. 124.

6. Barthes, *Mythologies*, pp. 135–6 and 140.

7. Carpenter, *Auden*, p. 72.

8. The term was coined by Louis MacNeice in 'Poetry', in Geoffrey Grigson, ed., *The Arts Today* (London: Bodley Head, 1935), p. 56. See Hynes, *Auden Generation*, p. 46.

9. I am referring to the poems up to and including *The Orators*. The case is a different one for some of Auden's later propagandist poems, of which 'Spain 1937' is the most problematic.

10. I have argued this point in *Modernism in Poetry*, pp. 121 and 129.

11. Barthes, *Mythologies*, p. 144.

12. Mendelson, *Early Auden*, p. 135.

13. Foucault, *Archaeology*, pp. 130–1.

14. Ibid., p. 131.

15. Mendelson regards this as a reference to the street fights between the police and Communists in Berlin in May 1929; *Early Auden*, p. 71.

16. Gutensberg might have been chosen for its association with 'good place', since its literal meaning is 'good mountain'. Auden's years in Berlin are documented in Norman Page, *Auden and Isherwood: The Berlin Years* (Houndmilk, Basingstoke and London: Macmillan, 1998). References to '1929' are on pp. 13, 21, 31, 34 and 173–4.

17. Foucault's 'authority of the creative subject'; *Archaeology*, p. 139.

18. Ibid., pp. 118–25.

19. The sanatorium setting itself is reminiscent of Thomas Mann's novel *The Magic Mountain* (1924).

20. Critics never seem to have problems identifying the threatening outside of the finale of '1929' as the Wall Street Crash of autumn 1929. Although the poem's eventual title may be seen as a hint, the poem does not contain clear allusions.

21. Auden tried to eliminate this poem from his *oeuvre*. It is most easily accessible in Robin Skelton, ed., *Poetry of the Thirties*, Penguin Modern Classics (Harmondsworth: Penguin, 1964), pp. 133–6.

22. Gilles Deleuze, *The Logic of Sense*, trans. Mark Lester with Charles Stivale, ed. Constantin V. Boundas (London: Athlone, 1990), p. 21.

23. 'Inside the Whale', quoted in Hynes, *Auden Generation*, p. 387.

24. Smith, *Auden*, p. 171.

25. Roland Barthes, 'The Death of the Author', in *Image, Music, Text*, trans. and ed. Stephen Heath (London: Fontana, 1977), pp. 142–8.

26. Linda Hutcheon summarises contemporary challenges to totalising and naturalising views of history in ch. 3, *The Politics of Postmodernism*, New Accents (London and New York: Routledge, 1989), pp. 62–92.

6. Displaced Voices: Post-War Auden

1. Jarfe, 'Wandern und Quest', p. 375, illustrates in greater detail the problem of individual fulfilment in a mass civilization.

2. The importance of homosexuality for Auden's poetics is discussed in Richard R. Bozorth, '"But Who Would Get It?": Auden and the Codes of Poetry and Desire', *English Literary History*, 62/3 (Autumn 1995), pp. 709–27.

3. I find myself in disagreement with David Pascoe here, who claims (in connection with 'Musée des Beaux Arts') that Auden reads surrealism 'as realistically as he could, investing it with the significance, the subject, of his own life'; '"Everything Turns Away": Auden's Surrealism', in Bucknell and Jenkins, *Language of Learning*, pp. 137–54 (p. 153). Pascoe bases this claim on biographical sources and (sometimes questionable) intertextual readings ('Auden's technique mirrors Brueghel's. Take his pronouns'; p. 150), but hardly a serious engagement with Auden's poetics.

4. Lacan, 'The Freudian Thing', in *Écrits*, pp. 114–45 (p. 137).

5. The poem's first line actually alludes to a Middle English homily, 'Sawles Warde'; Mendelson, *Early Auden*, p. 44.

6. Ibid., p. 46.

7. Spears, *Poetry*, p. 41.

8.   Mendelson, *Early Auden*, pp. 45–6.
9.   I have elaborated this point in 'Transgressive Travels: Homosexuality, Class, Politics and the Lure of Germany in 1930s Writing', *Critical Survey*, Special Issue on the Literature of the 1930s, 10/3 (1998), 48–55.
10. Eagleton summarises the function of 'Dover' in connection with Englishness as follows: 'To look beyond the edges of England is to know its pettiness, but also to confront a disorientating vision of general collapse – an image of planetary ruin which can be related to the particulars of Dover life only through the mediating device of the tides, which are at once local and global'; 'A Note on Auden', in *Exiles and Émigrés*, p. 187.
11. Carpenter, *W. H. Auden*, p. 226.
12. This sword, as John Fuller rightly remarks, is the one with which Charles Willcox accidentally kills Leonard Bast in Forster's *Howard's End*; *Reader's Guide*, p. 128. None the less, the inadequacy of Forster's novels as an illustration of the suffering of war and genocide is evident.
13. Kathleen Bell summarises the various aspects of the accusations in her preface to six letters from Auden to Professor and Mrs E. R. Dodds written at the beginning of the Second World War; 'A Change of Heart', in *'The Map of All My Youth': Early Works, Friends and Influences*, Auden Studies, 1, ed. Katherine Bucknell and Nicholas Jenkins (Oxford: Clarendon Press, 1990), pp. 95–115 (pp. 97–8).
14. Sigmund Freud, 'The Unconscious', *Metapsychology*, pp. 159–222. Lacan acknowledges his debt to, as well as departure from, Freud in the already-mentioned 'The Freudian Thing' (see n. 4). Julia Kristeva discusses the difference between the imaginary and the symbolic in *Revolution in Poetic Language*, trans. M. Waller (New York: Columbia University Press, 1984), pp. 19–106.
15. In the traditional annunciation story, Mary merely responds to the long declaration of what is to happen to her by asking for an explanation of modalities, 'How shall this be, seeing I know not a man?', in order to acquiesce quickly by declaring 'be it unto me according to thy word' (Luke 1: 26–38). One could hardly call this a dialogue.
16. This mistaken view is expressed, for example, in George W. Bahlke, *The Later Auden: From 'New Year Letter' to 'About the House'* (New Jersey: Rutger's University Press, 1970), pp. 117–32. Bahlke relies too much on (partially biographically motivated) simplifications, such as 'it [*For the Time Being*] is primarily an expression of faith embodying an analogy between present and past religious experience as well as between particular and universal problems' (p. 117), and even readings that have no textual basis, such as 'The "time being" may also refer to the years intervening between every man's birth and death' (p. 131).
17. Bahlke, *Later Auden*, p. 124.

7.   From Eros to Agape: The Philosophy of Auden's Later Works

1.   Charles Osborne's perceptive essay 'Auden as a Christian Poet' brings this to the point in the observation 'What is most interesting about

Auden's "conversion" is that he remained very much as he had formerly been. He had been an extremely eccentric Marxist, and he now became an equally eccentric Christian, one in whom the Audenesque outweighed the Christian elements': Bold, *The Far Interior*, pp. 23–46 (p. 28).

2. Auden mentions these events in his contribution to *Modern Canterbury Pilgrims*, ed. James A. Pike (New York: A. R. Mowbray, 1956); quoted in Osborne, 'Auden as a Christian Poet', pp. 26–8.

3. *Theology* (November 1950), p. 412; quoted in Carpenter, *Auden*, p. 300.

4. Auden's poem 'Some say that love's a little boy', written in 1938, which culminates in the refrain 'O tell me the truth about love' (*CP* 121–2) can be read as another attempt to multiply rather than essentialise the concept of love.

5. Callan, *Carnival*, p. 254.

6. The concept is outlined most comprehensively in Jürgen Habermas, *The Theory of Communicative Action*, trans. Thomas McCarthy (2 vols., Cambridge: Polity, 1986/1988).

7. Replogle, *Auden's Poetry*, pp. 57–8.

8. Edward Callan, 'Auden's New Year Letter', in Monroe K. Spears, ed., *Auden: A Collection of Critical Essays*, Twentieth Century Views (Eaglewood Cliffs, NJ: Prentice Hall, 1964), pp. 152–9 (p. 153).

9. Callan, 'Auden's New Year Letter', p. 158. In fairness, he also calls Kierkegaard's model non-restrictive, yet seems to miss the crucial problem that the non-restrictiveness is achieved at the cost of an obvious universalism.

10. Theodor W. Adorno, *Aesthetic Theory*, ed. Gretel Adorno and Rolf Tiedemann, trans. C. Lenhardt, The International Library of Phenomenology and Moral Sciences (London: Routledge & Kegan Paul, 1984), p. 412.

11. The parable is the starting-point of Nietzsche's influential essay 'On Truth and Lying in an Extra-Moral Sense', in *Friedrich Nietzsche on Rhetoric and Language*, trans. and ed. Sandel L. Gilman, Carole Blair and David J. Parent (New York and Oxford: Oxford University Press, 1989), pp. 246–57 (p. 246).

12. Edith Sitwell, *English Eccentrics*, revised edition (Harmondsworth: Penguin, 1971). The book was first published in 1933.

13. Auden himself acknowledged the influence of Williams' *The Descent of the Dove* in his notes to *New Year Letter*; see Hecht, *Hidden Law*, p. 210. Hecht also points out that Auden's attraction to Niebuhr's theology 'lay in his [Niebuhr's] dramatic sense of how theological matters presented themselves in the context of actual, practical life', p. 300. The titles of some of Niebuhr's books, *Christian Realism and Political Problems*, *Moral Man and Immoral Society*, and *Christianity and Power Politics* support this impression. Auden reviewed the last book in the *Nation*; see Carpenter, *Auden*, p. 306.

14. One of the rhetorically most forceful rejections of binary oppositions in postmodern thinking is Hélène Cixous' essay 'Sorties: Out and Out: Attacks/Ways Out/Forays', in Catherine Belsey and Jane Moore, eds., *The Feminist Reader: Essays in Gender and the Politics of Literary*

Criticism (Basingstoke and London: Macmillan, 1989), pp. 101–16. On p. 102 she states: 'And the movement whereby each opposition is set up to make sense is the movement through which the couple is destroyed. A universal battlefield. Each time, a war is let loose. Death is always at work.'

15. Adorno, *Aesthetic Theory*, p. 85.
16. Ibid., p. 194.
17. *Bricolage* is a term used by Claude Lévi-Strauss to characterise myth-making as an assemblage of pre-existent elements; *Structural Anthropology*, trans. Claire Jacobson and Brooke Grundfest Schoepf (New York and London: Basic Books, 1963). *Jouissance* is the term used by Roland Barthes for the 'pleasure of the text', a pleasure that can only be gained from interpretation and therefore from constructing as well as undoing, i.e. deconstructing, concepts, images, narratives, and characters: *The Pleasure of the Text*, trans. Richard Miller (New York: Farrar, Straus & Giroux, 1975).
18. Fuller, *Reader's Guide*, p. 162.
19. The theorist who has been most influential in introducing dialogue into the debates on aesthetics, culture and ideology is Mikhail M. Bakhtin. See in particular his *The Dialogic Imagination: Four Essays*, ed. Michael Holquist, trans. Caryl Emerson and Michael Holquist, Slavic Series, 1 (Austin: University of Texas Press, 1981). Although Bakhtin primarily refers to the novel, his concept of *heteroglossia*, a plurality of voices, is of great importance for the discussion of Auden's poetry, and is developed in the essay 'Discourse in the Novel', pp. 301–31.
20. The implications of this doubling are explored by some theorists of post-colonialism, for instance in Edward W. Said, 'Opponents, Audiences, Constituencies and Community', in Hal Foster, ed., *Postmodern Culture* (London: Pluto Press, 1985), pp. 135–59. The writings of Homi Bhabha also deal with this issue in terms such as 'hybridity'; see e.g. *The Location of Culture* (London: Routledge, 1994).
21. M. L. Rosenthal, 'Speaking Greatly in an Age of Confusion', *New York Herald Tribune* (20 July 1947), section 7, p. 3; reprinted in John Haffenden, ed., *W. H. Auden: The Critical Heritage*, The Critical Heritage Series (London *et al.*: Routledge & Kegan Paul, 1983).
22. 'The sexual act is only a symbol for intimacy'; quoted from a journal that Auden kept in 1929 in Mendelson, *Early Auden*, p. 7.
23. Auden had become a citizen of the US in 1946: Carpenter, *Auden*, p. 339.
24. The allusion is to *Confessions*, book viii, section 7, where Augustine prays: '*Da mihi castitatem et continentiam, sed noli modo*'; see Fuller, *Reader's Guide*, p. 232.

8. Last Things

1. Jean Baudrillard, *Fatal Strategies*, trans. Philip Beitchman and W. G. J. Niesluchowski, ed. Jim Fleming (London: Pluto Press, 1990), pp. 81–99.
2. Quoted in Callan, *Carnival*, pp. 241 and 254.

3. Carpenter, *Auden*, p. 375.
4. There were other pleasures as well, as Auden indicates in a letter: 'The sex situation [...] is from my point of view, exactly what it ought to be [...] It is so nice to be with people who are never shocked or psychologically insecure'; quoted in Richard Davenport-Hines, *Auden* (London: Heinemann, 1995), p. 258.
5. Spears, *Poetry*, p. 313.
6. Auden himself refers to the wind as 'a force which the conscious will cannot cause or control', in *The Enchafèd Flood or The Romantic Iconography of the Sea* (London: Faber and Faber, 1951), p. 69.
7. This idea (which has later echoes in Derrida and Levinas) is outlined in Martin Heidegger, *Being and Time*, trans. John Macquarrie and Edward Robinson (Oxford: Blackwell, 1962), pp. 227 and 235–41.
8. This is in fact the very first statement of Wittgenstein's treatise. Ludwig Wittgenstein, *Tractatus logico-philosophicus: The German text of Ludwig Wittgenstein's Logisch-philosophische Abhandlung, with a new translation by D. F. Pears and B. F. MacGuinness*, International Library of Philosophy and Scientific Method (London: Routledge & Kegan Paul, 1961).
9. One of these positions is that of Jürgen Habermas, as expressed, for example, in *Postmetaphysical Thinking*, trans. William Mark Hohengarten (Cambridge: Polity, 1992).
10. Fuller's otherwise perceptive reading sees the poem as a mere expression of these traditional frameworks; *Reader's Guide*, p. 225.
11. The idea finds an elaborate expression in Jean François Lyotard, *Libidinal Economy*, trans. Iain Hamilton Grant (London: Athlone, 1993), especially in its first section, 'The Great Ephemeral Skin', pp. 1–42.
12. In Adorno's words, the modernist work of art 'manifests intolerance of all externality and wants to transform itself into a reality *sui generis*'; *Aesthetic Theory*, p. 85.
13. Callan, *Carnival*, pp. 219–20.
14. Victor Shklovsky, 'Art as Technique', in *Russian Formalist Criticism*, trans. and ed. Lee T. Lemon and Marion J. Reis (Lincoln, Neb.: University of Nebraska Press, 1965), pp. 3–24.
15. Bataille calls the excessive elements on which culture is based 'unproductive activities: luxury, mourning ceremonies, wars, cults, the erection of representative monuments, games, theatre, the arts, perverse (i.e. non-genital) sexuality represent a similar number of activities which, at least originally, have their end in themselves'; Georges Bataille, 'La Nation de dépense', in *La Part maudite*, Collection 'critique' (Paris: Éditions de Minuit, 1967), pp. 27–54 (p. 33); my translation.
16. Jean Baudrillard, 'Simulacra and Simulation', in *Selected Writings*, ed. Mark Poster (Cambridge: Polity, 1988), pp. 166–84 (p. 170).
17. Odo Marquard, *Farewell to Matters of Principle: Philosophical Studies*, trans. Robert M. Wallace, Odéon (New York and Oxford: Oxford University Press, 1989), p. 90.
18. Fuller, *Reader's Guide*, p. 238.
19. Spears, *Disenchanted Island*, p. 320. He also points out that Auden had used the lines before, as the final chorus of the opera *Delia* in 1953.

20.   Carpenter, *Auden*, p. 63.

9. Auden's Postmodernism

1.   Callan, *Carnival*, p. 204.
2.   Gertrude Stein, 'Poetry and Grammar', in *Look at Me Now and Here I Am: Writings and Lectures 1909–45*, ed. Patricia Meyerowitz, Twentieth-Century Classics (London: Penguin, 1971), pp. 125–48 (p. 138).
3.   Adorno calls modernist works of art 'fragments disclaiming to be wholes, even though wholes is what they really want to be' (*Aesthetic Theory*, p. 184) and links this dilemma with art's attachment to rationality: 'Works of art cannot help continuing the work of repressive reason, for they contain that moment of synthesis which helps organise a totality', p. 423.
4.   One of the more balanced early challenges to the concept of postmodernity is Fredric Jameson's influential essay 'Postmodernism and Consumer Culture', reprinted in Foster, ed., *Postmodern Culture*, pp. 111–25. The recent years have seen a veritable explosion of more or less substantial attacks on the concept, among others from critics such as Christopher Norris and Terry Eagleton. See, for example, Christopher Norris, *What's Wrong with Postmodernism: Critical Theory and the Ends of Philosophy* (New York and London: Harvester Wheatsheaf, 1990).

Bibliography

PRIMARY WORKS

Auden, Wystan Hugh, *The Enchafèd Flood or The Romantic Iconography of the Sea* (London: Faber and Faber, 1951).
——, *The Dyer's Hand and Other Essays* (London and Boston: Faber & Faber, 1963).
——, *Collected Shorter Poems 1927–1957* (London and Boston: Faber & Faber, 1966).
——, *Secondary Worlds* (London and Boston: Faber & Faber, 1968).
——, *Collected Poems*, ed. Edward Mendelson (London: Faber & Faber, 1976).
——, *The English Auden: Poems, Essays and Dramatic Writings 1927–1939*, ed. Edward Mendelson (London and Boston: Faber & Faber, 1978).
—— and Christopher Isherwood, *Plays and Other Dramatic Writings by W. H. Auden 1928–1938*, ed. Edward Mendelson, *The Complete Works of W. H. Auden* (Princeton, NJ: Princeton University Press, 1988).
—— and Louis MacNeice, *Letters from Iceland* (London and Boston: Faber & Faber, 1985).
——, *Prose, Volume 1: 1926–1938*, ed. Edward Mendelson, *The Complete Works of W. H. Auden* (Princeton, NJ: Princeton University Press, 1996).

BIBLIOGRAPHIES

Bloomfield, B. C. and Edward Mendelson, *W. H. Auden: A Bibliography 1924–1969*, 2nd edition (Charlottesville, Va.: University of Virginia Press, 1972).
Gingerich, Martin E., *W. H. Auden: A Reference Guide* (Boston, Mass.: Hall & Co., 1977).
Mendelson, Edward, 'W. H. Auden: A Bibliographical Supplement', in *The Map of All My Youth: Early Works, Friends and Influences*, ed. Katherine Bucknell and Nicholas Jenkins, Auden Studies, 1 (Oxford: Clarendon Press, 1990), pp. 203–36.

AUDEN CRITICISM

Bahlke, George W., *The Later Auden: From 'New Year Letter' to 'About the House'* (New Jersey: Rutger's University Press, 1970).
Beach, Joseph Warren, *The Making of the Auden Canon* (Minneapolis: University of Minnesota Press, 1957).
Blair, John G., *The Poetic Art of W. H. Auden* (Princeton: Princeton University Press, 1965).
Bloom, Harold, ed., *W. H. Auden*, Modern Critical Views (New York: Chelsea, 1986).

Bold, Alan, ed., *W. H. Auden: The Far Interior*, Critical Studies (London: Vision Press, 1985).

Boly, John R., 'W. H. Auden's *The Orators*: Portraits of the Artist in the Thirties', *Twentieth Century Literature*, 27/3 (Fall 1981), 247–61.

——, 'Auden as a Literary Evolutionist: Wordsworth's Dream and the Fate of Romanticism', *Diacritics*, 12/1 (1982), 65–74.

——, *Reading Auden: The Returns of Caliban* (Ithaca and London: Cornell University Press, 1991).

Bozorth, Richard, '"Whatever You Do Don't Go to the Wood": Joking, Rhetoric, and Homosexuality in *The Orators*', in Bucknell and Jenkins, *Language of Learning*, pp. 113–36.

——, '"But Who Would Get It?": Auden and the Codes of Poetry and Desire', *English Literary History*, 62/3 (Autumn 1995), 709–27.

Bucknell, Katherine and Nicholas Jenkins, eds., *'The Map of All My Youth': Early Works, Friends and Influences*, Auden Studies, 1 (Oxford: Clarendon Press, 1990).

——, eds., *'The Language of Learning and the Language of Love': Uncollected Writing, New Interpretations*, Auden Studies, 2 (Oxford: Clarendon Press, 1994).

——, eds., *'In Solitude, For Company': W. H. Auden after 1940: Unpublished Prose and Recent Criticism*, Auden Studies, 3 (Oxford: Clarendon Press, 1995).

Buell, Frederick, *W. H. Auden as a Social Poet* (Ithaca, NY: Cornell University Press, 1973).

Callan, Edward, *Auden: A Carnival of Intellect* (Oxford and New York: Oxford University Press, 1983).

Carpenter, Humphrey, *W. H. Auden: A Biography* (London: Allen & Unwin, 1981).

Davenport-Hines, Richard, *Auden* (London: Heinemann, 1995).

Davidson, Dennis, *W. H. Auden*, Literature in Perspective (London: Evans Brothers, 1970).

Deane, Patrick, '"Within a Field That Never Closes": The Reader in W. H. Auden's "New Year Letter"', *Contemporary Literature*, 32/2 (Summer 1991), 171–93.

Duchêne, François, *The Case of the Helmeted Airman: A Study of W. H. Auden's Poetry* (London: Chatto & Windus, 1972).

Everett, Barbara, *Auden*, Writers and Critics (Edinburgh: Oliver & Boyd, 1964).

Fuller, John, *A Reader's Guide to W. H. Auden* (London: Thames & Hudson, 1970).

——, 'W. H. Auden's First Published Poems', *Notes and Queries*, 20 (September 1973), 333–4.

Grant, Damian, 'Verbal Events', *Critical Quarterly*, 16 (Spring 1974), 81–6.

Greenberg, Herbert, *Quest for the Necessary: W. H. Auden and the Dilemma of Divided Consciousness* (Cambridge: Harvard University Press, 1968).

Grigson, Geoffrey, 'Auden as a Monster', *New Verse*, 26–7 (1937), 13–17.

Haffenden, John, ed., *W. H. Auden: The Critical Heritage*, The Critical Heritage Series (London et al.: Routledge & Kegan Paul, 1983).

Hecht, Anthony, *The Hidden Law: The Poetry of W. H. Auden* (Cambridge, Mass. and London: Harvard University Press, 1993).

Hoggart, Richard, *Auden: An Introductory Essay* (London: Chatto & Windus, 1951).
——, *W. H. Auden*, Writers and Their Work, 93 (London: Longman, 1957).
Hooker, Jeremy, 'English Auden', *Poetry Wales*, 10/2 (1974), 5–18.
Isherwood, Christopher, 'Some Notes on Auden's Early Poetry', *New Verse*, 26–7 (1937), 4–9.
Jarfe, Günther, 'Wandern und Quest als Schlüssel zur Thematik in Audens Frühwerk', *Anglia*, 97/3–4 (1979), 376–97.
——, 'W. H. Auden und Sigmund Freud: Ein Versuch über den Einfluß Freuds auf Form, Bildlichkeit und Thematik in Audens fruher Dichtung', *Poetica*, 11/1–2 (1979), 176–206.
——, *Der junge Auden: Dichterische Verfahrensweisen und ihre Bedeutung in W. H. Audens Frühwerk* (Heidelberg: Carl Winter, 1985).
Kermode, Frank and John Hollander, 'W. H. Auden', in *Modern British Literature* (New York: Oxford University Press, 1973), pp. 583–6.
Mendelson, Edward, 'The Coherence of Auden's *The Orators*', *English Literary History*, 35 (1968), 114–33.
——, *Early Auden* (London: Faber & Faber, 1981).
Nelson, Gerald, *Changes of Heart: A Study of the Poetry of W. H. Auden*, Perspectives in Criticism, 21 (Berkeley: University of California Press, 1969).
Newman, Michael, 'The Art of Poetry XVII: W. H. Auden', *Paris Review*, 14/57 (September 1974), 32–69.
Norton, Dan S., 'Auden's Poetry', *Virginia Quarterly Review*, 21 (Summer 1946), 434–41.
Osborne, Charles, *W. H. Auden: The Life of the Poet* (London: Eyre Methuen, 1980).
Pascoe, David, '"Everything Turns Away": Auden's Surrealism', in Bucknell and Jenkins, *Language of Learning*, pp. 137–54.
Replogle, Justin M., 'Auden's Marxism', *PMLA* 80 (1965), 584–95.
——, *Auden's Poetry* (London: Methuen, 1969).
Rodway, Alan, *A Preface to Auden* (London and New York: Longman, 1984).
Smith, Stan, *W. H. Auden*, Rereading Literature (Oxford and New York: Blackwell, 1985).
——, 'Missing Dates: From *Spain 1937* to "September 1, 1939"', *Literature and History*, 13/2 (Autumn 1987), 155–74.
——, 'Loyalty and Interest: Auden, Modernism, and the Politics of Pedagogy', *Textual Practice*, 4/1 (Spring 1990), 54–72.
Spears, Monroe K., *The Poetry of W. H. Auden: The Disenchanted Island* (New York: Oxford University Press, 1963).
——, ed., *Auden: A Collection of Critical Essays*, Twentieth Century Views (Englewood Cliffs, NJ; Prentice Hall, 1964).
——, 'Auden and the Music of Time', *Southern Review*, 18/1 (1982), 25–43.
Spender, Stephen, ed., *W. H. Auden: A Tribute* (New York: Macmillan, 1975).
Turner, Daphne, 'Delight and Truth: Auden's *The Sea and the Mirror*', *Literature and Theology*, 3/1 (March 1989), 95–106.
Warren, Austin, 'The Poetry of W. H. Auden', *Southern Review*, 17/3 (1981), 461–78.
Wright, George Thaddeus, *W. H. Auden*, Twayne United States Authors Series, 144 (New York: Twayne, 1969).

GENERAL CRITICISM

Carter, Ronald, ed., *Thirties Poets: 'The Auden Group'*, Casebook Series (London and Basingstoke: Macmillan, 1984).
Eagleton, Terry, *Exiles and Émigrés: Studies in Modern Literature* (London: Chatto and Windus, 1970).
Emig, Rainer, *Modernism in Poetry: Motivations, Structures and Limits*, Studies in Twentieth-Century Literature (London and New York: Longman, 1995).
——, 'Transgressive Travels: Homosexuality, Class, Politics and the Lure of Germany in 1930s Writing', *Critical Survey*, Special Issue on the Literature of the 1930s, 10/3 (1998), 48–55.
Hynes, Samuel Lynn, *The Auden Generation: Literature and Politics in England in the 1930s* (London and Boston: Faber & Faber, 1976).
Nicholls, Peter, *Modernisms: A Literary Guide* (Basingstoke and London: Macmillan, 1995).
O'Neill, Michael and Gareth Reeves, *Auden, MacNeice, Spender: The Thirties Poetry* (Basingstoke and London: Macmillan, 1992).
Page, Norman, *The Thirties in Britain*, Context and Commentary (London and Basingstoke: Macmillan, 1990).
——, *Auden and Isherwood: The Berlin Years* (London and Basingstoke: Macmillan, 1998).

THEORY

Adorno, Theodor W., *Aesthetic Theory*, ed. Gretel Adorno and Rold Tiedemann, trans. C. Lenhardt, The International Library of Phenomenology and Moral Sciences (London: Routledge & Kegan Paul, 1984).
Bakhtin, Mikhail M., *The Dialogic Imagination: Four Essays*, ed. Michael Holquist, trans. Caryl Emerson and Michael Holquist, Slavic Series, 1 (Austin: University of Texas Press, 1981).
Barthes, Roland, *Writing Degree Zero*, trans. Annette Lavers and Colin Smith, Cape Editions, 3 (London: Cape, 1967).
——, *Mythologies*, selected and trans. Annette Lavers (London: Paladin, 1973).
——, *S/Z*, trans. R. Miller (New York: Hill and Wang, 1974).
——, *The Pleasure of the Text*, trans. Richard Miller (New York: Farrar, Straus & Giroux, 1975).
——, *Image , Music, Text*, trans. and ed. Stephen Heath (London: Fontana, 1977).
Bataille, Georges, *La Part maudite*, Collection 'critique' (Paris: Éditions de Minuit, 1967).
Baudrillard, Jean, *Selected Writings*, ed. Mark Poster (Cambridge: Polity, 1988).
——, *Fatal Strategies*, trans. Philip Beitchman and W. G. J. Niesluchowski, ed. Jim Fleming (London: Pluto Press, 1990).
Belsey, Catherine and Jane Moore, eds., *The Feminist Reader: Essays in Gender and the Politics of Literary Criticism* (Basingstoke and London: Macmillan, 1989).

Bernasconi, Robert and Simon Critchley, eds., *Re-Reading Levinas*, Studies in Contemporary Thought (London: Athlone, 1991).

Bhabha, Homi, *The Location of Culture* (London: Routledge, 1994).

Butler, Judith, *Gender Trouble: Feminism and the Subversion of Identity*, Thinking Gender (New York and London: Routledge, 1990).

Cixous, Hélène, 'Sorties: Out and Out: Attacks/Ways Out/Forays', in Belsey and Moore, *The Feminist Reader*, pp. 101–16.

Connor, Steven, *Postmodern Culture: An Introduction to Theories of the Contemporary* (Oxford: Blackwell, 1989).

Deleuze, Gilles, *The Logic of Sense*, trans. Mark Lester with Charles Stivale, ed. Constantin V. Boundas (London: Athlone, 1990).

de Man, Paul, *Blindness and Insight: Essays in the Rhetoric of Contemporary Criticism*, 2nd edition (London: Routledge, 1983).

Derrida, Jacques, *Speech and Phenomena and Other Essays on Husserl's Theory of Signs*, trans. David B. Allison, Studies in Phenomenology & Existential Philosophy (Evanston: Northwestern University Press, 1973).

——, *Writing and Difference*, trans. Alan Bass (London and Henley: Routledge & Kegan Paul, 1978).

Foster, Hal, ed., *Postmodern Culture* (London: Pluto Press, 1985).

Foucault, Michel, *The Archaeology of Knowledge*, trans. A. M. Sheridan Smith, World of Man (London: Tavistock, 1974).

——, *The Order of Things: An Archaeology of the Human Sciences*, World of Man (London and New York: Tavistock, 1974).

Freud, Sigmund, *On Metapsychology: The Theory of Psychoanalysis*, ed. Angela Richards, The Pelican Freud Library, xi (15 vols.; London: Pelican, 1984).

Habermas, Jürgen, *The Theory of Communicative Action*, trans. Thomas McCarthy (2 vols.; Cambridge: Polity, 1986/1988).

——, *Postmetaphysical Thinking*, trans. William Mark Hohengarten (Cambridge: Polity, 1992).

Heidegger, Martin, *Being and Time*, trans. John Macquarrie and Edward Robinson (Oxford: Blackwell, 1962).

Hutcheon, Linda, *A Poetics of Postmodernism: History, Theory, Fiction* (New York and London: Routledge, 1988).

——, *The Politics of Postmodernism*, New Accents (London and New York: Routledge, 1989).

Kristeva, Julia, *Revolution in Poetic Language*, trans. M. Waller (New York: Columbia University Press, 1984).

Lacan, Jacques, *Écrits: A Selection*, trans. Alan Sheridan (London: Tavistock, 1977).

Lemon, Lee T. and Marion J. Reis, eds., *Russian Formalist Criticism*, (Lincoln, Neb.: University of Nebraska Press, 1965).

Lévi-Strauss, Claude, *Structural Anthropology*, trans. Claire Jacobson and Brooke Grundfest Schoepf (New York and London: Basic Books, 1963).

Lyotard, Jean-François, *The Postmodern Condition: A Report on Knowledge*, trans. Geoff Bennington and Brian Masumi, Theory and History of Literature, 10 (Manchester: Manchester University Press, 1984).

——, *Libidinal Economy*, trans. Iain Hamilton Grant (London: Athlone, 1993).

Marquard, Odo, *Farewell to Matters of Principle: Philosophical Studies*, trans. Robert M. Wallace, Odéon (New York and Oxford: Oxford University Press, 1989).

Nietzsche, Friedrich, *Friedrich Nietzsche on Rhetoric and Language*, trans. and ed. Sandel L. Gilman, Carole Blair and David J. Parent (New York and Oxford: Oxford University Press, 1989).

Norris, Christopher, *What's Wrong with Postmodernism: Critical Theory and the Ends of Philosophy* (New York and London: Harvester Wheatsheaf, 1990).

Ricoeur, Paul, *Interpretation Theory: Discourse and the Surplus of Meaning* (Fort Worth: Texas Christian University Press, 1976).

Riffaterre, Michael, *Text Production*, trans. Terese Lyons (New York: Columbia University Press, 1983).

Saussure, Ferdinand de, *Course in General Linguistics*, trans. Roy Harris (London: Duckworth, 1983).

Welsch, Wolfgang, *Unsere postmoderne Moderne*, 2nd edition, Acta Humaniora (Weinheim: VCH, 1988).

Wittgenstein, Ludwig, *Tractatus logico-philosophicus: The German text of Ludwig Wittgenstein's Logisch-philosophische Abhandlung, with a new translation by D. F. Pears and B. F. MacGuinness*, International Library of Philosophy and Scientific Method (London: Routledge & Kegan Paul, 1961).

Young, Robert, ed., *Untying the Text: A Post-Structuralist Reader* (London: Routledge & Kegan Paul, 1987).

MISCELLANEOUS

Mann, Thomas, *The Magic Mountain*, trans. H. T. Lowe-Porter, 3rd edition (London: Secker & Warburg, 1961).

Sitwell, Edith, *English Eccentrics*, revised edition (Harmondsworth: Penguin, 1971).

Skelton, Robin, ed., *Poetry of the Thirties*, Penguin Modern Classics (Harmondsworth: Penguin, 1964).

Stein, Gertrude, *Look at Me Now and Here I Am: Writings and Lectures 1909–45*, ed. Patricia Meyerowitz, Twentieth-Century Classics (London: Penguin, 1971).

Index

231

Auden, Wystan Hugh (*Contd.*)
'Hong Kong', 126
Horae Canonicae, 177, 188–96, 206
'I chose this lean country', 80, 87
'In Memory of Sigmund Freud', 109–10
'In Memory of W. B. Yeats', 107–9
'In Praise of Limestone', 7, 132, 171–3, 175, 183
In Time of War, 127–8
'In Transit', 170–1
'Ischia', 175–6
'Island Cemetery, An', 176–8
'Islands', 177, 182
'It was Easter as I walked in the public gardens', 6, 57, 80, 88–100, 155, 165, 219n.
'It's no use raising a shout', 22, 84
'Journal of an Airman', 57, 65, 68–75
Journey to a War (with Christopher Isherwood), 6, 125–6
'Journey to Iceland', 125
'Lakes', 177, 181–2
'Lauds', 195
'Letter, The', 85, 184
'Letter to a Wound', 57, 60, 67–8, 77
Letter to Lord Byron, 121–4, 126–7
Letters from Iceland (with Louis MacNeice), 6, 121–2, 124
'Look there! The sunk road winding', 23
'Love by ambition', 116, 184
'Love Feast, The', 173–4
'Lullaby', 147–9, 151, 159, 160
'Luther', 134
'Macao', 126–7
'Major Port, A', 127
'Makers of History', 111
'Masque, The', 167
'Massacre of the Innocents, The', 142–3
'Meditation of Simeon, The', 140–1
'Missing', 87–8
'Misunderstanding, A', 184

'Montaigne', 134
'Mountains', 7, 177, 180–2
'Musée des Beaux Arts', 128–9, 150, 154, 219n.
New Year Letter, 132, 148–57, 159, 171
Night Mail, 6, 102–3
'1929', 6, 57, 80, 88–100, 155, 165, 219n.
'No Change of Place', 14, 19, 84
'Nones', 192–3
'No trenchant parting this', 70, 80–4, 184
'Novelist, The', 130
'Objects', 186–7
'Ode to Gaea', 173
'Ode to Terminus', 174
On the Frontier (with Christopher Isherwood), 5, 45–51, 124
Orators: An English Study, The, 5–6, 19, 31, 42, 52–79, 118, 164, 212
Oxford Book of Light Verse, The, 136
Paid on Both Sides, 5, 29–35
'Permanent Way, A', 211–12
'Pick a quarrel, go to war', 23
'Plains', 177, 182
Poems (1928), 5, 9, 80
Poems (1930), 12, 29, 80
Poet's Tongue, The, 213n.
Portable Greek Reader, The, 140
'Postscript', 198
'Precious Five', 184–6, 188
'Prime', 189–90
'Prologue', 53–5, 62
'Quest, The', 131–3, 169
'Question, The', 17–18
'Questioner Who Sits So Sly, The', 14
'Schoolboy making lonely maps', 24
Sea and the Mirror, The, 157–64, 166, 171
'Secondary Epic', 112
'Secret Agent, The', 22, 24
'Sentries against inner and outer', 22
'September 1, 1939', 110–11, 137, 148, 165, 191

234

Index

Shakespeare, William, 156, 162, 199
works by:
As You Like It, 210
Macbeth, 120
Romeo and Juliet, 29, 47
Tempest, The, 11, 157, 161–2
Shklovsky, Victor, 190
Sitter, Willem de, 152
Sitwell, Edith
works by:
English Eccentrics, 153
Spanish Civil War, 50, 105–7, 124, 146
Spender, Stephen, 1, 5, 14
Stalin, Joseph [Dzhugashvili, Iosif
Vissarionovich], and Stalinism,
59, 123
Stein, Gertrude, 66, 207
Stoker, Bram
works by:
Dracula, 181
Strindberg, August, 35
Structuralism, 207
Sunday Express, The, 75
Surrealism, 5, 21, 29, 31–2, 56, 69, 74,
117, 219n.
Swift, Jonathan, 199

Tennyson, Alfred, 151
Thomas, Dylan, 3
Thucydides, 110
Tiberius [Tiberius
Claudius Nero], 182
Tolkien, John Ronald Reuel, 12
'trickster', 71
'truly strong man', 43–4, 47, 96, 120,
132, 148, 154–5, 169–70

Upward, Edward, 1, 75

Virgil [Publius Vergilius Maro],
112, 165
Voltaire, François Marie Arout de,
151
Vorticism, 183

Wagner, Richard, 154
'Wanderer, The', 118
Warner, Rex, 75
War Poets, 39
Washington, George, 154
Weimar Republic, 6
Welsch, Wolfgang, 4
Whitehead, Sarah, 153
Williams, Charles, 153
works by:
Descent of the Dove, The, 221n.
Wittgenstein, Ludwig, 49, 207
works by:
Tractatus logico-philosophicus,
182, 223n.
Wordsworth, William, 23, 154
'Wulf and Eadwacer', 215n.

Yeats, William Butler, 1, 4, 12, 22–3,
86, 103, 104, 107–9, 129, 204
works by:
'Byzantium', 86, 147
'Circus Animals' Desertion,
The', 178
'Irish Airman Foresees His Death,
An', 108
'Lapis Lazuli', 181
'Sailing to Byzantium', 86